WILD fishing

Britain's 700 most beautiful, secluded & affordable places to fish

Kevin & Jill Adams

WILD THINGS PUBLISHING

Liddel, p151

WILD fishing

Ystwyth, p213

Contents

Regions

Hury Reservoir p142

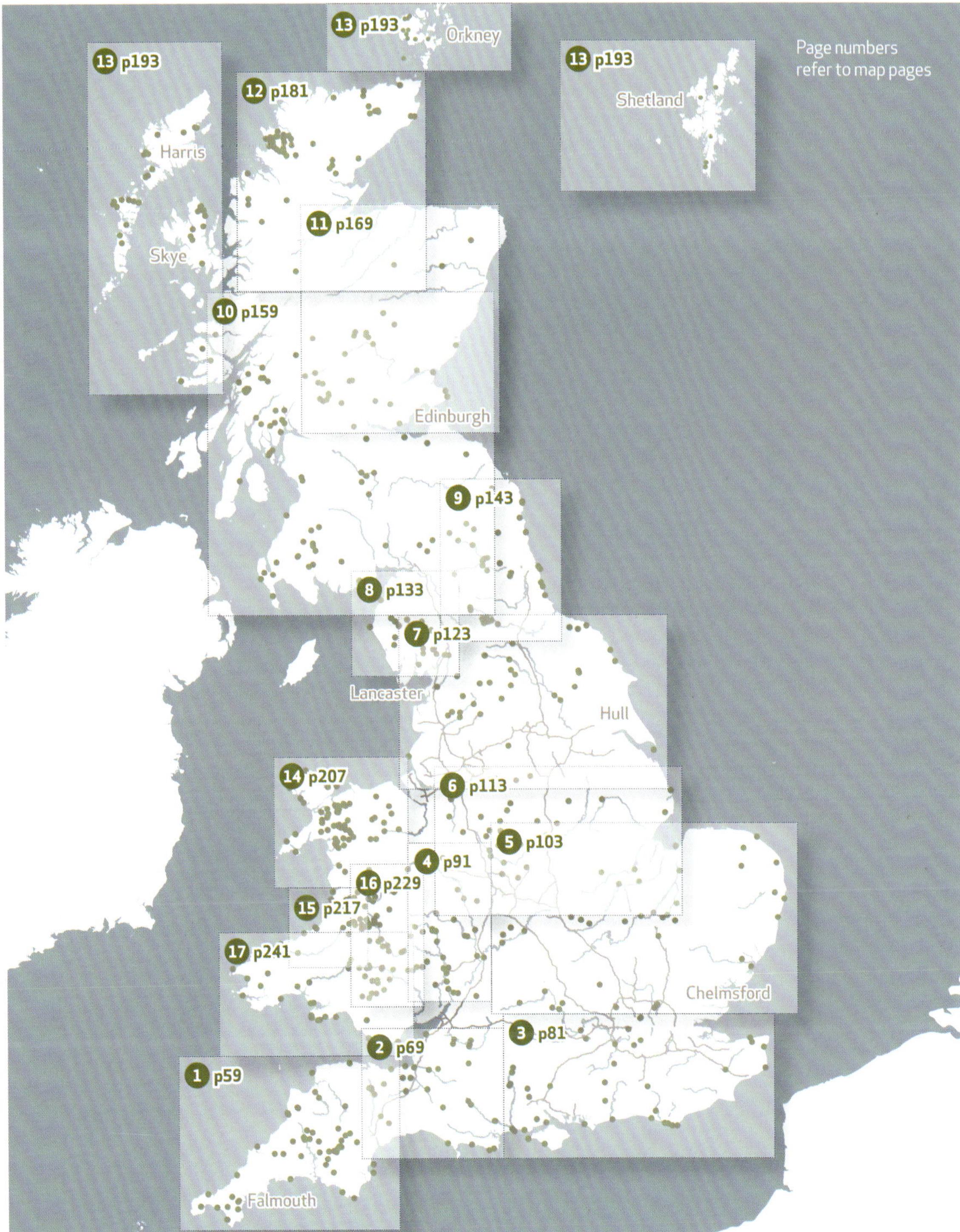
Page numbers refer to map pages
13 p193
Orkney
13 p193
13 p193
Shetland
12 p181
Harris
11 p169
Skye
10 p159
Edinburgh
9 p143
8 p133
7 p123
Lancaster
Hull
14 p207
6 p113
5 p103
4 p91
16 p229
15 p217
17 p241
Chelmsford
3 p81
2 p69
1 p59
Falmouth

River Mease, p112

Introduction

What is Wild Fishing

A pike! It must have been a pike. On my third ever cast as a young boy, I was reeling in a worm when something exploded around my feet – the violent surge of the attack flooding my wellingtons with river water. Sitting on the bank by the Old Bridge in Hereford, emptying my boots and lamenting the loss of my tackle, my angling journey began. It eventually took me to America, where you can roam the vast country and fish almost anywhere with just a local fishing licence. That scale of freedom doesn't exist here in the UK, and this book sets to redress that in part.

We define *Wild Fishing* as fishing for native species in beautiful, remote surroundings. Many of these spots are free or at least very inexpensive. With growing ecological awareness there is increasing resistance to the costly practice of stocking rivers with fish. It's surely far better to fish for non-invasive species. Stocking started about 200 years ago when rainbow trout were shipped over from the US, but we suggest that apart from in limited areas around the Home Counties, this practice should stop.

Catch-and-release fishing once seemed a ridiculous practice – Why catch a fish and let it go? Now, firmly established among game anglers, it's widely accepted that a game fish is far too valuable to be caught only once. As Lee Wulff said, "The finest gift you can give to any fisherman is to put a good fish back, and who knows if the fish that you caught isn't someone else's gift to you?" Of course, coarse anglers have long practised catch-and-release, leading the way for their game-fishing counterparts.

Upper Wye, p. [illegible]

Many skilled game anglers, accustomed to fishing for stocked trout on manicured banks, are now seeking out wild fishing at much more reasonable prices. It may involve harder work and smaller returns, but the satisfaction is far greater.

Wild Fishing doesn't just mean trout. The Lady of the Stream, the grayling, once dismissed as a nuisance during trout fishing, is now rapidly gaining in popularity with anglers keen to target a fish that actually belongs in our native rivers. The grayling is also becoming a 'gateway fish': inspiring many to ask: why limit ourselves to just grayling on a fly? What about chub, carp, roach, and, of course, pike? A pike is surely one of the most exciting fish to have on the other end of your rod.

In the past, all caught pike were killed to preserve precious game stocks, but no longer. Pike in clear waters are just as visually exciting to fish for as any brown trout. Cast your fly past a bed of reeds and watch as a pike ambushes it with a swirl and a splash. The entire tranquillity of the river is shattered as the battle begins.

The River Wye is one of the UK's premier coarse fishing rivers, though it was once famous for its salmon. My uncle told me that in the 1970s, his beat on the Wye earned more income from salmon than his entire farm. Those days are long gone, but other opportunities are rising. Barbel fishing is fast becoming popular and why not? It's a beautiful fish that responds well to a fly and fights as hard as any salmon.

Irfon, p224

There's a noticeable shift among anglers away from landscaped riverbanks and expensive fishing enclaves stocked with non-native, overgrown species. This practice is starting to feel outmoded, ecologically ignorant and wasteful in its extravagance. In our new dynamic landscape, Wild Fishing is emerging as a testament to the angling community's awakening awareness about the need to conserve, protect, and restore our aquatic ecosystems.

These wild, natural species can be fished for without the excessive environmental and financial burden that stocked fish and landscaped riverbanks entail. We hope our book, which showcases 700 native fishing spots in the UK, will help promote this new approach to an ancient pastime.

We're aiming to not only share these favourite spots, but also hopefully inspire a shift towards a modern way of fishing that reflects how we can live today. We hope it serves as a helpful guide, encouraging you to explore our wildernesses – carpe diem (and no, that doesn't mean 'fish of the day').

Kevin Adams

Getting Started

Do I need a licence to go fishing?

This is a common question – and the short answer is, if you are over 12 years of age and fishing in freshwater in England and Wales, then yes, you do. Sea fishing does not require a licence, but for all rivers, canals, ponds, and lakes, you need a licence, regardless of whether these are public or private, even if you own the lake!

Young people, however, can fish for free. Under 13s don't need any licence, and 13 to 16s are free but must register. A fishing licence for a day, week, or year can be bought easily online, but do use the official *Gov.uk* site to avoid online tricksters.

Fishing Licence cost

Licence type	Trout & coarse up to 2 rod	Trout & coarse 3 rod	Salmon & sea trout
1-day	£7.30	Not available	£13.50
8-day	£14.70	Not available	£30.50
12-month	£36.80	£55.30	£93.10
12-month 66 + over & disabled	£24.50	£36.80	£62.00
12-month Junior aged 13-16	Free, but must be registered	Free, but must be registered	Free, but must be registered

Prices correct as of 2025. For the most up-to-date information check *Gov.uk*

Can I fish all year round?

This depends strictly on where you are fishing. On rivers with coarse fish (i.e. all species except trout and salmon), there is a 'close season' in the spring (from 15th March to 15th June inclusive) to protect coarse fish while they spawn. This means it is illegal to fish for coarse fish during this period on any river in England and Wales.

Weaver River, p107

River coarse fishing season

Rivers are closed for coarse fishing from 15th March to 15th June. You can still fish many other venues such as man-made lakes at this time, but always check first! For trout and salmon fishing, the season is different, as these fish breed in the winter. The regions vary, but typically you can fish for trout and game fish from 16th March to 30th September.

However, most other waters, such as lakes and canals, can be fished year-round as long as you have permission from the owner, with the exception of some waters designated as Sites of Special Scientific Interest where the coarse fish close season still applies. You can fish in the sea all year round, too.

Can I fish where I like?

Once you have your rod licence, you will still need permission to go fishing from whoever owns or has the fishing rights to that particular bit of water. Normally this involves buying a day ticket or joining the fishing club that owns or leases the lake.

Tackle shops are a great source of information on local fishing and often sell day tickets and club memberships. They have local knowledge you won't always find online! Don't be afraid to ask them directly when you buy your tackle and bait. Most are incredibly helpful.

What other rules are there that I need to follow?

Almost all club waters and fisheries have a set of rules which you need to follow. These will often be on a sign at the fishery, on your day ticket, or on the website of the club. Make sure you read these and understand them before you begin fishing. Most rules are there to ensure everyone enjoys themselves and that the fish are looked after properly.

Respect for nature

One of the key things to remember is that you must leave no trace that you have been fishing once you have left. Don't cut down trees or branches, don't have BBQs or fires, and don't leave any litter behind. Every angler sometimes gets tangles or manages to get their line caught in a tree or bush. If this happens to you, do everything

Lower Wye, p85

possible to retrieve the line safely, then wind it up and take it home with you. We highly recommend that any old line you want to get rid of is recycled via the Anglers National Line Recycling Scheme, but if this is not possible, cut it into small pieces and dispose of it in your rubbish bin at home. Similarly, be very careful how you dispose of old hooks that you don't want anymore.

Also, be mindful of not disturbing others while you are fishing. Loud music, shouting to mates, and running around will disturb others; most people are out in the countryside to enjoy the peace and tranquillity, so please respect this.

Can I keep the fish I catch in the UK?

Coarse fishing in the UK is based on a catch-and-release ethic, which means that beautiful perch like these are returned alive and well.

Getting out there

Day ticket fisheries: Some of the best places to begin fishing are small lakes with plenty of fish and easy access.

Fishing clubs: For affordable, friendly fishing, your local fishing club is very often the best place to start. See if there's one near you to join and contact them about finding easy waters to get started. They're always keen to get new members and kids fishing.

Free fishing events and fishing lessons: Perfect for families and beginners, they are often free to attend and allow you to ask any questions you might have. Indeed, an hour with a friendly coach could be worth several weeks of trying to suss things out for yourself!

Take a look at *Anglingtrust.net/getfishing* for loads of useful ideas.

Abbreviations

- Directions/web
- Location
- Cost
- Fishing method

Fly	Fly fishing
Spin	Spinning
Bait/deadbait	Either/or
Led	Ledger
Shore/kayak	Either/or
Worm	

- Quarry type

BT	Brown trout
RT	Rainbow trout
TT	Tiger trout
Gr	Grayling
ST	Sea trout
FT	Ferox
Pe	Perch
Pi	Pike
Sa	Salmon

Moriston River, p173

Equipment to get started

Fly rod: a basic, lightweight fly rod for wild fishing would be seven foot four weight, you could go lighter, to a 3 weight and smaller, to a six footer.

Fly line, leader, and tippet: together, these create your fly fishing line. All angling suppliers will help you with your selection.

Fly reel: drag reels help you control the fly line and help you play the fish, so it's essential for fly fishing.

Fly and hook: your fly is your bait. Make sure you have a sharp hook and an appetising fly for the fish you're trying to catch.

Beyond a rod, you'll need a landing net to land fish safely, and a tool to remove hooks. 99% of fish must be released these days by law, so it's important to be equipped properly.

Fishing with a fly in small brooks and streams is relatively easy, and once you find the rhythm of fly casting, you'll soon be catching fish.

Why is it easier in these tumbling streams? Because, unlike larger sedate rivers or lakes, the denizens of these streams have no more than a split second to inspect your fly before it rushes past them. Plus, they're hungry, and the tumbling river masks your presence downstream of the trout.

Finding out more

Read up a few books, watch a few YouTube videos on fly casting and fly selection and you'll be good to go fly fishing.

The redoubtable Andy Rigg, founder of Rigged & Ready in the Lake District has put together a few pages to introduce you into coarse fishing – see *Riggedandready.net*. Many of the skills cross over into fly fishing, some do not.

And remember, all fishing disciplines should employ Issac Walton's dictate: *Study To Be Quiet*.

Don't forget

1. You need to buy a fishing licence before you go fishing in freshwater in England and Wales.
2. The coarse fish close season means that you cannot fish for coarse fish species between 15th March – 15th June inclusive on rivers and a small number of still waters and canals.
3. You must have permission before you fish in any freshwater in England and Wales. This usually means buying a day ticket or club membership. You cannot simply start fishing and hope for the best – it is up to you to check first!
4. You need to make sure you are using the right sort of tackle and have proper unhooking equipment.
5. Fish should be returned to the water after capture. Virtually all coarse fish must be released by law (there are some occasional exceptions to this, such as the capture of small fish for bait that are to be used in the same water body; however, you must always check that you have permission before permanently removing any fish).

River Avon, p73

England

Henry David Thoreau captured the essence of the wilderness best when he said: "Many men go fishing all of their lives without knowing it is not fish they are after." This rings so true – fishing is about memories and experiences. Sticking to the same fishing spots is limiting.

Some might imagine that Wild Fishing in England cannot compare to the rugged Scottish Highlands or North Wales, but I disagree. Consider large parts of the southwest, the Lake District, or the Peak District. England's version of Wild Fishing has its own charm. We've uncovered hidden gems – secret fishing spots tucked away from the beaten path. Whether it's the remote reaches of the River Wye or the peaceful solitude of a Dartmoor stream, the wilderness here is about finding your own sanctuary in nature.

We've explored all these areas and can assure you there's plenty of dramatic, exciting fishing here. The call of a lonesome loch in the Lake District or the tranquil reaches of a secluded river in the Yorkshire Dales can provide a gorgeous canvas for your angling adventure. Here, the surroundings aren't just a backdrop – they're an integral part of the experience.

We've also included a section on Urban Fishing, primarily focused on England. Today, it's often referred to as 'Street Fishing'. These are fishing spots within town centres, usually completely overlooked and therefore unfished. In most cases, they're free. Perhaps the most famous example is the River Wandle in London, where Nelson once angled. It is said that Halford got the technique of dry fly fishing here, though without giving due credit to the local anglers. In these urban oases, you can lose yourself for a few hours, fishing alongside the city hustle and bustle.

England's extensive coastline along the North Sea and English Channel offers many opportunities for sea angling. From the rugged beauty of Cornwall's shores to the tranquil bays of Devon, the coastlines here are every bit as wild as Orkney's.

It's all right here, waiting for you.

Wales

For the Wild Angler, Wales offers a treasure trove of opportunities, rivalled in the British Isles only by Scotland and, debatably, the southwest of England. With a topography that ranges from majestic mountains to lonely isolated lakes and dramatic coastal regions, Wales provides a breathtaking backdrop for those seeking the thrill of Wild Fishing.

The inland lakes, called llyns, sparkle like shards of sapphire amidst the rolling landscapes. Each llyn in Wales has its own character; no two are alike. Some are boggy, peat-stained pools while others are clear moorland waters. The brown trout in these lakes vary as much as their habitats. Some only hold small fingerlings, starved of sustenance. Others are filled with golden trout, as fat and happy as the small fingerlings seem sad and bereft. Occasionally, some of the llyns can hold the trout of your dreams – a monster. These rare, fabled fish might weigh up to five pounds, perhaps not a fish of a lifetime but certainly for your year. Or, if your skills are like mine, your decade. However, mainly assume fish in the half-pound category, with a large one topping a pound and a half. Most of the llyns mentioned in our book will be, at the correct time, swarming with fly life. Some llyns, with food for the larger predatory trout, such as minnows and sticklebacks, are where you'll find the real specimens.

Take, for example, Llyn Trawsfynydd on the Llyn Peninsula, known for its pike, perch, and eels, or the mythical Llyn Ogwen, cradled by the dramatic peaks of Snowdonia – a haven for specimen trout and perch hunters. Admittedly, some of the trout in these lakes are stocked.

Wild Sea Angling enthusiasts can cast their lines into the Bristol Channel, Irish Sea, and beyond, chasing the elusive thrill of sea bass, mackerel, and, even the shark. The sea bass, in particular, deserves a book all on its own. Many anglers spend their lives chasing these elusive fish. Does much else compare to casting for sea bass as they hunt in a school – the waves crashing around you, the sea birds diving in to scoop up the floating remnants of their prey fish? Truly wild fishing.

Llyn Trawsfynydd, p204

River Esk, p149

Scotland

A land of untamed beauty and rugged landscapes, perfect for Wild Fishing. Simply tie on a pair of hiking boots and set off into the wilderness – at least if you're bank fishing. Hiking miles in waders gets tiresome very quickly. Most lochs are free to fish for brown trout or coarse fish such as pike and perch. However, larger rivers that carry salmon or sea trout (migratory species) require a permit. The bailiffs here have the same powers as the police, able to arrest anyone caught fishing illegally.

Scotland's rivers are the lifeblood of its angling legacy. From the River Tay to the Spey, these waterways are sanctuaries for salmon and trout. Fly fishing, spinning, or whatever method is practical and legal is deeply woven into Scotland's cultural fabric, arguably reaching its ultimate expression in some of these pristine waterways. Anglers who cast a line here become part of a lineage that stretches back centuries, joining the ranks of those who have fished these waters for generations

The lochs, like mirrors reflecting the sky, are made for Wild Fishing. The fish here are seldom stocked – no need for it. These lochs can be as remote as you're willing to hike, or if you're feeling lazy or unable, many are accessible from the roadside. Either way, you'll have an experience that's rarely be duplicated in the British Isles, save for the upper Welsh llyns. Pike fishing in Scottish lochs is an exciting trend, with some angling outfitters offering specialised services. Generally, the larger the loch, the larger the pike. Spinning or dead bait from the shore or boats are typical methods, but live bait is illegal in Scotland.

Then there's the Scottish coastline, where Wild Sea Anglers, can confront the North Sea's roaring embrace, or the tumultuous waves of the Atlantic Ocean. From the Orkney Islands to the Outer Hebrides, this rugged coastline creates an opportunity to chase mackerel, cod, and even the mighty Atlantic salmon.

Wherever in Scotland you choose to fish you'll be guided by the seasons: Spring heralds the return of salmon, summer's warmth entices anglers to the rivers and lochs to fish for trout, and autumn creates a new chapter as the salmon embark on their upstream pilgrimage. Not even the winter chill can deter dedicated anglers seeking the promise of a grayling or two.

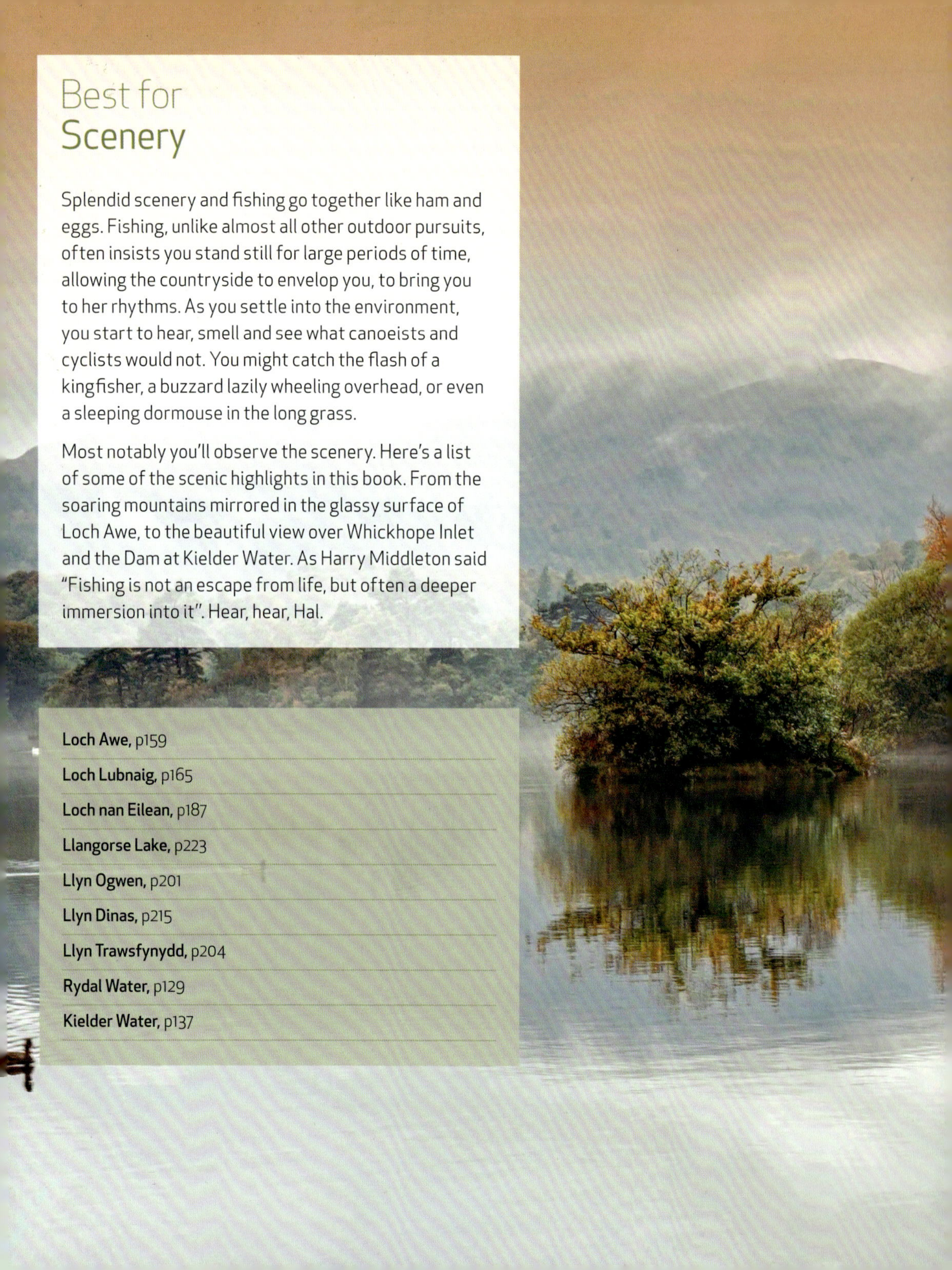

Best for Scenery

Splendid scenery and fishing go together like ham and eggs. Fishing, unlike almost all other outdoor pursuits, often insists you stand still for large periods of time, allowing the countryside to envelop you, to bring you to her rhythms. As you settle into the environment, you start to hear, smell and see what canoeists and cyclists would not. You might catch the flash of a kingfisher, a buzzard lazily wheeling overhead, or even a sleeping dormouse in the long grass.

Most notably you'll observe the scenery. Here's a list of some of the scenic highlights in this book. From the soaring mountains mirrored in the glassy surface of Loch Awe, to the beautiful view over Whickhope Inlet and the Dam at Kielder Water. As Harry Middleton said "Fishing is not an escape from life, but often a deeper immersion into it". Hear, hear, Hal.

Rydal Water, p129

Best for
Wild Pike Fishing

Ted Hughes, the late Poet Laureate, was a pike obsessive, or Pikeman as he would probably like to be called. He once recalled, "When I was feeling good I'd have dreams full of giant pike that were perhaps also leopards... They'd become symbols of deep, vital life... My obsession with pike maybe was my obsession with those energies."

The record pike caught on a fly in UK waters weighed 43lb, taken on a remarkable size 10 Woolly Bugger. The angler had been fishing with a guide for trout – quite a surprise I imagine. Several of the entries below could yield pike that exceed this. Llyn Ebyr, for example, is rarely fished and spans thirty acres – who knows what it might hold? The others are known pike waters, and you would expect, if the fishing gods are with you, to haul out something large – whether it's on a fly, live, or dead bait.

Llyn Trawsfynydd, p204

Best for
Urban Wild Fishing

Urban Fishing, or as I've just recently discovered it's called, Street Fishing (love the name) is, attracting a younger fishing demographic, according to *The Guardian*. It's most popular in Europe, with Paris being the epicentre. When one of the movement's pioneers, Fred Miessner, died suddenly in a car crash recently, hundreds of French youth turned out for a fishing vigil.

Below are our UK Urban, or Street Fishing, suggestions. Each offers you a chance to escape the city for a while and descend into a green oasis away from the hubbub. Some are well-known, especially the granddaddy of them all – The Wandle. Others may offer solitude, aside from perhaps a few people kipping in the undergrowth. It's a nimble form of fishing, you can scoot around your town discovering spots, mapping them on a bike, or in London, on the Tube.

The *London Evening Standard*, writing about Urban Angling quotes a Mr. Tim James who says "In London, time goes by and you don't notice the seasons changing. But when you're fishing regularly, you do notice. You'll return to a spot a week later and there'll be a bird that wasn't there the week before. Or flowers will have bloomed. You chime in with nature's body clock, which really focusses your mental health."

London/Wandle, p77

Bude/Neet, p52

Winchester/Itchen, p75

Stroud/Frome, p85

Leominster/Lugg, p89

Ludlow/Teme, p89

York/Ouse, p121

Edinburgh/Water of Leith, p153

River Wandle, p77

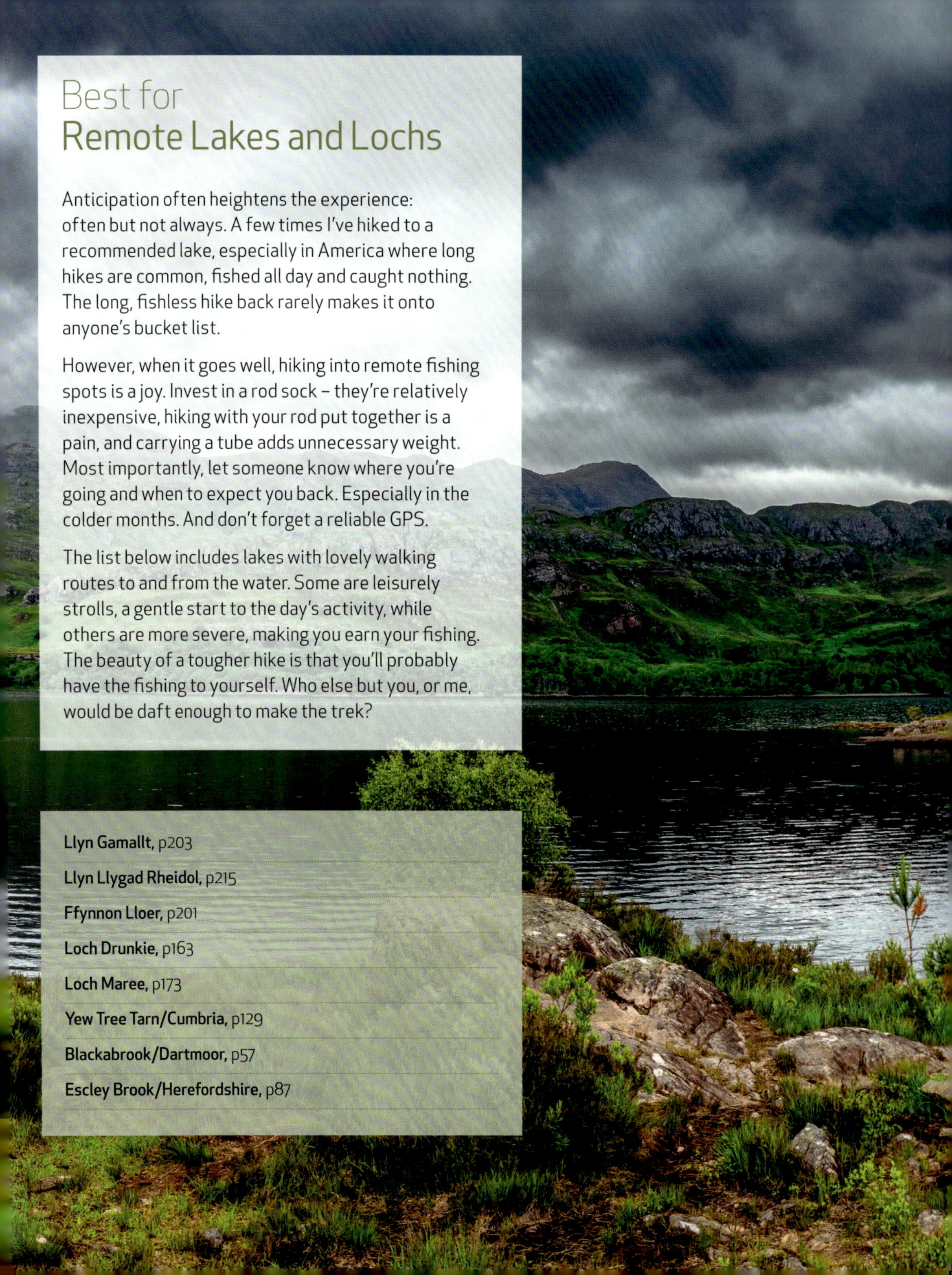

Best for
Remote Lakes and Lochs

Anticipation often heightens the experience: often but not always. A few times I've hiked to a recommended lake, especially in America where long hikes are common, fished all day and caught nothing. The long, fishless hike back rarely makes it onto anyone's bucket list.

However, when it goes well, hiking into remote fishing spots is a joy. Invest in a rod sock – they're relatively inexpensive, hiking with your rod put together is a pain, and carrying a tube adds unnecessary weight. Most importantly, let someone know where you're going and when to expect you back. Especially in the colder months. And don't forget a reliable GPS.

The list below includes lakes with lovely walking routes to and from the water. Some are leisurely strolls, a gentle start to the day's activity, while others are more severe, making you earn your fishing. The beauty of a tougher hike is that you'll probably have the fishing to yourself. Who else but you, or me, would be daft enough to make the trek?

Llyn Gamallt, p203

Llyn Llygad Rheidol, p215

Ffynnon Lloer, p201

Loch Drunkie, p163

Loch Maree, p173

Yew Tree Tarn/Cumbria, p129

Blackabrook/Dartmoor, p57

Escley Brook/Herefordshire, p87

Loch Maree, p173

Best for
Wild Rivers for Trotting

Trotting is a lovely way to fish rivers and highly efficient too. It's how most of us began fishing. It's not for the lazy though – it requires float control, good rivercraft skills and plenty of patience. You can buy a centrepin reel and do it properly, though a good centrepin isn't cheap and will takes time to master. Alternatively, you can do what most of us do and use the ubiquitous fixed spool reel – cheaper and far, far easier.

The goal of trotting is for the bait to trundle along the bottom, so float selection is crucial. I typically use an Avon float. When targeting smaller species, 2lb to 3lb line is adequate, but if you're after chub or barbel, move up to 4lb line. As for bait? Maggots, bread or worms are all ideal.

Here are our recommended wild rivers for this delightful, reflective way of fishing.

Wye, p85

Irfon, p224

Dee, p207

Severn, p228

Chew, p65

Dochart, p163

Ouse, p121

Neet, p52

Itchen, p75

River Irfon, p224

Best for
Coarse Fly Fishing

In recent years, there has been a dramatic increase in fly anglers turning to coarse species to get their fly fishing fix. The growing movement of 'Fly For Coarse' sets itself firmly against fly fishing's inherent snobbery toward coarse fish, offering a fresh set of techniques and species for the open-minded fly angler. Each species of coarse fish presents a unique challenge (since all freshwater fish rely on similar food sources), though each requires a bit of thought and a tweak to your technique to target them successfully.

While all coarse fish can be targeted, pike, perch and chub are the most popular for this relatively new form of fishing.

Perch is a swaggering, and handsome fish. Small perch are gluttons of the highest order: attacking any fly you put in front of them without hesitation. Larger specimens, however, are far more cautious and tricky, which is precisely why they grow to be bigger fish.

Izaak Walton called chub "the fearfullest of fishes" and that's certainly true of larger ones. A minor stream side disturbance and they're gone. However, like small perch and sheep, the smaller chub can be suicidal, but both large and small will take flies and are a worthy quarry.

River Dove , p111

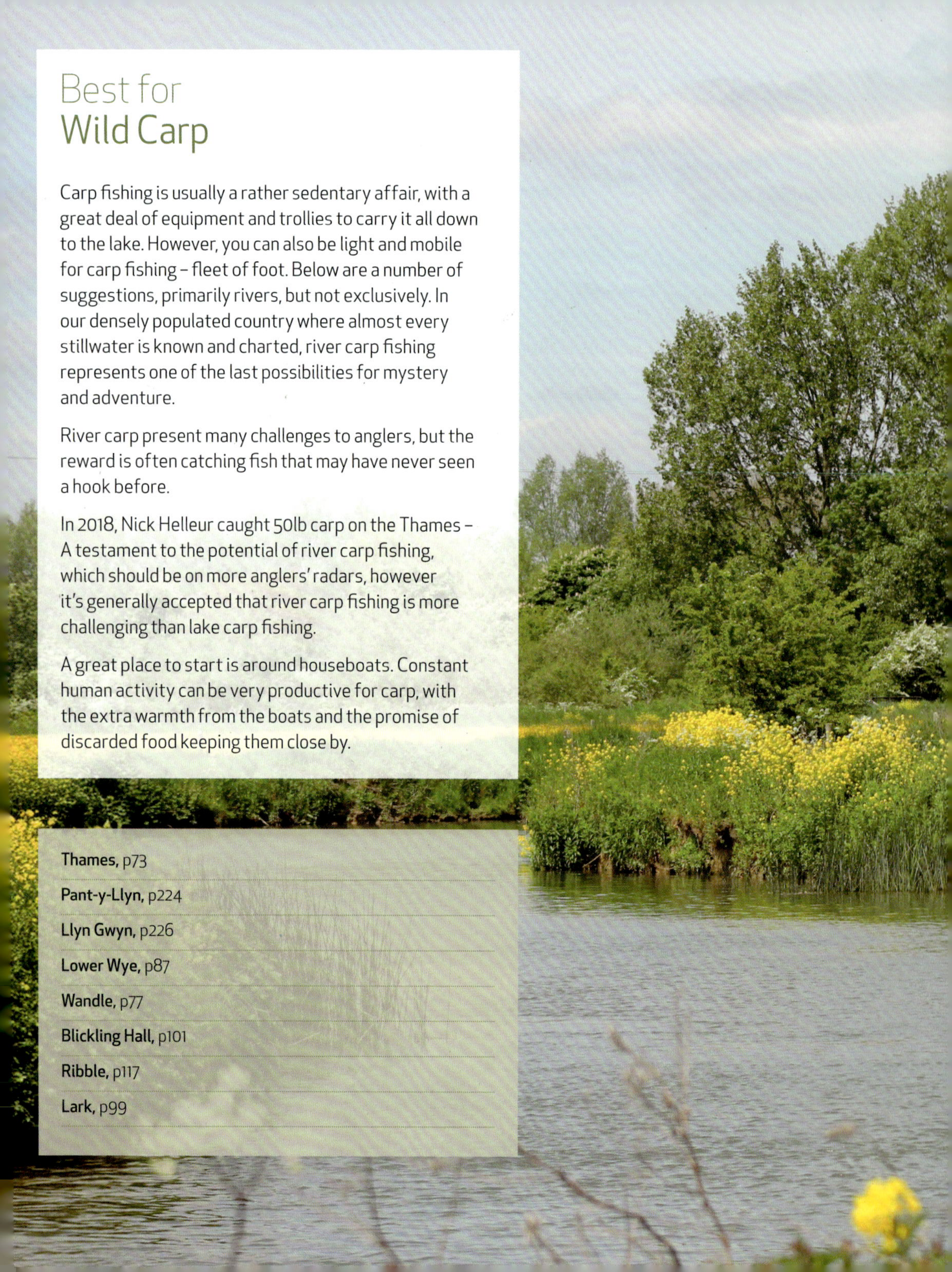

Best for
Wild Carp

Carp fishing is usually a rather sedentary affair, with a great deal of equipment and trollies to carry it all down to the lake. However, you can also be light and mobile for carp fishing – fleet of foot. Below are a number of suggestions, primarily rivers, but not exclusively. In our densely populated country where almost every stillwater is known and charted, river carp fishing represents one of the last possibilities for mystery and adventure.

River carp present many challenges to anglers, but the reward is often catching fish that may have never seen a hook before.

In 2018, Nick Helleur caught 50lb carp on the Thames – A testament to the potential of river carp fishing, which should be on more anglers' radars, however it's generally accepted that river carp fishing is more challenging than lake carp fishing.

A great place to start is around houseboats. Constant human activity can be very productive for carp, with the extra warmth from the boats and the promise of discarded food keeping them close by.

Thames, p73

Pant-y-Llyn, p224

Llyn Gwyn, p226

Lower Wye, p87

Wandle, p77

Blickling Hall, p101

Ribble, p117

Lark, p99

Thames, Oxfordshire, p73

Best for
Fishing Inns

What could be better than a hard but successful day's fishing, followed by retiring to a famous old fishing pub where you can regale the bar with your tales of angling derring-do? Perhaps not so great for those in the bar but certainly for you – provided they stay long enough to listen. And why shouldn't they? It is an angling pub, after all.

Few pleasures in life are as profound as soaking in a hot bath for an unfeasibly long time, reviewing your successes after tramping the banks of a remote river. That, and perfecting your fishing tale for the pub.

Most inns have guides on staff who, if you have deep enough pockets, are usually well worth the additional cost. They can put you on fish from the start, rather than you relying on your rivercraft. That said, rivercraft is, once you know it, relatively easy – to me, first and foremost on any river is the flow of foam, bringing food to the waiting fish. That's where they are.

All of the inns listed below offer superb fishing opportunities alongside a comfortable stay, although few offer budget fishing options. Instead, cheaper nearby rivers are listed in the relevant chapters.

The Arundell Arms, Lyd, Tamar, thearundell.com, p55

The Inn at Whitewell, Hodder, Innatwhitewell.com, p116

Trigony House, Nith, Dumfries, trigonyhouse.co.uk, p146

Alt Motel, Loch Borrallan, altnacealgachmotel.co.uk, p174

Bron y Graig, Llyn Brenig, bronygraig.com, p206

The Half Moon Inn, Devon, halfmoonsheepwash.co.uk, p55

Devonshire Arms, Wharfe, devonshirehotels.co.uk, p119

Dolffanog Fawr, Llyn Mwyngil, dolffanogfawr.co.uk, p205

The Peacock, Derbyshire, thepeacockatrowsley.com, p116

The Inn at Whitewell p116

Best for
Remote Beaches

Remote fishing beaches have their own rugged charm. The haunting quality of a beach that seems at the end of the world, with only you around is a lovely way to spend a day, or a week. While almost all beaches around the British Isles offer the opportunity to catch fish it is generally beaches that are steeply sloping and creating access to deeper water to cast into which are most productive. Shallower beaches generally yield fewer and smaller fish, such as flatfish species adapted to feed in very shallow water, along with undersized school bass. Like in all fishing, differentiation is key. Any obstruction is likely to be a source of interest to smaller sea creatures, and in turn, the fish that feed on them.

So, with that in mind, here is our list of the wild and rugged beaches where you can enjoy one of the most exciting fishing experiences in the UK. All this and it's free – aside from perhaps the odd car park charge.

Newport Beach, Nevern, p233

Cornwall & Devon

1

3

5

"There in the fen five rivers began," wrote Williamson in his 1927 classic *Tarka the Otter*, noting that these were the Taw, Torridge, Teign, Tavy, and Dart. For almost forty years, Ted Hughes, surely our greatest poet of Wild Fishing, called this area his home. The granite slab that bears Hughes's name was placed in the area where Dartmoor's rivers rise: the Taw, Dart, East Okement, and Teign. In all of England, nowhere else has the wealth of Wild Fishing that the South West has.

The main rivers, the Exe, Dart, and Camel, weave through the landscape, offering anglers a choice of fishing for brown trout, sea trout, and the occasional salmon. All this and excellent coarse fishing too, in spectacular countryside. The South West Lakes Trust has thousands of acres of water with fisheries ranging in size from two to 900+ acres, all affordable and all with exciting fishing, both coarse and game.

Devon has over 125 miles of rugged, rocky coastline, so almost all of the shore fishing here is from rocks. Due to the exposure to the Gulf Stream, the waters are warmer than most, which gives a greater choice of angling species for you to target. Whether you're after bass or mackerel with spinners or flies, or chasing rays with beach casting gear, the fish are all here. My favourite, the bass, are best fished for at night when they come closer to the shore, hoping (praying?) to avoid seabirds under the cover of darkness.

Cornwall, with its skinny landmass sandwiched between two seas, has over four hundred miles of coastline, most of which is suitable for beach fishing. Again, due to the Gulf Stream, Cornwall is regarded as having some of the best sea fishing in Europe. For me, beach fishing in Cornwall is mackerel (I can hear the purists howl), but really, who can beat the spectacle? Seabirds in screaming frenzies as they dive-bomb churning bait balls the size of a football pitch and you casting into the middle of it all. What could be better?

7

CORNWALL

1 DRIFT RESERVOIR

65-acre clear water Drift Reservoir is located in an area of outstanding natural beauty just two miles west of Penzance. The reservoir is stocked with rainbow and wild brown trout. During lulls in the action, keep an eye out for ospreys. They're infrequent visitors here, but they'll gladly show you how fishing should be done.

→ Permits can be obtained by the boathouse at the water. 50.1043, -5.586 £12 Fly, bait, spin, led RT

2 BUSSOW RESERVOIR

At seven acres and close to St. Ives, this is a peaceful carp fishery but ideal if you are holidaying in the South West. Carp over thirty pounds are here in these comparatively shallow waters. It's also teeming with coarse fish, so you needn't be limited to carp.

→ Swlakestrust.org.uk 50.1988, -5.5023 £10 Fly, bait, spin, led Carp, coarse

3 PRAA SANDS

This beach could be in the Caribbean with its long sweep of sandy beach. The best bet, we're told, for Praa Sands is frozen sand eels, the bigger the better. You could be lucky with a ray on this beach, but most likely you should expect a bass, or two.

→ Car Park immediately behind the beach. 50.1023, -5.3867 Free Beach Ray, bass

4 COBER/HELSTON

Medium-sized river running through the centre of Helston. The brown trout are around a pound in size and perch are here too. Apparently, the best place to fish is in the Lowertown area, over the stepping stones. These are free-rising trout, so the best bet is various dries, probably Klinkhammers. At least, that's what I would start with if there's no visible hatch.

→ The fairground car park would be best. 50.1109, -5.2614 Free Free BT, Pe

5 MULLION COVE

All you really need to enjoyably fish this and the rest of the Cornwall coast is a light lure rod and a 10lb line. You can catch mackerel and pollock around the wall and, occasionally, you can catch one of my favourite fish, the bass - although they are becoming less common.

→ The Mullion Cove car park is a 5-minute walk up Nannsmelleyon Road from the beach and it's far cheaper than the Mullion Cove NT car park. 50.0151, -5.2579 Free Shore Mackerel, pollock, bass

6 STITHIANS RESERVOIR

Situated in the darkest depths of Cornwall, the 274-acre reservoir offers some brilliant rainbow trout fishing, and there is also a good head of brown trout in the lake. Boats and float tubing are allowed, and day and season tickets are available. The season runs from March to the end of November.

→ Swlakestrust.org.uk 50.188, -5.2095 £25 Fly BT, RT

7 HELFORD ESTUARY

The lower Helford River is known for decent mullet and large bream. You can also catch various flatfish with good-sized plaice. Bass, pollock, and mackerel can also be caught in the river. However, if you are targeting bass, please be aware that Helford is a spawning area, and there is a size limit on estuarine bass of 36cm – you are not allowed to keep bass caught in the river under this size.

→ Helford car park is a short walk to the estuary. 50.0956, -5.1328 Free Shore Bass, pollock, mackerel

7

12

4

9

13

8 ARGAL RESERVOIR

Hidden in a valley just above Penryn, this 65-acre coarse fishing venue is situated close to the Cornish town of Falmouth. There are carp, pike, tench, bream, roach, rudd, perch, and eels in the lake, with carp going up to a massive 40lb in size. Day and season tickets are available. The pike fishing season runs from October to the end of February. It also has good provisions for disabled anglers.

→ Swlakestrust.org.uk 50.1528, -5.1338 £10 Fly, bait, spin, led Carp, coarse

9 COLLEGE RESERVOIR

This 40-acre reservoir is situated next door to Argal Lake and is run as a syndicate. There are carp, pike, bream, tench, perch, roach, and rudd present in the lake. Predominantly run as a carp syndicate through October to the end of February, 10 pike tickets a month are available. This water is home to 'The Secret' - 40lbs of carp in one enormous package.

→ Swlakestrust.org.uk 50.1606, -5.124 £10 Fly, bait, spin, led Carp, coarse

10 PERRANPORTH

Named after St. Pirin, the patron saint of Cornwall. You'll be sharing the beach with kite surfers, but it's several miles long, so you'll be fine. This area provides excellent bass beaches and all species of flatfish. In the autumn, you will also catch codling and whiting in this area.

→ The car park overlooks Perranporth beach and is called the car park on the promenade. 50.3517, -5.1569 Free Led Flatfish, codling, whiting

11 POLZEATH BEACH

If you have a sea kayak, this would be a great place to try. The beach is well exposed to swell, so launching is only possible in low swell but once out, you can expect to encounter bass and pollock towards and around Pentire Point and the occasional gilthead bream at the entrance to the River Camel.

→ The car park overlooks Polzeath Beach. 50.575, -4.9179 Free Shore/kayak Bass, pollock

12 CAMEL/TRESARRETT

A stunning section of the River Camel with six named, accessible pools providing excellent salmon and sea trout fishing. The beat also offers spectacular dry and nymph fly fishing for wild brown trout, with plenty of varied waters to be explored. I invariably prefer beats with varied waters because

10

11

18

15

22

it gives you more choice with our highly variable weather.

→ Fishpassapp.co.uk 50.5266, -4.6983 £12 Fly BT, ST, Sa

13 TALLAND BAY

A well-known spot for smugglers, according to local legend. Talland Bay is, in fact, two sheltered shingle beaches, Talland Sands and Rotterdam Beach. It has also been the scene of many shipwrecks, including that of a French trawler, the Marguerite, in March 1922. Good spinning for bass and bait fishing with sand eels works well too.

→ The car park overlooks Talland Bay. 50.3378, -4.4976 Free Shore Bass

14 INNY/COOMBE

An intimate and dynamic beat offering excellent small stream fly fishing for wild brown trout, grayling, and the occasional daytime sea trout. Much of this water is suited for close-range casting, but, apparently, almost all the other casts in your arsenal are required to cover the water fully, and you certainly should be open to wading to fully appreciate this delightful water.

→ Fishpassapp.co.uk 50.6238, -4.4803 £6 Fly BT, ST, Sa, Gr

15 COLLIFORD LAKE

The largest lake of The South West Lakes Trust portfolio. At a whopping 911 acres on Bodmin Moor, the lake offers some fantastic brown trout fishing. Surprisingly, to me at least, it's only an 8km hike around the entire perimeter. So you could cover all the bank water within a day. Day and season tickets are available for this venue. The season runs from 15th of March to 12th of October.

→ Swlakestrust.org.uk 50.5275, -4.593 £21 Fly BT

16 CROOKLETS BEACH

Victorian ladies used Crooklets Beach for bathing while the gentlemen were segregated to Summerleaze. The best time to fish is two hours before low water and on the incoming tide. Typically for skate and flatfish. You should also be able to pick up bass at night.

→ The car park overlooks Crooklets Beach. 50.8359, -4.554 Free Shore Skate, flatfish, bass

17 NEET/BUDE (URBAN ANGLING)

From the Rugby Club to the sea, you can fish here completely free. It's Urban Angling, but nothing wrong with that, and the price is excellent. You will be targeting trout

and mullet primarily, and all fishing styles are acceptable - ruling out dynamite and electricity, of course - or trout tickling, which I think is now illegal.

→ Crescent long-stay car park is best to fish the Neet. 50.8242, -4.5433 Free Fly, bait, spin, led Mullet, trout

18 UPPER TAMAR LAKE

An 81-acre venue situated on the Devon and Cornwall border. The bird life here is spectacular, including a Glossy Ibis - shouldn't they be in Florida? It is a prolific match, specimen carp, and big perch venue and is run by day ticket or season ticket. The species present are carp, bream, roach, rudd, perch, and eels. Carp to mid 30s, perch to near 5lb, and big bags of silvers can be expected.

→ Swlakestrust.org.uk 50.8801, -4.4353 £10 Fly, bait, spin, led Carp, eels, perch

19 LOWER TAMAR LAKE

A 35-acre reservoir that sits on the Devon and Cornwall border. It offers some truly amazing carp and bream fishing. Carp go well into the 30 pounds and there is a big head of double-figure bream. Good stocks of roach, perch, and rudd are also present in the lake. It can get weedy, so ideally, plan your visit with that in mind.

→ Swlakestrust.org.uk 50.8755, -4.4245 £12 Fly, bait, spin, led Carp, tench, eels

20 LYNHER/BERRIO MILL

This stretch of the Lynher has riffles and pocket water with occasional deep pools. Five of the pools are excellent holding water, creating the chance of sea trout and salmon through the season. The brown trout fishing is productive throughout the year but is at its best in May-July and again in September.

→ Fishpassapp.co.uk 50.5151, -4.3744 £6 Fly BT, ST, Sa, Gr

21 OTTERY/TAMAR, HAM MILL

A highly prolific brown trout river, with some anglers reportedly catching 26 in a session, which, given my angling skills, will never happen to me. You can also catch late season sea trout too. The river system is also very productive in supporting wildlife. It has everything you would expect to see, plus the lovely Marsh Fritillary butterfly.

→ Fishpassapp.co.uk 50.6571, -4.3476 £12 Fly BT, ST, Sa, Gr

22 LOWER DUTSON FARM

We chanced upon this delightful farm pool while photographing the nearby Tamar where we met Alfie and his dad, Dave. There is something so right about a father and son fishing together. I wish it was more common and that fathers took the time to pass on their fishing skills to their children. It's a great way to create lifelong memories.

→ lowerdutson.co.uk 50.6515, -4.3447 £12 Bait Coarse, carp

23 KENSEY/ST. LEONARDS

Small river which needs to be fished with a small rod. You'll be targeting brown trout in gorgeous surroundings in a lightly coloured river which fishes best after some rain to bring the water levels up a notch. The deeper parts generally hold the larger fish who tend to hold on the riverbed.

→ Fishpassapp.co.uk 50.6393, -4.3349 £6 Fly BT, ST, Gr

24 TAMAR/NETHERBRIDGE

This is a classic stretch of the middle Tamar, with long runs and large pools. Netherbridge generally experiences a prolonged and plentiful mayfly hatch, with notable caddis and midge hatches too. In May, salmon can be caught almost anywhere in the Tamar system.

→ Fishpassapp.co.uk 50.65, -4.3349 £12 Fly BT, ST, Sa, Gr

26

31

25

WOOLADON
ARUNDELL ARMS
FISHING
BEATS 7A, 7B
& 8A
26

30

DEVON

25 CAREY/MIDDLE BRIDGE

The river is not overly wide (10-20ft) and is relatively shallow, meaning lighter tackle is favourable. To fish this beat, we recommend using the various small access points into the river to fish individual pools, or wade freely up or downstream to cover all the water. However, you'll cover more river if you zip in and out of the access points.

→ Fishpassapp.co.uk 50.7103, -4.3086 £6 Fly BT, ST, Sa, Gr

26 THRUSHEL/ARUNDELL ARMS

Ah, The Arundel Arms. The inn, I feel, is an exemplar of how to do commercial wild fishing correctly. Not expensive, great waters and knowledgeable staff who 'get it'. Great waters, great people, great part of the world. The Thrushel has good brown trout pools and sea trout pools between the two bridges. Fine for wading.

→ Thearundell.com 50.6458, -4.2732 £45 Fly BT, ST, Sa

27 ROADFORD LAKE

Weighing in at an impressive 738 acres, Roadford Lake is a renowned brown trout fishery. It's fed by the River Wolf, which is a good wild fishing spot in its own right. Boats and float tubing are available. The lake is run on day tickets and season tickets. The season runs from 15th of March to 12th of October. The Wolf is always a good bet when the weather turns nasty.

→ Swlakestrust.org.uk 50.6952, -4.2379 £21 Fly BT

28 BAGGY POINT

This can be a dangerous place to fish in poor weather but in good weather it's spectacular. You need to be as nimble as a mountain goat to access the best fishing marks here, and, again, this should never be attempted in bad weather. You have a plethora of fish species to target, too innumerable to list here. Mackerel, bass, and pollock are the favourites.

→ The NT car park overlooks Baggy Point. 51.1432, -4.2605 Free Shore Mackerel, Bass, Pollock

29 JENNETTS RESERVOIR

Big carp water. You can, if the Fishing Gods are with you, catch multiple twenty-pound carp here in a single day, with even larger, over thirty-pounders, turning up occasionally. The fish can be caught off the bottom or the surface. There are also significant tench here, up to 8lb.

→ Swlakestrust.org.uk 51.0008, -4.2192 £12 Fly, Spin, Dead Bait Carp, tench, roach

30 TORRIDGE/ROTHERN BRIDGE

The beat offers the chance of an early salmon or a sea trout throughout the season and also has some large brown trout. Good old Bernard Venables wrote: "The Torridge has a beauty of a special Devon kind, to enchant and still a troubled mind. In its deep valley, under the tree-hung crests, there is a seclusion as gently rurally perfect as is to be found in England". Sounds about right.

→ Fishpassapp.co.uk 50.958, -4.17 £12 Fly BT, ST, Sa

31 LYD/ARUNDELL ARMS – BEAT 19

Lovely water, heavily wooded, deep in a typical Devon valley. You'll fish this 1.5-mile beat all day. Careful, it can be slippery on the rocks. But deeply tranquil, apart from your occasional curse when you slip on a rock (which you will). We've seen reports of Ephemera Danica hatching here. Never seen it ourselves but for the lucky few...

→ Thearundell.com 50.6292, -4.1588 £45 Fly BT, Gr, ST, Sa

38

37

40

32 TAVY/TAVISTOCK (URBAN ANGLING)

Free as per Tavistock council from the Plymouth bridge to the Packhorse Bridge at Vigo Street. Some good pools here and, during a spate, you'll have company from the locals. Typically, everybody is worming or spinning. Flies would obviously work too.

→ Whitchurch Road parking is the closest to the Tavy. 50.5471, -4.146 Free Fly, bait, spin, led BT, ST

33 PLYM/CAD

The Cad is best fished from late May/early June onward, with upstream dry and duo set-ups being particularly effective, although deep pockets of fast water are also good for modern nymphing styles. Later on in the season, you might want to try plopping a terrestrial in with a big splash, just as if it's been blown onto the water.

→ Fishpassapp.co.uk 50.4541, -4.0672 £12 Fly BT, ST, Sa

34 BURRATOR RESERVOIR

A 150-acre reservoir that offers some fantastic rainbow trout fishing, with the odd wild brown trout thrown in as well. Boats can be booked, and float tubing is available too. Tickets for this are either day or season tickets. The season runs from March to the end of November. I wouldn't want to float tube too late into the season; it can get very cold.

→ Swlakestrust.org.uk 50.4986, -4.0432 £25 Fly BT, RT

35 YEALM

This is a lovely beat which combines two distinct sections of water. The upper section displays typical moorland river features, with a mix of runs and pools suiting dry fly/nymph fishing. The lower section is more open and has five holding pools which provide good brown trout and, with the right water, excellent sea trout fishing.

→ Fishpassapp.co.uk 50.396, -3.9697 £15 Fly BT, ST, Sa

36 COWSIC

It features a number of baffles which have created long smooth glides, ideal for dry flies as they bob down the river. It can be tough walking, we're told, so, again we're told, start upstream first - it's easier. Flies have got to be small, as you would imagine, 14 would be the largest and progressively going ever smaller until neither you nor the fish can see them.

→ Westcountryangling.com 50.5606, -3.9706 £12 Fly BT

37 WEST DART

Somewhat larger than the East Dart but offering the same idyllic fishing. Gorgeous open countryside unfurling mile after mile. Good opportunity to fish a small rod set-up, 3 or 4 weight. Stealth is the name of the game here, I assume it's apocryphal, or at least I hope so, but we've been told that wthe fish scarper as soon as they hear a car door slam.

→ Westcountryangling.com 50.5585, -3.9659 £12 Fly BT

38 BLACKABROOK

Good wild brown trout fishing, with the best fishing lying between the West Dart and the Oakery Bridge. Classic open moorland fishing, with hard-won angling involving small and spooky trout. There's no point fishing unless you're prepared to really embrace the ethos of staying far, far back and very, very quiet.

→ Westcountryangling.com 50.5514, -3.9411 £12 Fly BT

39 WALKHAM RIVER

For a weekly permit price of £15, you can fish five beats on the River Walkham, which is an excellent way to spend your week in the South West. Be on your toes when dry fly fishing here, the takes are immediate and if you doze off the fish will be gone. You can also, on the same permit, fish the Egg River, a tumbling, rough and ready brook that used to provide hydroelectricity and now, when the time is right, supports sea trout.

→ Twpfishing.net 50.5561, -4.0334 £15 Fly, Spin BT

40 CHERRYBROOK

The best-known trout fishery in Dartmoor. One you simply must fish. The Cherrybrook and the other Duchy waters are frequently written about by angling writers such as Mike Weaver and Pete Tyjas, and the salmon fishing by Charles Bingham.

→ Westcountryangling.com 50.5766, -3.9304 £12 Fly BT

41 UPPER EAST DART (POSTBRIDGE)

Miles upon miles of wonderful brown trout fishing set in moorland. Really, what more could you ask for? Can be boggy and tricky to hop across the river after wet weather. We normally stick to the bridges when it's been raining. It's exceedingly windswept up here, so casting can be tricky.

→ Westcountryangling.com 50.5943, -3.9114 £12 Fly BT

34

36

42

43

42 TAW RIVER (STICKLEPATH)

In the local pub, the regulars talk about catching small brown trout in their youth on the Taw which runs just outside but nobody seems to be doing it now. Get down there and fish, we suggest. This is a lovely tumbling stream and would repay somebody taking the time to clamber over the rocks and down into the dells to see what they can catch.

→ Plenty of parking on the road in Sticklepath. 50.7295, -3.9255 Free Fly BT

43 WALLABROOK

A small tributary with difficult fishing for wild and frequently spooked brown trout. You need to creep up on 'em. Small flies are crucial and no splashy presentations. Fish fine and far off. The lightest leader you dare and, obviously, small rods. The fish you will catch here will be memorable and the equivalent of a six-pounder, or more, in a stocked lake.

→ Westcountryangling.com 50.5908, -3.8811 £12 Fly BT

44 FERNWORTHY RESERVOIR

A 78-acre brown trout-only reservoir situated in the stunning Dartmoor National Park. The lake is run on either day or season tickets, and float tubing is allowed on this venue with prior permission. The season runs from the 15th of March to the 12th of October. If you want to indulge your inner antiquarian, the Fernworthy Cairn Circle and Fernworthy Assycombe Stone Row are awaiting your inspection.

→ Swlakestrust.org.uk 50.64, -3.8845 £21 Fly BT, RT

45 LITTLE DART/BLUE FOX GLADE

Usually lightly fished, this secluded stretch has a nice mix of riffles, runs, and some lovely big pools. Trout fishing is mainly what you'll be doing here, but you have a chance of a sea trout or even possibly a salmon, given good water, which means after some rain to bring the water level up.

→ Fishpassapp.co.uk 50.8987, -3.8446 £6 Fly BT, ST

46 WATERSMEET

Lovely spot where you can fish for trout, salmon, and sea trout. The National Trust have a list of regulations which will need to be followed. Gorgeous scenery and abundant wildlife are here to keep you occupied. They're keen that you fish with barbless hooks to minimise harm to the fish.

→ Nationaltrust.org.uk 51.2234, -3.7997 £15 Fly, bait, spin, led BT, ST, Sa

47 HOPE COVE

Fish with live prawns and little gobies under a float, and you'll have a great time catching pollock, wrasse, and maybe a bass, or two. The wrasse fishing is excellent here, but you must expect to lose some tackle. It's a cost of fishing this spot (and many other UK coastal spots). If you're not losing tackle, you're not fishing hard enough.

→ Hope by-pass is the closest to Hope Cove. 50.2486, -3.8597 Free Shore Pollock, Wrasse, Bass

48 UPPER TEIGN

The Upper Teign is comprised of a delightful mix of pools, glides, and riffles and, although good nymph water, the dry fly is king once things get going. The best time for brown trout is considered to be May and June. We've heard it can be a phenomenally productive fishery with anglers catching sixty fish in a few hours.

→ Fishpassapp.co.uk 50.6792 -3.8344 £15 Fly BT

49 TEIGN/FINGLE BRIDGE

Sea trout fishing is best in late spring and throughout summer, with night-time fly fishing accounting for most of the fish. But you can fish for, and expect to catch, wild brown trout in all their glory throughout the day and fishing season here. Lovely spot and great angling.

→ Upper-teign-fishing.org.uk 50.6953, -3.781 £25 Fly BT

50 GAMMONS HEAD BEACH

It's a trek to get down to this site, but worth it. People have been fishing and farming in the immediate area for thousands of years and it feels like it. It has a feel of permanence. Excellent bass fishing on a lure, surface, or sub-surface, depending on the tide. Best avoided during peak tourist season as it can get quite crowded.

→ East Prawle car park is closest but it's a bit of a walk. 50.2052, -3.7131 Free Shore Beach

51 TRENCHFORD RESERVOIR

Excellent pike fishing. The reservoir is very deep in places, and there are plenty of large features for the pike to hide in and around, all the better to ambush their prey. Fish up to and over 30lbs have been reported. I doubt I would fly fish these waters for pike; they're just too large, but spinning would be marvellous.

→ Fishpassapp.co.uk 50.63, -3.691 £9 Spinner, Deadbait Pike, Pe

52 HOPES NOSE

A well-known mark that allows short casting into deep water. This can get too popular when the fish are running, and the local council has been paying attention, meaning there are restrictions on how many mackerel can be kept. It's a hike to get here from your car, so bear this in mind when you plan your trip.

→ The Harbour car park is closest to Hopes Nose, but it is a bit of a walk. 50.4635, -3.4807 Free Shore Mackerel

53 BERRY HEAD

The UK record shore-caught mackerel was landed near here in Berry Head Quarry in 1982. It was almost six pounds. I don't know anybody who targets specimen mackerel, but this would appear to be a very good place to do it. If I were a specimen mackerel hunter, this is where I would start my campaign.

→ Dedicated Berry Head car park on Gillard Road. 50.3997, -3.4827 Free Shore Mackerel

54 CULM/CHAMPERHAIES

This beat of the River Culm provides good brown trout fishing during the spring and summer and usually produces fish over 1lb. There is also a lovely mix of coarse fish present, with chub, dace, roach, perch, and pike all year round. So, year-round sport in one location: provided you can locate them.

→ Fishwwsapp.co.uk 50.8282, -3.4017 £9 Fly BT, ST, Sa, Gr, Pe, Pike

55 TALE/ESCOT PARK

The clean, non-silted gravels in this wonderful little river of glides and deep pools support a significant number of river invertebrates, with cadd is, mayflies, and stoneflies being commonplace. Great fly fishing in all levels of the water column. I would probably start with a dry and see how I got on. Reverting to wets and nymphs only if required.

→ Fishpassapp.co.uk 50.7767, -3.2998 £9 Fly BT

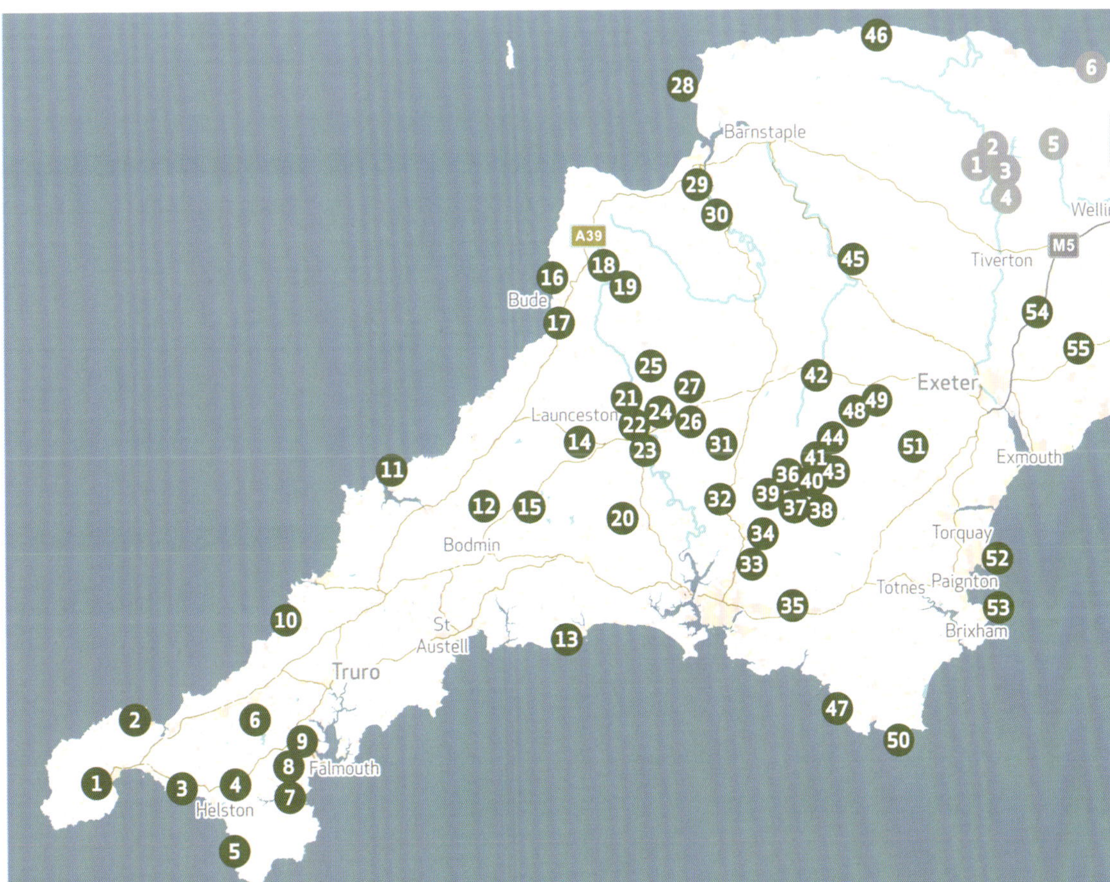

Somerset & Dorset

Famous for the Somerset Levels, which in recent years attracted national publicity when they were severely flooded, Somerset offers the angler sea fishing along its northern coastline on the Severn Estuary and the Bristol Channel, as well as river fishing for trout and coarse fish in its rivers, lakes, reservoirs, canals, and commercial fisheries. In addition to the River Avon, Somerset's truly wild fishing rivers include the Axe, Brue, Chew, Cary, Parrett, Sheppey, Tone, and Yeo.

In Dorset, Chesil Beach is one of the best shore fishing destinations in England, with anglers travelling from all over the country to fish from its shingle banks. During the weekends, you'll see tents lined along the shore as people fish through the day and into the night. So, if you want the wild fishing experience, go to the same place but during the week; it's far, far quieter. You can see why weekend anglers cram the banks. Thanks to deep shelving ledges just metres from the shoreline, the water is extremely deep and can be fished at any stage of the tide. This means it throws up a mixed bag of species and has been responsible for some record-breaking fish in recent years. One of the biggest ever shore-caught English fish was landed on Chesil Beach in 2015. It was a w weighing in at a whopping 78.6lbs. Not only was it caught, but it was also released back carefully into the water, unharmed. Take a bow, Mr Guy Spriggs. A true gent.

There are several rivers of note to tempt the wild angler to Dorset, with plenty of opportunities for trout fishing, including the River Frome, the Tarrant, the Allen, and the River Piddle (which is also, more politely, known as the Trent or North River). Using the Piddle as an example for the wild fishing in Dorset, you can expect to fish for trout but also sea trout and occasionally salmon. The Piddle's fly life is superb, with the best of the fishing starting with early Olives and Hawthorns, followed by the Mayfly. It picks up again in the autumn, with late hatches of Olives and Sedges.

SOMERSET

1 BARLE

The Dulverton Association does not promise you manicured banks for your money, but this is gorgeous Wild Fishing. The Barle here is a very attractive water with a number of large pools and broken passages. Both a downstream nymph or upstream dry can be very effective and often result in a good number of offers and fish caught. Many of these tend to be in the 4 to 6-inch category, but there are also some bigger brown trout hovering around.

→ Dulvertonanglingassociation.org.uk
51.0387, -3.5526 £35/year Fly
BT, Gr, Sa

2 EXE

The Exe has three beats on this permit. At 2km in length, the Hollam is the longest of the DAA beats, and with its variety of pools, riffles and glides, it provides some challenging but rewarding fishing. The flies recommended, apart from the usual GRHE and Pheasant Tails, include a Copper John, sized 14-16.

→ Dulvertonanglingassociation.org.uk
51.0397, -3.5231 £35/year Fly
BT, Gr, Sa

3 HADDEO RIVER

A wildly diverse river. We're told you're just as likely to catch a salmon smolt as a brownie. Sounds good to us. Wading is easy, and a short rod is best. Due to the dam holding back the water, it's probably best not to fish this water during a long, dry spell, unless it's so hot you would welcome a dunking.

→ Dulvertonanglingassociation.org.uk
51.0286, -3.5183 £35/year Fly
BT, Gr, Sa

4 BATHERM/WESTONS

This attractive beat runs through open pasture and is probably best approached with a short 7-8ft 3/4 weight rod; wading is required to access some of the deeper pools and runs. Otters are here: some relish fishing in their footsteps, others less so.

→ Fishpassapp.co.uk 50.9921, -3.4811
£6 Fly BT, Ga

5 CLATWORTHY RESERVOIR

We're told the trout in this reservoir are always looking up and most of the time can be found cruising just under the surface. A well-presented dry fly is often enough to produce a take. The area near the dam is popular with boat anglers, especially during summer when lots of fish gather in this area.

→ Wessexwater.co.uk/fishing 51.0715, -3.3685 £10 Fly BT, RT

6 ST. AUDRIE'S BAY

A pebble and rock beach, muddy in parts. Expect codling and bass. Most anglers choose to fish at high tide from the main pebble beach, which offers comfortable fishing and casting to a reasonably clean ground. Also, there is a remarkable waterfall. After fishing, if you have time, step into the waterfall and feel its mist, or strip off for a cold bracing shower.

→ The Home Farm Holiday Centre overlooking St. Audrie's Bay has inexpensive P&D parking for day visitors. 51.1833, -3.2791 Free Beach Codling, bass

7 HAWKRIDGE RESERVOIR

A smaller reservoir stocked with almost all known varieties of trout on these shores; rainbows, browns, tigers, golden and blue trout. It's an angling lucky dip. Not truly wild because it's stocked but still great fun to attempt to catch the various varieties. We

19

8

13

shouldn't be too po-faced about Wild Fishing.
→ wessex-water-fishing 51.1199, -3.1335 £10 Fly BT, RT, tiger, blue

8 TONE/TAUNTON (URBAN ANGLING)

We accessed the water via a small walkway beside Dunelm. Delightful, reed-fringed water, well worth visiting. Most riverine species are present and, we're told, salmon have been caught up to 5lb. Fishing to the rear of Dunelm is a peaceful and delightful spot. We saw a kingfisher too, which always heightens the fishing experience.

→ Taunton station is very close to the Tone. 51.0201, -3.0929 Free Fly, bait, spin, led BT, chub, barbel, roach

9 PARRET RIVER

Lovely little club that have their annual membership set at a bargain £20. Or, the £4 day ticket will have you fishing on the River Parret. Expect to catch skimmer bream, chub and perch. Maggots seem to be the bait of choice. At Bow Bridge, a massive 6lb plus chub was caught. It might be worth bringing a fly rod too. It seems a good opportunity to fly fish for coarse species.

→ Langportaa.com 51.0354, -2.8307 £4 Fly, bait, spin, led Coarse

10 STOLFORD BEACH

Backed by a storm bank of pebbles, with the lower shore consisting of bands of shale and limestone. This is a well-known cod area, but you can also find Thornback rays, whiting, pouting, poor cod and smoothhounds. Bass are in the warm water outlets too. It's also a good spot for fossils, so keep an eye out while fishing.

→ Stolford sea front car park overlooks Stolford Beach. 51.2082, -3.1054 Free Beach Cod, rays, smoothound

11 DURLEIGH RESERVOIR

Apparently, this reservoir was built to provide water for the newly built British Cellophane factory in 1938. Durleigh Reservoir is renowned as a superb carp water with both mirror and common carp available to be caught. Although fishing is not allowed from the dam wall, anglers can fish from both banks where the water is as deep as 26ft.

→ Wessexwater.co.uk/fishing 51.1199, -3.0387 £12.50 Spinner, bait Carp

12 HUNTSPILL RIVER

This venue became quite famous during the '80s and early '90s for the national competitions held here. There were some huge shoals of bream, and bags in excess of 100lb were quite common. Although the bream are not as prolific as they were in the venue's heyday, there are still reports of very good catches. If bream aren't your thing, you could do well here targeting perch, or even pike.

→ Bridgwaterangling.co.uk 51.1995, -2.9957 £6 Fly, bait, spin, led Coarse

13 BRUE RIVER

A wonderful, mature river: the fishing feels really wild. Roving along the beats with a worm set up, casting to the large perch this river holds, can be a perfect day's sport. There are, of course, other fish here too; chub, roach and bream being dominant.

→ Fishinginsomerset.com 51.1821, -2.8125 £45/year Fly, bait, spin, led Coarse

14 SHEPPEY RIVER

There are some double-figure carp and pike in these waters. Often, fish from the River Brue will wander up to the Sheppey to eat, so it's well worth spending some time here. You should expect to encounter chub, roach, bream and perch. It's a lovely spot to while away a few hours.

→ Fishinginsomerset.com 51.1893, -2.6966 £45/year Fly, bait, spin, led Coarse

15 LADYE BAY

Park on the road overlooking the bay, which in turn is overlooked by grand Victorian houses. Near the turnaround at the top of the road are small stone steps leading down to the bay. Slippery rocks and strong currents make for a daunting mix, so be careful. Dogfish, rays, codling and flounder are the main quarry.

→ When we've visited, we've parked along the road. 51.4516, -2.852 Free Shore Dogfish, rays, codling

16 CHEW RIVER

The name Chew apparently has Celtic origins that means 'the moving, gushing water'. Seems apt. The water is mainly fly only but at certain times of the year, other methods can be employed. This means you can target many species with your fly.

→ Bathampton.org 51.3801, -2.5085 £40/year Fly BT, Gr, coarse

17 CHEW RIVER/KEYNSHAM

Another good trotting water with the additional benefit of being free, provided you fish at the Keynsham Memorial Park. A lot of chub here but also plenty of other species too. Roach and dace appear to be dominant alongside the chub.

→ Keynsham train station is very close to the Chew. 51.4148, -2.4948 Free Fly, bait, spin, led Coarse

18 KENNET & AVON CANAL

The club has some eight miles of fishing on this water. I'm not sure why I don't feature more canals in this book. Provided you're prepared to walk a little, you can fish in gorgeous surroundings and in splendid isolation. There are large fish in here; roach to 2lbs, bream to 5lbs, tench to 3lbs and perch to 4lbs plus. There are also some very big chub in the Claverton area, and quality carp to 20lbs plus.

→ Bathampton.org 51.361, -2.309 £40/year Fly, bait, spin, led Coarse

19 AVON/CLAVERTON

Good trotting waters above and below Bath, with a variety of species on the Avon. The Avon is teeming with fish; bream, chub, roach, carp, pike, barbel, perch, tench, trout and dace. Good fishing all year round and there are some specimen fish to try for here.

→ Bathampton.org 51.3747, -2.3001 £40/year Fly, bait, spin, led Coarse

20 BOX BROOK

The Box, or By Brook, is a tributary of the Bristol Avon. The only maintenance work that we could see was access to the river: perfect. True Wild Fishing. A lovely spring-fed limestone river, supporting an abundance of insect life with (usually) an amazing mayfly hatch and a thriving population of free-rising wild trout.

→ Bathampton.org 51.4076, -2.2862 £40/year Fly BT, Gr

21 FROME RIVER/RODDEN MEADOW

We know very little about this small fishing beat on the river Frome at Rodden Meadow, but it looks attractive. This ancient meadow has supported Frome in its textile business, with sheep grazing and teasel cultivation. We believe the fishing here to be free, at least we can't find the owner. It would be best to contact Frome town council to make sure.

→ Frometowncouncil.gov.uk 51.2322, -2.3147 Free Fly, bait, spin, led BT, Gr, coarse

27

DORSET

22 SUTTON BINGHAM RESERVOIR

The remains of Sutton Mill lurk under the water here while you fish. Both bank and boat fishing for brown trout and rainbows is available. Yes, it's stocked but it's very well done and in lovely surroundings. Fish at around 2lb are the most common but you might chance upon something much larger too.

→ wessex-water-fishing 50.9003, -2.6315 £10 Fly BT, RT

23 STOUR/CUT MILL

This is a delightful and serene place to fish away from the madding crowd. You might encounter the occasional walker following the Stour Valley Way, and good luck to them - it's 64 miles long. All the usual coarse species are here waiting to inspect your angling enticements. They'll let you know what they think of your presentations.

→ S-haa.co.uk 50.9486, -2.3174 £5 Fly, bait, spin, led Coarse

24 STOUR/FIDDLEFORD MILL POOL

The banks of Fiddleford Mill Pool can be slippery in the winter, or after heavy rain. Be cautious. The pool is good for perch, roach, dace, bream, chub and pike. It can throw up the odd surprise: hard-fighting carp or tench, but these are rare exceptions.

→ S-haa.co.uk 50.9215, -2.2848 £5 Fly, bait, spin, led Coarse

25 STOUR/LEAZE

This is a lightly fished stretch which can be very productive with good deep pools. Given the size of the beat, it's well worth walking a distance to locate the fish. There are big roach, chub and perch here, with very large pike mixed in. Given its lightly fished, it's a good opportunity to see if you can bag a specimen pike.

→ Christchurchac.org.uk 50.7999, -1.9964 £70/week Fly, bait, spin, led Coarse

26 ALLEN/WIMBORNE MINSTER (URBAN)

Very little fly life has been observed, but it's a good mixed chalk stream fishery. With trout around half a pound and grayling, chub and dace too. Given the lack of obvious fly life, I would spin these waters or worm. I love worm fishing and regard it as a neglected art.

→ All accessible spots through Rising Sun pub to Walford Bridge. 50.7981, -1.9854 Free Fly, bait, spin, led BT, Gr, dace, chub

27 CHESIL BEACH

The scene of many shipwrecks, Chesil Beach was named "Dead Man's Bay" by Thomas Hardy, in his usual romantic fashion. Nowadays, this eighteen-mile strip of land is better known for fishing. A huge range of species can be caught here. Cod and big whiting are caught in the winter, along with flounder. Summer sees smooth-hound, thornback rays, Dover sole and gurnards. Pouting and dogfish can be caught all year round, and other species which can be caught here include triggerfish, turbot, brill, scad, dab and bull huss. The area around the Dragon's Teeth (anti-tank defences left over from the Second World War) is a top winter cod mark.

→ Chesil Beach car park is next to Portland Castle. 50.631, -2.5662 Free Shore Rays, sole, turbot, brill

28 MAN O' WAR BEACH

Not named after the jellyfish as you would expect but named after the cliff face which, apparently, resembles 17th-century warships. You're sheltered from the wind here, which is a blessing, but it is snaggy, so be philosophical about equipment losses. Expect conger eels, mackerel on feathers, or bass. As usual, early morning, or evening, is the best.

32

30

28

→ Durdle Door car park is a short walk up the coastal path to Man O'War beach. 50.6225, -2.2726 Free Shore Bass, congers, mackerel

29 ST. ALDHELM'S HEAD

To fish here successfully, you'll be scrambling over rocks, so don't bother coming in bad weather; it's not worth the barked shins (or worse). Using spinners and plugs for bass and pollock can be very productive here, and some very good wrasse take float-fished worm and mackerel baits.

→ Best bet is to park at Renscombe, a brisk walk of 2000 metres to St. Aldhelm's Head. 50.5792, -2.0579 Free Shore Bass, congers, mackerel

30 DANCING LEDGE

A great spot to fish from shore, but use light equipment. You'll be spinning for bass here and a good job too. The bottom is hungry for fishing equipment and makes it almost impossible to contemplate any other kind of fishing. Stick with spinning for bass, or float fishing.

→ The Spyway car park is probably best to park at. It's 1000 metres from Dancing Ledge. 50.5915, -2.0058 Free Shore Bass

31 AVON/THE ROYALTY

This is one of the main mixed fisheries in the UK. You can catch salmon here and also barbel - but really most species are present. It's the sort of place every angler should fish at least once in his life. It's a special experience, especially if you land one of the specimen barbel, or a salmon.

→ southernfisheries.com 50.7385, -1.7788 £25-£75 Fly, bait, spin, led BT, Sa, ST, coarse

32 CHRISTCHURCH HARBOUR

Two rivers, the Avon and the Stour, flow into the Harbour at its northwest corner. The harbour is generally shallow and due to the tidal harmonics in the English Channel, has a double high water on each tide. An area of Special Scientific Interest, Christchurch Harbour offers some of the best sea trout fishing in England, and even the occasional salmon! Other species are specimen mullet, and it's a very high-quality bass fishery too.

→ swlakestrust.org.uk 50.7215, -1.7532 £21 Shore Mullet, ST, bass

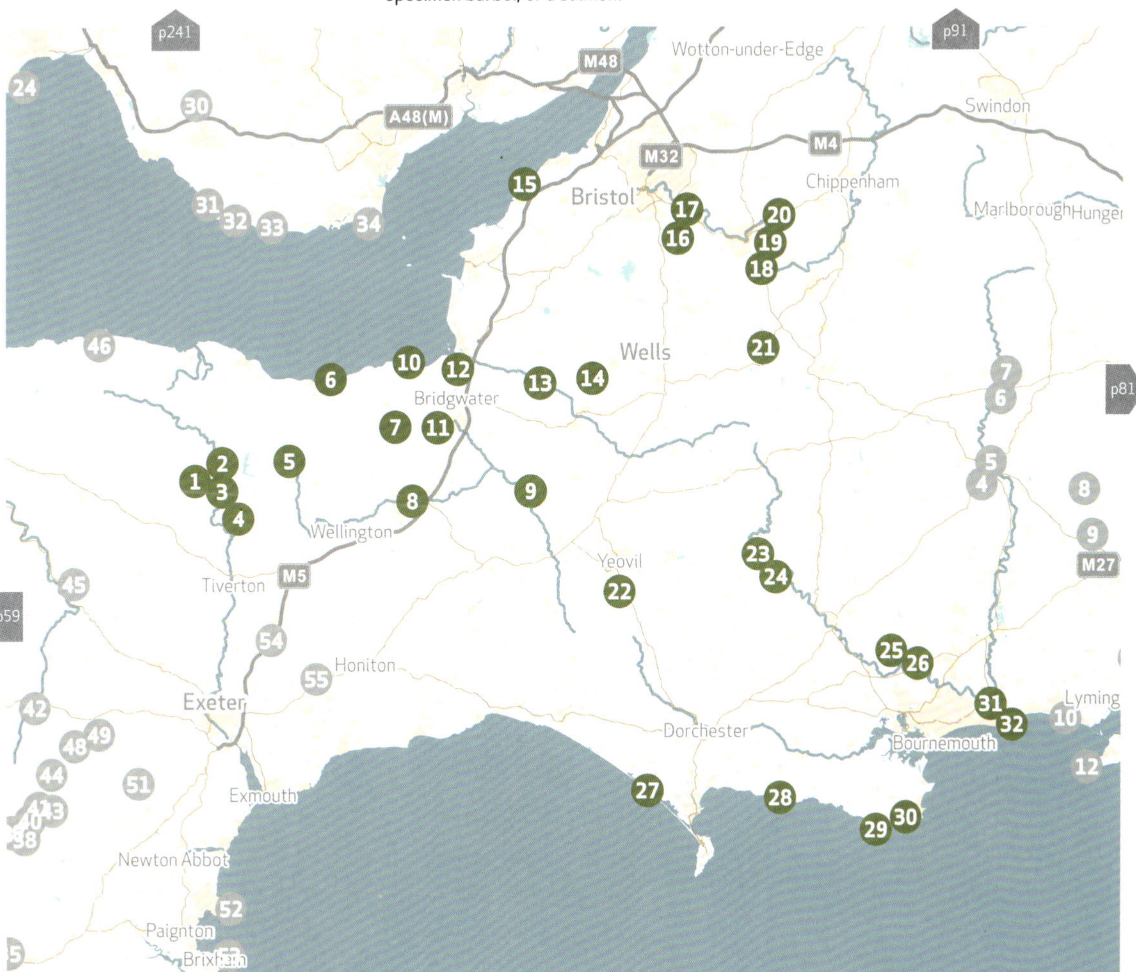

Southern England

All anglers know that Hampshire is the home of chalk streams. All anglers also know that F.W. Halford developed, codified, and promoted the dry fly fishing code on these streams, which then swept around the world. Fewer people know that Halford, this staunch Victorian, as stiff as a board in his starched shirt and fishing tie, went under the pseudonym "Detached Badger," which sounds like a 1970s prog rock group.

The fancy-dan rivers, Test and Itchen, with their manicured lawns, rusticated fishing huts and stocked trout, are outside the purview of this book. Mottisfont on the River Test is regarded as the birthplace of fly fishing by some, although the wild, northern river anglers have a more substantial claim. And I've even read that Halford was copying anglers on the Wandle in London, who were fishing with dry flies long before his books came out.

Although there are few natural lakes in Wiltshire, the county has several diverse rivers, including the River Kennet, a classic chalk stream which rises on the Marlborough Downs near Silbury Hill, the Bristol Avon which flows west to the Bristol Channel, and the Hampshire Avon which rises in the Vale of Pewsey and carves its way through Salisbury Plain. In addition to the Kennet and the two River Avons, there are several tributaries which provide some of the best wild trout fishing in England, with the River Nadder, the River Bourne, the Ebble, and the River Lambourn all providing opportunities for anglers.

The entire region of Surrey, Sussex, and Kent is in the thrall of the Great Wen, London. Yet even here nature and wilderness peek through. In the very heart of the sprawling metropolis, you can practise wild fishing on the Thames at London Bridge. An oasis of calm surrounded by the hubbub of metropolitan life. A record ten-pound trout was hauled out of the Thames at Putney in 2012 – proof that the river is coming back to life. Venturing slightly further away, the ponds at Hampstead Heath can be productively fished, and Epping Forest is a delight with fishing for carp, roach, and perch in romantic, solitary splendour. Best of all, in our opinion, is the Wandle, offering chalk stream fishing of high quality, where you can fish in Nelson's footsteps.

As we venture out, rod in hand, to try our luck in the great suburbs surrounding London: Sussex, Surrey, and Kent, we could despair at finding truly wild fishing. However, while the suggestions within this section are not full-on wild fishing, they represent an excellent day's fishing and great fun.

5

BERKSHIRE

1 EMM BROOK/WOKINGHAM

Small brook that holds an array of coarse fish which connects to the River Loddon. All methods of fishing here are welcome, and it's free. It's usually quite overgrown, so it's difficult fishing, but during the winter months when the vegetation dies down, the river opens up.

→ Winnersh train station is very close to the Emm river. 51.4107, -0.85 Free Fly, bait, spin, led Coarse

2 THAMES/SONNING

Deeply lovely spot but due to its proximity to London is difficult to get a peaceful day's fishing. Further, it's very popular with the boating community, so your fishing will, at the wrong times, be interrupted by pleasure barges and the local boys doing depth charges from the bridge. To the admiration of the local girls.

→ Gov.uk/guidance/river-thames-lock-and-weir-fishing 51.476, -0.9132 £34/year Fly, bait, spin, led Coarse

3 PANG RIVER

Small free-rising brown trout on a beautiful chalk stream, with plenty of insect life. You can catch both rainbow and brown trout. As far as I'm aware, you can fly fish how you like. So, for a change, perhaps you could forget Halford and his strictures and go American and fish a nymph downstream. Cast to the far bank and let the fly swing around, occasionally lifting the rod as it does so. Deadly.

→ Barnelmsfishery.co.uk 51.4538, -1.1215 £38 Fly BT, RT

WILTSHIRE

4 NADDER/CONSTABLE FISHERY

Three separate fisheries provide two miles of varied water suitable for both Coarse and Game Fishing. Only 10 minutes from the Salisbury Railway Station, yet in the heart of the countryside with 'Constable' views of the Cathedral and surrounding water meadows. Fishing is on both the River Avon and River Nadder providing excellent roach, chub, perch, dace, grayling, specimen pike, and brown trout. Although not in great numbers, barbel are also occasionally caught from some of these stretches.

→ Salisburydistrictac.co.uk 51.0652, -1.8128 £10/£12 Fly, bait, spin, led Coarse, BT

5 AVON/SALISBURY (URBAN ANGLING)

A one and a half mile stretch of the River Avon running from within the Salisbury City boundary taking you upstream into the countryside. This is an excellent fishery with Coarse and Game Fishing available on both banks; it is noted for specimen roach and dace but also holds good heads of grayling, chub, pike, and brown trout. There is a possibility of catching a roach above the magical 2lb mark from this fishery.

→ Salisburydistrictac.co.uk 51.0776, -1.8004 £10/£12 Fly, bait, spin, led BT, pike, coarse

6 AVON/LORDS WALK (URBAN ANGLING)

This is a half-mile stretch of the River Avon in Amesbury that is noted for its specimen grayling fishing and is one of the few places on the Avon above Salisbury where Coarse Fishing is permitted. The stretch is

9

7

14

popular as a winter trotting venue where there is a real chance of catching a 2lb grayling.

→ Salisburydistrictac.co.uk 51.1645, -1.7788 £8/£10 Fly, bait, spin, led BT, Gr, Roach, Dace

7 UPPER AVON/DURRINGTON

The paths are maintained by a local residents' group and, in the majority of the fishery, there are no trees or shrubs to obstruct casting. Please be aware of non-fishers walking when casting. The wading section at the bottom of the beat benefits from a good growth of ranunculus each year and varies in depth from between mid-calf to waist. Much above the waist, and I find I get increasingly uncomfortable, so it's good to know.

→ Salisburydistrictac.co.uk 51.1995, -1.7664 £10 Fly BT, Gr

HAMPSHIRE

8 HOLBURY LAKES

The River Dun winds between the four lakes in this tranquil setting. The water can become cloudy with heavy rain but is normally clear. You'll need to fish fine and far off, especially on their Willow Lake - longer, fine leaders with small to tiny dry flies (hook size 18 to 22).

→ Holburylakes.co.uk 51.0408, -1.5884 £48 Fly BT

9 WOODINGTON LAKES

Family-run trout fishery. Three lakes, plus a tributary of the Test called the Blackwater, which has sea trout running through and some brown trout. The main fishing, however, is on the lakes. The trout are frequent risers to surface flies here, especially at the usual times: dawn and dusk. The Leat has good fly activity too.

→ Woodingtonlakes.co.uk 50.9787, -1.5701 £30 Fly RT

10 TADDIFORD GAP BEACH

A sheltered beach with a view of The Needles and well known for fossils, especially for crocodile fossils. The ground is generally clean sand and shingle. Sole and small turbot are quite commonly caught here along with the occasional smoothhound. Mackerel and gar show up too. It's quite isolated, so you should be able to ply your fishing trade in peace.

→ The parking for Taddiford Gap is five hundred feet from the beach. 50.73, -1.6315 Free Shore Sole, turbot, mackerel

11 HATCHET POND

A shallow lake but with some patches of deep water, surrounded by heathland. Most of the usual coarse fish are here; roach, bream, tench, pike, perch, eels, and rudd. It's equally of interest due to its rare freshwater plants and animals. It's in the very highest category of protection afforded by both Site of Special Scientific Interest and a Special Area for Conservation.

→ Forestryengland.uk 50.8109, -1.4789 £20 Fly, bait, spin, led Coarse

12 ALUM BAY

Probably the most scenic beach on the Isle of Wight with an excellent view of The Needles. Mainly shingle. You can catch big congers here if that floats your boat. Or bass. Lots and lots of mackerel too - chasing the fry towards the beach. Access via stone steps or if you're feeling very lazy, a chairlift.

→ The Needles car park is very close. 50.6636, -1.584 Free Shore Wrasse

13 BRIGHSTONE BAY

A sandy beach that's off the beaten track, so usually you can fish in seclusion. Ballan wrasse are caught from Atherfield ledge, congers on the rougher ground, and rays from cleaner sections. Also, expect bass, pouting, and dogfish to show up too. Also, a good spot for finding fossils, which you can do while waiting for that big ray to show up.

→ Chiton Chine car park is very close to Brighstone Bay 50.6245, -1.3839 Free Shore Rays

14 LEPE BEACH

A stony beach that forms part of Lepe Country Park, situated in an Area of Outstanding Natural Beauty, and boy, is it ever! Relatively unknown and unfished but has good fishing from July right through to February. A fairly shallow venue, but a good cast will put you into the depths of the Beaulieu River, especially at low water when you can get closer.

→ Lepe's car park overlooks the beach. 50.785, -1.3609 Free Shore Bass, smoothound, rays

15 ITCHEN/WINCHESTER (URBAN ANGLING)

Grayling are prolific here and offer the best chance of a catch. We're told shrimp and caddis patterns work best. It's rare to see rising trout in these town waters of Winchester except, we are told, it does happen during the mayfly season. So, fishing for free during the Mayfly season on The

10

11

12

13

19

20

22

15

Itchen. As my American wife would say, "beat that with a stick". Not sure what it means, but it sounds accurate.

→ All accessible spots through Wharf Mill to City Mill, Winchester Council. 51.0581, -1.3085 Free Fly, bait, spin, led Gr, BT

SURREY

16 VALE END

Two lakes and river beats offer varied fly fishing for rainbow and brown trout in a beautifully landscaped setting. Mill Pool and Belmont are stocked with brown and rainbow trout of an average weight of 2lb 8oz up to in excess of 10lb.

→ Alburyestatefisheries.co.uk 51.2185, -0.5054 £51 Fly RT

17 BOURNE RIVER/ADDLESTONE

The river through Addlestone is about fifteen feet wide, so it's a small river. Free fishing is on the north bank, Crockford Bridge to Sayers Court. Trotting and ledgering are generally regarded as the best techniques to start catching some fish.

→ Facebook.com/BourneAnglers 51.3663, -0.4894 Free Fly, bait, spin, led Coarse

LONDON

18 HOGSMILL RIVER

Delightfully, this urban river issues out from a chalk spring in Ewell, and it meanders through London to eventually join the Thames. Much less fished than its cousin, The Wandle, and far more modest and discrete. You can fly fish for trout here, but it's chub fishing with bread flakes that will provide the vast majority of the action.

→ Malden Manor train station is very close to the river. 51.3548, -0.2525 Free Fly, bait, spin, led BT, carp, coarse

19 SYON PARK

Exquisite setting set within the 200 acres of Syon Park, home of the Duke of Northumberland. All within eight miles of central London. Fishing is not too challenging, provided you move around and keep casting. You'll see crowds around the house, but you will be kept separate in your own fishing enclave.

→ Alburyestatefisheries.co.uk 51.4782, -0.3162 £51 Fly RT

20 WANDLE (URBAN FISHING)

Fish where Nelson fished. Fish where FW Halford copied the idea of dry fly fishing from the local fishermen. Is this the most famous free fishery in the UK? I suspect it is. Look at the well-done and researched website, which will tell you exactly where to fish and what to expect. It can get crowded during the weekends in the summer months.

→ Wandlepiscators.net 51.3907, -0.1684 Free Fly, bait, spin, led BT, carp, coarse

21 HAMPSTEAD, NUMBER 2 POND

The main fishing is on the south bank, but there are a few swims on the north side. East side is residential, and the west bank is very steep. Highly recommended to go early in the morning or later in the evening when the crowds have dispersed. If you fish in the main part of the day, you will be constantly asked if you have caught anything.

→ Cityoflondon.gov.uk 51.5596, -0.1658 £11 Fly, bait, spin, led Coarse

22 MEN'S POND, HAMPSTEAD HEATH

A green oasis. If you find yourself in London with fishing rods, or, indeed, if you live there, the Hampstead Heath ponds are relatively unfished and are well worth a shot. These ponds were dug in the 17th and 18th centuries to provide the growing London with fresh water. Plenty of coarse fish to catch; carp, bream, roach, rudd, tench, gudgeon, perch, and pike.

→ Cityoflondon.gov.uk 51.5634, -0.1581 £11 Fly, bait, spin, led Coarse

SUSSEX

23 EAST/WEST WITTERING

I've tried fly fishing here a number of times with friends to no avail. However, others have (claimed) to have done well and caught numerous bass. It should also be noted the depths vary considerably, so a wading stick would be a good addition. Slack tides at night appear to be frequently cited as the most productive.

→ The car park overlooks West Wittering beach. 50.7694, -0.8876 Free Shore Bass

24 DUNCTON MILLS FISHERY

A beautiful trout fishery located in Duncton, near the small town of Petworth. Well managed and picturesque. The fishery is made up of 4 trout fishing lakes that are stocked with hard-fighting rainbow trout, brown trout, and tiger trout that weigh 2lb upwards.

→ Dunctonmilltroutfishery.co.uk 50.9412, -0.6289 £30 Fly BT, RT, Tiger

22

17

23

24

25 SHILLINGLEE FISHERY

A very pleasant commercial fishery with feisty pike and cautious carp. It's been run for almost thirty years and is a very smooth operation. The main action is on the specimen lake. It's also a Tench Fishery with fish caught up to ten pounds - look for the bubbles. We're told luncheon meat fished at two feet works well on the carp.

→ Shillinglee.co.uk 51.0799, -0.6273 £15 Fly, bait, spin, led Carp, pike, coarse

26 WEST BEACH/LITTLEHAMPTON

After a good blow, slipper limpets can be washed up, and they provide good bait. Expect mullet, stingrays, and some bass here. West Beach can be busy during the summer but barren and windswept during the winter. An SSI, West Beach has one of only 3 sand dune systems in West Sussex. It's a laid-back beach.

→ The West Beach car park overlooks the beach. 50.8011, -0.5424 Free Shore Bass, eels, flounders

27 ARDINGLY RESERVOIR

Surprisingly new reservoir, which was created in 1978 to keep the local area in water and to regulate the flow of the River Ouse. The reservoir is deep, so the favored method has always been tip fishing with a ground bait feeder. This is still the best method for the omnipresent bream shoals: heavy feeding with crumb. Also, excellent for winter pike fishing.

→ Ardinglyactivitycentre.co.uk 51.0421, -0.0968 £15 Fly, bait, spin, led Pike, carp, tench

28 ROTTINGDEAN CLIFFS

Great fishing area but can be snaggy. Excellent spinning for pollack, mackerel, bass, and garfish. Given the snags, you must be philosophical about tackle losses that will occur, but hopefully, the fishing will outweigh the losses. If you're not losing some equipment, you're not fishing hard enough. Or so say the equipment manufacturers.

→ The Marine Cliffs car park overlooks Rottingdean Cliffs 50.8026, -0.0592 Free Shore, kayak Pollock, mackerel, bass

29 SWANBOROUGH FARM FISHERY

These three little secluded lakes are a gem in the Sussex Downs. When we've been there, it's entirely empty, creating a haunting, peaceful atmosphere with views of chalk

30

cliffs and modernist chalets on the hill. Plenty of parking. Eel and roach are here too, but it's known for its carp fishing.

→ Swanboroughfishinglakes.com 50.856, -0.004 £15 Fly, bait, spin, led Carp, coarse

30 SEAFORD HEAD BEACH

This small cove is divided from the main beach by a large groyne and a jetty. Backed by the sheer chalk cliffs of Seaford Head Nature Reserve, care should be taken when fishing in the area, as rockfalls are not unknown.

→ South Hill Barn car park is a brisk walk of one km to the beach. 50.7639, 0.1088 Free Shore Bass

31 CUCKMERE HAVEN BEACH

Good bass waters. Fishing for bass is pretty straightforward and involves a basic setup of an 8ft spinning rod, a reel with 8-10lb line, and a bunch of silver spinners, preferably Toby spoons. Sea bass tend to feed on small fry close to rocks, and it is quite common to catch them almost under your feet. The best way to locate a shoal is to watch the surface of the water for any disturbance, which is usually the bass chasing small fish and/or seabirds dive bombing the cornered bait fish.

→ Best to park at the free parking at South Hill Barn and walk over, a little over a km. 50.7587, 0.1495 Free Shore Bass

32 BIRLING GAP

Where the South Downs meet the sea. Do not go in the tourist season; it's far too crowded but has spectacular scenery (hence the crowds). As long as it's not too rough, you can take whiting, bass, and the odd codling. Lug seems to work best. Also, like almost everywhere else on the south coast, this area was known for its smuggling.

→ Billing Gap car park is next to the seafront. 50.7427, 0.2026 Free Shore Whiting, bass, codling

33 COW GAP SHORE

Good bass fishery. Spring, bottom fish. Summer, lures, plugs, and surface poppers. Autumn, if water is clear, same as summer, if not, bottom fish. Conger eels are also around from spring through to autumn. You'll need large fish or squid baits, fished after dark, on a 5/0 hook to catch them.

→ Heathy Brow car park is the closest to Cow Gap, about 1km away. 50.7423, 0.2635 Free Shore Bass, congers, Dover sole

31

32

34

34

37

38

KENT

34 RECULVER BEACH

The twin sisters are two towers built within a Roman fort. The Romans settled here for the harbour, it is believed. I'm further told that the Bouncing Bomb was tested where you'll be fishing. You'll need a twelve-foot beach casting rod to be successful here. Lugworms will work for the mackerel and peeler crabs for the bass.

→ Parking within sight of the towers
51.3799, 1.2071 Free Shore
Mackerel, bass

35 WANTSUM RIVER

This is a very prolific river; if a fish swims in England, it should be here, apart from barbel. Maggots appear to be the best bait. Sadly, it seems the river is little fished anymore. In Roman times, this was a sizeable river and was capable of accommodating ocean-going vessels. Much diminished now.

→ wantsumaa.co.uk 51.3468, 1.2284
£5 Fly, bait, spin, led Coarse

36 STOUR/ASHFORD (URBAN ANGLING)

Ashford Borough Council lets anglers fish the Stour on their patch for free. An enlightened view, not shared by Canterbury Council, who discourage angling on their part of The Stour. You'll encounter the usual coarse fish and perhaps a trout or two. Please fish the river, or else the Ashford Stour might follow the fate of the Canterbury Stour. A joyless and puritanical fate.

→ kentishstour.org.uk 51.1475, 0.88
Free Fly, bait, spin, led BT, Coarse

37 ST MARGARET'S BAY

At either end of the bay, you can find live prawns in the rock pools. Use them to float fish for bass. St. Margaret's is in the Domesday Book as "Sancta Margharita". The Victorians developed St Margaret's as a holiday resort. Lord Byron, Ian Fleming, and Noel Coward are amongst its famous former residents and visiting guests. Not sure if any of them scrambled around in the rock pools looking for prawns to catch bass. History is silent (as far as I know).

→ Parking overlooking St. Margaret's Bay
51.1497, 1.3845 Free Shore Bass

38 SANDWICH BAY

The coastal area consists of sand flats with their associated salt marshes and coastal sand dunes. The Sandwich Flats stretch for about five miles along the coast. It's fishable on all tides, and you can catch most of the standard UK sea species during the winter and summer months, depending on their specific seasons. Lovely sandy bottom which means you get to retain your kit.

→ You can park at the Borrow Pitt car park for free. 51.3069, 1.3757 Free Shore
Sole, bass, rays

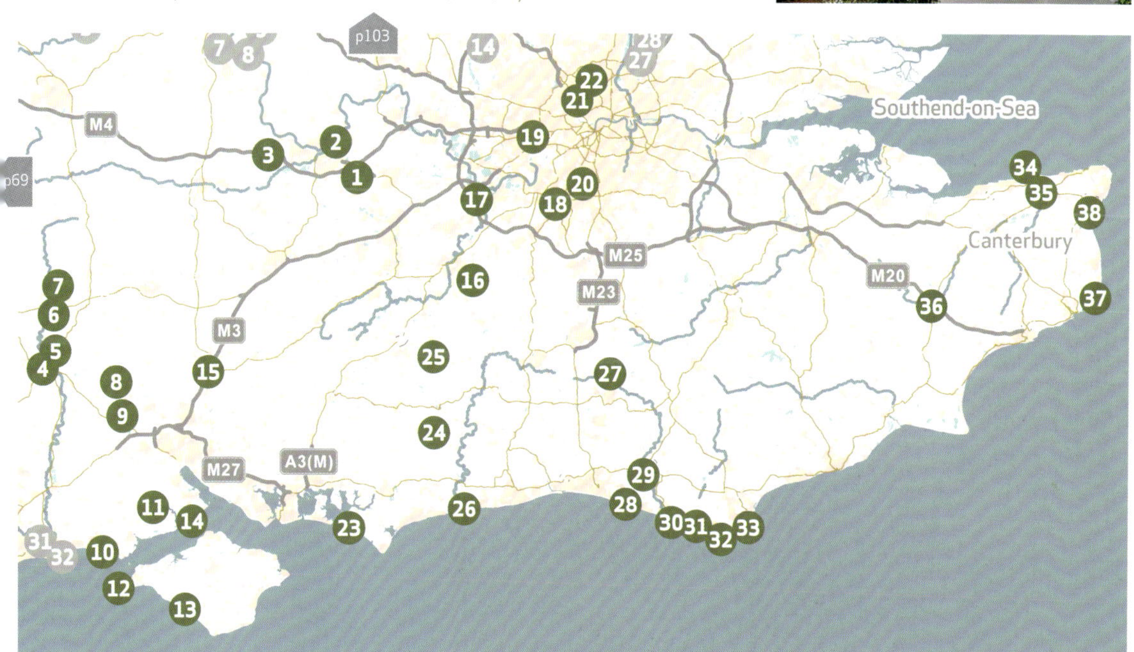

West Midlands

Herefordshire, a county of hills and valleys, apple orchards and hop fields lies on the border with Wales. Famous for the majestic River Wye and the deep-cut Teme, both of which offer fishing for everything from salmon and trout to barbel, pike, and silver fish. It is also home to a mass of lakes and pools, including the famous and mysterious Redmire Pool, whose three acres are considered the temple of carp fishing. The water first came to angling attention in 1951 when a British record carp of 31lb was caught by Bob Richards. Followed by Richard Walker in 1952 with 44lb, then Chris Yates with 51lb 8oz in 1980. A word to the wise: the bait for Yates' fish was sweetcorn bought from the Spar in Ross On Wye.

On the banks of the River Arrow in Worcestershire, Redditch became the most important town in the world for making angling the global, mass-participation sport it is now. The town dominated the supply of early recreational tackle, with businesses producing handmade hooks, lines, reels, rods, and lures since the late 1600s. Redditch should start a fishing museum; I'm unsure why they haven't.

However, we also think of Worcestershire for specimen barbel in the Avon and the Severn. For those so inclined, there are world records to be broken with catching barbel on a fly. There doesn't yet appear to be an official record-keeping for coarse fish on a fly, but I'm hoping to encourage the British Record Fish Committee to consider doing so.

The tributaries of the Severn and Avon are also worthy of our angling consideration: the Avon's are the Arrow and the Isbourne and the Severn's feeders the Salwarpe, Stour, and Teme. They all hold excellent stocks of fish.

Gloucestershire has a variety of fishing, with the obvious exclusion of sea fishing, just like Herefordshire and Worcestershire above. Gloucestershire fishing is dominated by the Severn, which flows large and wide throughout the county, and the tributaries that run off her or are in the same catchment area: the Boyd, the Bybrook, the Cam (which flows into the Gloucester and Sharpness Canal), the Chelt (from which Cheltenham gets its name), the Coln (which joins the River Thames near Lechlade), the Churn (another Thames tributary), the Evenlode, the Leadon, and the Tetbury Avon.

GLOUCESTERSHIRE

1 FROME/STROUD (URBAN ANGLING)

Not easy water, but it's recovering from its industrial past. There is fly life present, and the trout are in the small range, but we're told the potential for larger exists. Well worth having a go if you're in Stroud or the surrounding area. Classic urban fishing, so a shorter rod (which will roll cast) will be your best bet.

→ All accessible spots through Stroud, Stroud District Council. 51.7418, -2.2174 Free Fly, bait, spin, led BT, Gr

2 BIDEFORD BROOK

Only a couple of miles from the Severn, this stream is a typical example of a small lowland stream. The trout are what you would expect in such a setting, all about 12" and hidden in the deep pools. Wading will be best in felt waders.

→ Fishingpassport.co.uk 51.7634, -2.4486 £11 Fly BT

3 BLACKPOOL BROOK

Not dissimilar to Cannop Brook, this is another small stream that runs through the Forest Of Dean. Wading can be tricky over the boulder riverbed, and care should be taken when wading and fishing through the short, dark tunnels, but it's a unique fly fishing experience and should not be missed.

→ Fishingpassport.co.uk 51.7674, -2.5027 £11 Fly BT

4 CANNOP BROOK

Ideal for a couple of hours of fishing when you find yourself in the Forest Of Dean. Although the river is fairly straight, there are a couple of meanders that will provide holding places for the trout. A six or seven-footer rod is all that you will need.
Or perhaps a bit longer if you'll be doing a lot of roll casting.

→ Fishingpassport.co.uk 51.7944, -2.5681 £11 Fly BT

HEREFORDSHIRE

5 WYE/WYEBANKS

Not very wild, but it's excellent coarse fishing. The flow is quite fast for this part of the Wye, and the barbel and dace fishing is particularly good. Chub fishing can be superb, with specimens to 5 and 6lb. That's a large chub.

→ Fishingpassport.co.uk 51.8503, -2.5869 £27.50 Fly, bait, spin, led BT, chub, dace

6 MONNOW VALLEY

Spectacular mayfly hatches make this one of the best fly fishing spots in the country during the summer months. This stretch of the Monnow is also host to a variety of coarse species, including chub and grayling. The best of the coarse fishing is towards the downstream end of the fishery, where the river is slower and deeper.

→ baa.uk.com 51.824, -2.7342 £22.50 Fly, bait, spin, led BT, coarse

7 WYE, ROSS-ON-WYE (URBAN FISHING)

Here's a chance to do some Urban Fishing in the picturesque town of Ross On Wye. There are some lovely runs for you to get back into trotting, perhaps to pick up a chub or two and some perch. It's a great place to catch barbel (over 10lb every year) and chub (to 6lb+). Luncheon meat does well, but the local barbel

7

10

particularly like bacon grill! If you fancy a proper wild experience you can pay to camp on the river bank outside the White Lion Pub just the other side of Wilton Bridge.

→ Rossanglingclub.co.uk 51.9137, -2.5919
£10 Fly, bait, spin, led Coarse

8 WYE/FOY BRIDGE

Barbel and chub provide good sport for coarse anglers here throughout the season, particularly from swims on the left bank and the croy on the bottom left bank. For salmon anglers, the beat has a good fly fishing pool with numerous boulders and potential lies.

→ Fishingpassport.co.uk 51.9556, -2.5688
£23 Fly, bait, spin, led BT, chub, barbel

9 WYE/STRANGFORD

With distinct bends in the river, this beat offers a good variety of waters to try, and at a variety of heights. Access is good, but when wet, it will require a walk of approx 500m to the river. All of the usual Wye species are here, including Salmon, Barbel, and large and plentiful Chub.

→ Fishingpassport.co.uk 51.947, -2.6278
£23 Fly, bait, spin, led BT, chub, dace

10 WYE/LOWER CARROTS

The best months for salmon fishing are April, May, and June, or late September. The beat also offers excellent coarse fishing for all the usual species, including barbel, chub, and pike. The salmon fishing has dropped off over the decades. My uncle told me that at one point, it was in the balance as to which provided the most income: his farm or the salmon fishing - no more.

→ Fishingpassport.co.uk 52.0308, -2.6361
£28 Fly, bait, spin, led BT, Gr, chub

11 TRELOUGH POOL

This shallow four-acre lake provides plenty of cover for the carp. On a summer's day, you can watch them cruising the shallows and, by the same token, you can watch them feeding. A lovely way to spend the day within The Whitfield Estate set deep in the Herefordshire countryside.

→ Fishingpassport.co.uk 51.9987, -2.8451
£17.50 Fly, bait, spin, led Carp

12 DULAS BROOK

Delightful little stream with some very deep passages which you wouldn't expect in such a diminutive waterway. This stream can run red in a flood, like the Usk. Meant to have a great Mayfly hatch, but I've never been here to see it. You need to be very, very stealthy to be successful here. These are easily spooked wild fish.

→ Fishingpassport.co.uk 51.9584, -2.9027
£11 Fly BT

13 ESCLEY BROOK

The Escley is a fast-flowing, tumbling upland trout stream that flows off the Black Mountains. It's a mixture of riffles and deep pools. There's an excellent Mayfly hatch, which makes the trip worthwhile when you time it to coincide with the hatch. It's a fast-flowing bedrock stream, so studded soles to your waders are highly recommended.

→ Fishingpassport.co.uk 51.9571, -2.9751
£13.50 Fly BT

14 WYE/WARREN

An excellent coarse fishery nearby to the famed Hay-on-Wye, town of books. A slippery walk down to the river via a small track next to the church of St. Mary. Some of the caught fish have been truly remarkable; Barbel 13lb 8oz, Pike 28lb 8oz, and Chub 6lb. All this in a mile or so of water.

→ Haywarren.org.uk 52.0761, -3.1369
£10 Fly, bait, spin, led BT, coarse

15 ARROW/KINGTON

Unknown to most, I was born in Kington but don't let that put you off. Meandering through farmland, this stretch of The Arrow is ideal for those looking for wild brown trout in a small upland stream. Wading is relatively easy over a gravel and silt riverbed. Just like walking up Hereford Broad Street, as somebody told me.

→ Fishingpassport.co.uk 52.1894, -3.0544
£13.50 Fly BT, Gr

16 LUGG/HINDWELL-COOMBE

The setting is fantastic – meandering along the floodplain and shadowed by Wapley Hill. It's easy wading over the gravel riverbed (always a blessing to not need a staff), and the Lugg here will hold its flow even in summer. Good numbers of trout and grayling.

→ Fishingpassport.co.uk 52.2595, -2.9984
£11 Fly BT, Gr

17 ARROW/LEEN

You'll need chest waders to get the most out of this fishery, but it's easy wading with a gentle stretch of the Arrow with a gravel bed. A number of good-sized grayling are here, and a recommendation is to trot with maggots in the winter months. Sounds good to me.

→ Fishingpassport.co.uk 52.2228, -2.9042
£17.50 Fly, bait, spin, led BT, Gr

27

21

18

18 LUGG/EYTON BEAT

We're told that the river is becoming renowned as excellent for winter grayling. I've fished when the ferrules have to be blown on to remove the accumulating ice. It's potentially an easier option than the Wye. Apparently, the catch returns show a number of specimen fish. Note the day price quoted is for winter grayling fishing.

→ Fishingpassport.co.uk 52.2435, -2.7797 £22.50 Fly BT, Gr

19 PINSLEY BROOK

The Pinsley has many characteristics of a southern chalk stream, and although very small in places, it has a very healthy population of trout. Early in the season is the best time to fish the brook, before the bankside vegetation is at its most dense, making fishing a frustrating affair.

→ Fishingpassport.co.uk 52.2327, -2.7774 £11 Fly BT

20 KENWATER/LEOMINSTER (URBAN ANGLING)

The Kenwater comes directly off the Lugg in town. Lots of highly spooky small trout, but you can occasionally get lucky with a grayling or two. Full confession: I never have succeeded on The Kenwater, and that's through a number of attempts.

→ Plenty of parking in Leominster 52.2307, -2.7327 Free Fly, bait, spin, led BT, Gr

21 LUGG/LEOMINSTER (URBAN ANGLING)

I grew up fishing the Lugg, where trout of a few pounds are not rare. Best flies? Try a Barret's Bane or Professor. I believe these are flies local to the area. Parts of this river are idyllic, running through the quiet market town of Leominster. You can also fish the Kenwater while still staying in the town.

→ Plenty of parking in Leominster 52.228, -2.7307 Free Fly, bait, spin, led BT, Gr

22 LUGG/DINMORE

Lovely little stream that I have fished all my life. However, it's having problems caused by the chicken farms further up in the catchment area. Still, you can catch the usual coarse fish and the occasional trout. I was fishing it Tenkara style last year with very little success. The water was grey.

→ Baa.uk.com 52.1495, -2.719 £40/year Fly, bait, spin, led BT, coarse

SHROPSHIRE

23 MERRINGTON CARP FISHERY

A man-made lake and well done. We're told there are two hundred or so carp in the lake. There's a shallow depression in the middle which is about six inches deeper than the rest of the lake, and that's where the carp frequently congregate.

→ Merringtoncarpfishery.co.uk 52.7881, -2.8055 £15 Fly, bait, spin, led Carp

24 WYTHEFORD/RODIN RIVER

Close to the Ironbridge Gorge, this is a rural Shropshire lake of some three acres. A classic farm lake with all the major coarse fish present. This venue also offers fishing on a stretch of the river Rodin too; the river contains silvers, barbel, and chub.

→ Nantwichangling.com 52.7815, -2.6446 £20/year Fly, bait, spin, led Coarse

25 WOODLANDS LODGE

Two pools; one for the members and one for the day ticketers. The day ticket pool has some seriously large carp, roach, and large perch. I'm not sure why the perch grow so large here in this part of the country, but they do. The smaller ones are relatively easy to catch on a fly, the larger ones, not so much.

→ Kfac.co.uk 52.5436, -2.4562 £6 Fly, bait, spin, led Carp, perch, roach

26 SEVERN, UNICORN INN

This is serious barbel water, and barbel are just starting to be appreciated as a fish to hunt with a fly (down deep, of course, so probably a nymph of some description). Barbel prefer oxygen-rich waters and are therefore often found in strong currents in the middle reaches of rivers. Unlike trout and grayling, barbel cope well with higher water temperatures, so are a good alternative in the dog days of summer.

→ Kfac.co.uk 52.4773, -2.3747 £8 Fly, bait, spin, led Barbel, perch, chub

27 TEME/LUDLOW (URBAN ANGLING)

The weirs can be successfully fished for large trout and grayling that abound throughout the Ludlow Teme. This is classic wild urban fishing, and the fish will have rarely encountered an angler. Marvellous stuff. Small rod and stealth might, just might, produce results.

→ All accessible spots through Ludlow to Dinham Bridge, Plymouth Settled Estates. 52.3659, -2.7256 Free Fly, bait, spin, led BT, Gr

19

20

21

26

33

WORCESTERSHIRE

28 TEME/EASTHAM BRIDGE

There are reports of pike over 25lbs and barbel over 10lbs caught in these waters. To me, that's very tempting to try my luck on both of them in a single day fishing on a fly - obviously fishing a different fly for each. I've never heard of an angler catching both a pike and barbel on a fly within the same day.

➔ Baa.uk.com 52.3187, -2.5019
£40/year Fly, bait, spin, led Pike, barbel, coarse

29 TEME/BROADWAS

You'll need to plan your fishing carefully - it's a popular match fishing venue. I would certainly check on the BAA website before travelling any distance. A good number of the standard coarse fish are represented here, so a number of angling disciplines can be utilised, but the ledger would make the most sense.

➔ Baa.uk.com 52.1943, -2.3613 £40/year Fly, bait, spin, led Coarse

30 TEME/LEIGH

This stretch can be a little daunting with its fast current and steep banks, so care must be taken. There are plenty of other stretches on The Teme which the BAA has in their portfolio. However, if you are minded and nimble of foot, this is an excellent fishery with specimen barbel and chub. The UK record chub on a fly could well come from these waters.

➔ Baa.uk.com 52.1906, -2.3289
£40/year Fly, bait, spin, led Chub, barbel, coarse

31 SALWARPE/CLAINES

This little beauty fished best when the Severn is in flood and/or later in the year. Dexter cattle will be gazing at you in your exertions the way that only cattle can. To my mind, slightly stunned looking but are friendly and inquisitive. Most coarse fish are here, plus, we're told, the occasional carp.

➔ Baa.uk.com 52.2393, -2.2309
£40/year Fly, bait, spin, led Coarse

32 SEVERN/BUSHLEY

It's deep here, very deep. Specimen barbel can be found, as well as large pike. It also holds shoals of bream, but it's the pike that intrigue me in these waters. I'm thinking rather than dead bait, a spinner could be productive. In wet weather, the track to the carpark can be impassable, unless you have a 4x4.

➔ Baa.uk.com 52.0446, -2.207
£40/year Fly, bait, spin, led Coarse

33 AVON/BREDON

This is a languid stretch, slow and deep. Ideal for contemplative angling, watching your float continue its stately progression downriver. Large shoals of bream abound here, and also all their other coarse fish brethren. Near Bredon Hill with its Iron Age fort and megaliths.

➔ Baa.uk.com 52.032, -2.1211
£40/year Fly, bait, spin, led Bream, coarse

28

29

31

32

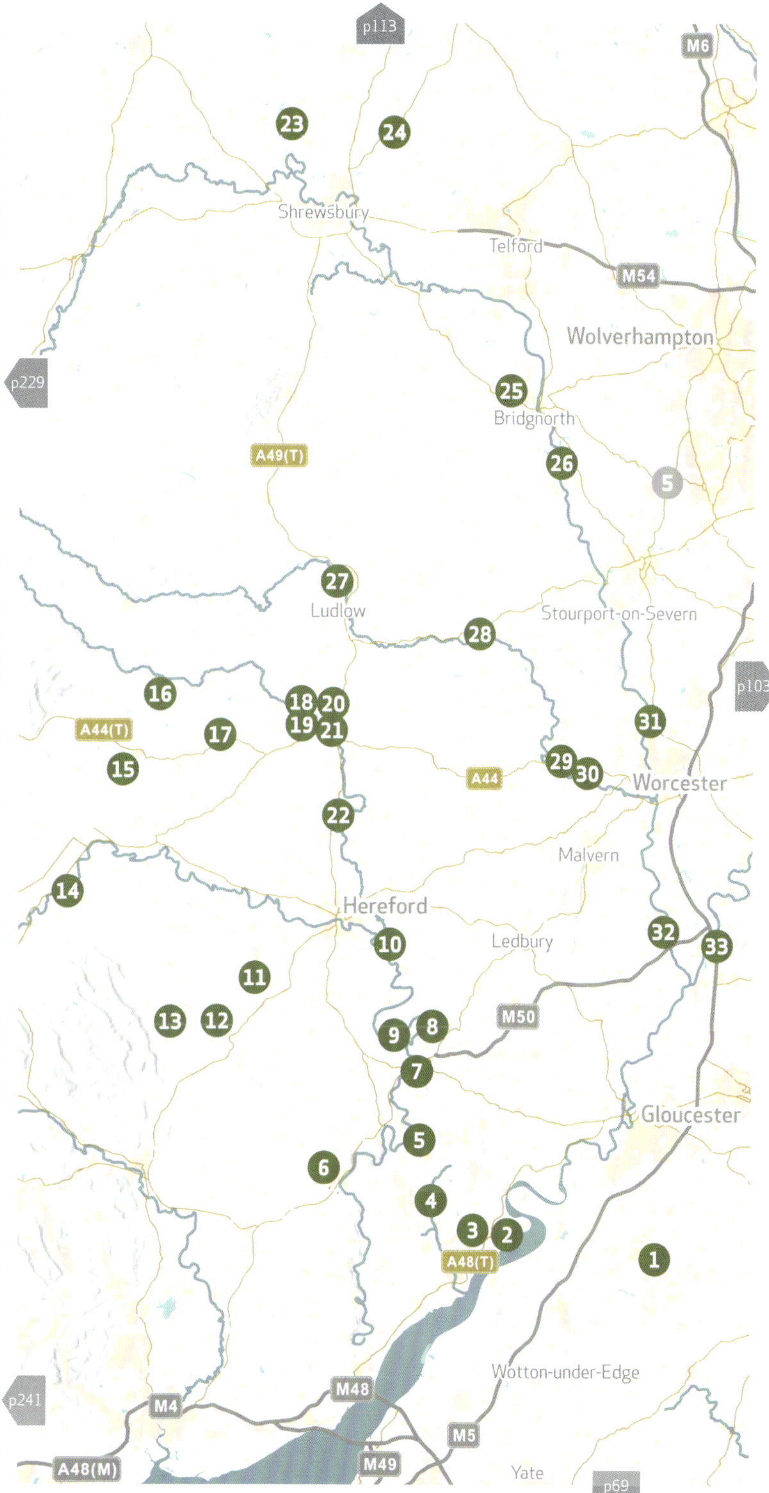
p113
M6
Shrewsbury
Telford
M54
Wolverhampton
p229
Bridgnorth
A49(T)
Ludlow
Stourport-on-Severn
p103
A44(T)
A44
Worcester
Malvern
Hereford
Ledbury
M50
Gloucester
A48(T)
Wotton-under-Edge
p241
M4
M48
M5
A48(M)
M49
Yate
p69
1
2
3
4
5
6
7
8
9
10
11
12
13
14
15
16
17
18
19
20
21
22
23
24
25
26
27
28
29
30
31
32
33

2

Central & East England

1

4

5

Warwickshire is mainly known for coarse fishing on lakes with some rivers, primarily the Avon, an excellent barbel fishery. There are also a host of smaller streams and rivers running off the Avon, such as the Blythe and the Alne. The Alne is a tributary of the River Arrow, which also holds wild brown trout, while other coarse rivers in the county include the Leam, the River Stour, the Sowe, the Anker, and the River Dene. Warwickshire also gives me an excuse to mention Shakespeare and fishing by way of the Reverend Henry Nicholson Ellacombe, who delightfully argues that, in fact, Shakespeare fished. In his book entitled Shakespeare as an Angler, first published in 1883, he argues that Shakespeare was indeed a successful angler. Ellacombe goes on to hypothesise that Shakespeare had probably enjoyed many a day's fishing on the Warwickshire and Gloucestershire streams. In fact, Shakespeare mentions fishing some eight times in his plays, hardly proof positive, but it's the best we can muster.

The central part of Oxfordshire contains the River Thames and several of its tributaries, including the River Thame, and a clutch of fishable reservoirs.

Hertfordshire boasts Dame Juliana Berners, who was the prioress of the Priory of St Mary of Sopwell, near St Albans. She wrote *The Treatyse on Fysshynge with an Angle* (1496), the world's first-ever fishing book. It includes a fly fishing section with instructions on the rod, line, and hook's construction as well as how to make trout fishing flies for the different seasons.

Cambridgeshire is synonymous with the River Cam. Unusually, the river was named after the town, which in turn named the county. There's a stretch of the River Cam in Cambridge city centre that offers free coarse fishing for chub and pike. We also outline a number of other free fishing (urban fishing) spots throughout British towns and cities within this book.

The Suffolk and Norfolk Broads are Britain's largest protected wetlands. The Broads are a historic and unique angling destination, home to a variety of fish species including bream, rudd, tench, roach, perch, carp, and most famously, large pike. These pike will take a fly, and frankly, there is not much to compare on Britain's inland waterways to a pike taking your fly.

To hunt large pike, it pays to be mobile and search out the hotspots. These predators seldom stray too far from their next meal, often lurking in wait near overhanging trees with submerged roots or close to bridges and other structures that provide cover for their prey fish, such as roach, especially in winter when they may form large groups.

WARWICKSHIRE

1 AVON/CLEEVE PRIOR

The beat starts at the picturesque Cleeve Prior and is a quintessential Warwickshire Avon beat. Nothing dramatic, an even flow and a consistent depth. This allows for good float fishing for an array of coarse fish. We're told maggots are the best bait.

→ Baa.uk.com 52.142, -1.8902 £40/year Fly, bait, spin, led Coarse

2 ARROW/ARROW MILL

With the Arrow's abundant fly life, expect good mayfly hatches from this stretch of water in late May and June. Although not the longest of beats, it will provide an angler with a few hours of first-class small river trout and grayling fishing on both dry fly and nymph.

→ Fishingpassport.co.uk 52.2027, -1.8801 £11 Fly BT

3 ALNE/PENNYFORD HALL

This is a shallow stretch but within it are deep pools. The BBA suggests fishing with a float and that it lends itself well for roving fishing (covering as much ground as you can seeking the fish and when you find them staying put). A very enjoyable style of fishing.

→ Baa.uk.com 52.2561, -1.7822 £40/year Fly, bait, spin, led BT, Pike, Coarse

4 AVON/WASPERTON

Wasperton is best fished with light float tackle. It's quite shallow with a deeper section downstream. Occasional trout are caught but it's primarily a coarse fishery. There are barbel here too, perhaps try a spot of fly fishing with a nymph, especially in the oxygenated waters of this beat.

→ Baa.uk.com 52.2295, -1.6109 £40/year Fly, bait, spin, led BT, Coarse

OXFORDSHIRE

5 THAMES/BUSCOT/TROUT INN

The river is fairly narrow here and has lots of features, from thick beds of rushes, streamer weed, gravel runs and an abundance of overhanging trees and bushes. So it's rich in fish-holding features. You can find roach and perch to barbel and chub with pike and carp too – all in the Thames up here. Ancient Fishery Rights granted by Royal Charter to the Brethren are still held by The Trout Inn, which controls two miles of trout and coarse fishing waters. You cannot fish directly from the Trout land these days, but the stretch of water on the south bank between the lock and Lechlade can be used during the open season, and a bailiff patrols this and collects the fees from the bank.

→ Abingdon.gov.uk 51.6896, -1.6778 £40/year Fly, bait, spin, led Coarse

6 THAMES/SWINFORD TOLL BRIDGE

Idyllic spot to fish for perch, roach, and pike and, while you're at it, keep half an eye out for the various birds; kingfishers, herons, and crested grebes, I've spotted them all here. The bridge was put up for auction in 2009 and sold for a little over £1 million.

→ Gov.uk/guidance/river-thames-lock-and-weir-fishing 51.7745, -1.3594 £34/year Fly, bait, spin, led Coarse

7 THAMES/CULHAM

Culham village is curled around the Thames here and has always done so, hence Cula's hamm, referring to the village's position in a bend of the Thames. You can expect to have excellent fishing for chub, roach, bream, perch, and pike (providing all goes well).

→ Gov.uk/guidance/river-thames-lock-and-weir-fishing 51.6503, -1.2678 £34/year Fly, bait, spin, led Coarse

13

8

10

14

12

8 THAMES/DAY'S LOCK

This is an important site, it's the main spot to gauge the flow of the Thames. As in all EA lock fishing sites, of which there must be twenty, all for the cost of £34 a year, they are strict about exactly where you can fish. They designate each fishing site with a sign, so there's not much excuse if you get it wrong.

→ Gov.uk/guidance/river-thames-lock-and-weir-fishing 51.6382, -1.1794 £34/year Fly, bait, spin, led Coarse

9 THAME RIVER

The fishing has stretches of the beautiful River Thame in and around the Chiselhampton, Cuddesdon, and Drayton St Leonards areas of Oxfordshire. Coarse fishing is a long and glorious tradition on The Thame, and for these prices, it will continue on into the next century and beyond.

→ Cmvaa.org.uk 51.6839, -1.1389 £5 Fly, spin, worm Coarse

NORTHAMPTONSHIRE

10 RAVENSTHORPE RESERVOIR

Far smaller than Grafham or Rutland, the fish here are still in excellent condition. It takes no more than forty-five minutes to walk the entire circumference. We're told nymphs and buzzers on a slow retrieve will have the best results.

→ Anglianwaterparks.co.uk 52.3343, -1.0094 £28 Fly, bait, spin, led Trout, pike, perch

11 PITSFORD WATER

The clear Pitsford Water is well-regarded by anglers the world over. It's a tranquil scene, well stocked with rainbow and brown trout, and attracting anglers of all abilities and ages. A good place to try a popper and skitter it over the weed beds. If you get lucky with a large fish, you should have a slashing take that you'll never forget.

→ Anglianwaterparks.co.uk 52.3108, -0.886 £26 Fly, bait, spin, led Trout, pike, perch

12 SYWELL LAKE

A sixty-seven-acre Victorian reservoir. It's no longer supplying drinking water, but it's one of the best tench fisheries available. Fish up to 12lb have been caught, with the average being around the 7lb mark. It can occasionally be smitten with a blue-green algae, so always check before going.

→ Northnorthants.gov.uk 52.2803, -0.7808 £5 Fly, bait, spin, led Tench, pike, coarse

HERTFORDSHIRE

13 TRING RESERVOIRS

The waters are well known for specimen-sized bream, carp, catfish, tench & pike, and also contain good numbers of quality roach & perch. I'm told that they hold five UK records. The reservoirs are also well known for their birds. Great Crested Grebes, swans, and herons are usually around, and in winter, ducks abound.

→ Tringanglers.org.uk 51.8182, -0.6665 £10 Fly, bait, spin, led Coarse

RUTLAND

14 CHESS RIVER (URBAN ANGLING)

Delightful, small chalk stream. Apparently, they have breeding rainbow trout which is a hallmark of a very healthy river, alongside large grayling and brown trout. Half a mile of fishing, and when we've been there, nobody else was fishing. You have it all to yourself.

→ Fee parking at the fishing site. 51.6452, -0.4633 Free Fly, bait, spin, led BT, Gr, Ch

15

17

fishing methods apply. I would suspect that the most action would come from a float and hook adorned with a maggot, worm, or piece of corn.

→ Nationaltrust.org.uk 52.3309, -0.1206 £ Free Fly, bait, spin, led BT, chub, barbel, dace

19

15 RUTLAND WATERS

It's all about understanding the wind at the famous Stillwater fishery. If you are a right-handed fisherman, you want a gentle breeze blowing from left to right. This way you can let your flies drift along naturally with the wind. Or, find a bank where the wind is blowing onto the shore. Provided it is coming in at a bit of an angle, you will still be able to cast to trout that have run down the wind or are moving up the bank to face the drift current. Rutland has large numbers of smaller zander but some truly enormous pike.

→ Anglianwaterparks.co.uk 52.665, -0.6133 £29 Fly, bait, spin, led Trout, pike, zander

CAMBRIDGESHIRE

16 NENE RIVER

The name Nene is ancient. Probably pre-Celtic, so the scholars think. The river does have an ancientness about it as it slowly rolls along. If you want to avoid the bream to concentrate on the carp instead, you'll need to deploy large baits; boillies and nuts.

→ Deepingstjamesanglingclub.co.uk 52.576, -0.3892 £5 Fly, bait, spin, led Coarse

17 GRAFHAM WATER

This reservoir is nestled in bucolic countryside. Excellent for trout and predator fishing. However, Grafham has always lived in the shadow of Rutland Water. Hard-fighting Rainbows are common up to 5lb. They're feasting on Daphnia, which means they put on weight quickly. One of the best places in the country to target massive zander and perch, both with lures and flies.

→ Anglianwaterparks.co.uk 52.2907, -0.3255 £29 Fly, bait, spin, led Trout, Pike, Zander, Perch

18 EAST DELPH LAKES

These are carp lakes run by very knowledgeable and passionate carp anglers. East Delph Lakes are a very special place with reviews from carp anglers that are almost always five-star. At two acres, the front lake has two islands and nine swims, covering three banks. The lake has a strict six-angler policy, which makes for calm fishing.

→ Eastdelphlakes.com 52.5905, -0.1325 £25 Spinner, bait Carp

19 GREAT OUSE

Potential for massive roach and perch with good bags of bream and chub. The usual

20 100 FOOT DRAIN

How can you not love the name? The 100 Foot Drain. The section here is tidal, which means you can get the odd flatfish or sea trout to spice up your fishing day. Float fishing is the norm here, and, of course, it flows both ways.

→ Cambridge-fpas.co.uk 52.353, 0.044 £45/year Fly, bait, spin, led Coarse

21 HERITAGE LAKE/COTTENHAM

A peaceful and still lake of some three acres with markedly different depths from a few inches to feet, or so. Roach, rudd, and carp are all successfully breeding here with a few supplemental carp added. It can get weedy at times.

→ Cambridge-fpas.co.uk 52.3135, 0.1625 £45/year Fly, bait, spin, led Coarse

22 THE OLD WEST

Yet another great name of a fishery on the CFPAS books. Tench can grow to a large size here, 7lb and above, but they are not numerous. Most other coarse species are present. Reports suggest that this is a good all-year-round fishery.

→ Cambridge-fpas.co.uk 52.3328, 0.2209 £45/year Fly, bait, spin, led Coarse

23 BURWELL

The Cambridgeshire Lodes are a series of man-made waterways, believed to be Roman in origin. The Burwell Lode is good for pike and zander in the winter months, and the summer sees the bream and roach anglers trying their luck. The depth is uniformly between six and ten feet deep. We're told the best bet is to stay mobile until you hit fish.

→ Cambridge-fpas.co.uk 52.2862, 0.3189 £45/year Fly, bait, spin, led Coarse

24 LARK RIVER/PRICKWILLOW

A delightful little fenland river, and, very polite: it's a very gentle, sedate flow. Not really a lark at all, a misnomer. Expect bags of tench, roach, and bream in the summer months. The Club suggests fishing in the winter, where matchmen can get fabulous hauls of small silverfish.

→ Cambridge-fpas.co.uk 52.4168, 0.3487 £45/year Fly, bait, spin, led Coarse

23

24

28

25 CAM/BYRON'S POOL

Byron's Pool was named after Lord Byron, who used to swim at the weir pool. No mention if he ever fished here, and he probably didn't. Byron, no stranger to hyperbole, is quoted as saying "The art of angling, the cruelest, the coldest and the stupidest of pretended sports." Thanks, Byron. Anyway, biggish chub, roach, and pike abound here.

→ Cambridge-fpas.co.uk 52.1713, 0.0986 £45/year Fly, bait, spin, led Coarse

LINCOLNSHIRE

26 WELLAND RIVER

All the coarse fish that you can possibly think of are here to be caught, but we're told this is regarded as a hard river to fish. Anglers concentrate on the bream and tench during the summer months, but the winter is regarded as prime piking time. A lovely pursuit on a frosted winter morning.

→ Deepingstjamesanglingclub.co.uk 52.6799, -0.1843 £5 Fly, bait, spin, led Coarse

ESSEX

27 EPPING FOREST/LOWER FOREST LAKE

We have Mr. Yarburgh, a local brewer, to thank for this lake, which he commissioned to provide a swimming pool and work for the local residents in the exceptionally cold winter of 1893/4. I'm assuming Mr. Yarburgh didn't expect the locals to swim in the winter months. Predominately carp and gudgeon.

→ Cityoflondon.gov.uk 51.6329, 0.0186 Free Fly, bait Coarse

28 EPPING FOREST/WAKE VALLEY POND

In the past, we've heard that it's been tough fishing for carp and tench. There was even speculation of fish theft. However, I know that this is a very well-managed fishery with frequent spot checks of angling ID, so I think theft is highly unlikely.

→ Cityoflondon.gov.uk 51.6516, 0.0444 Free Fly, bait Coarse

29 EPPING FOREST/BALDWINS HILL POND

We hear reports of pike being caught in this pond, which was originally built in 1874, or so. Tench are more common. It's a pretty spot, dammed at one end and fed by a stream on the other.

→ Cityoflondon.gov.uk 51.6584, 0.0588 Free Fly, bait Coarse

30 IRLAM'S BEACH

Expect bass and eels from the end of March, peaking in summer, and then flounders and mullet at the top of the tide around the mouth of the creeks. Big bass from September to November on evening tides. Winter then goes into whiting and flounders.

→ Parking at West End Lane car park 51.9181, 1.261 Free Beach Bass, flounder

NORFOLK

31 THE WASH

As every school child knows, The Wash is where King John lost his crown jewels. On the Norfolk side of this enormous expanse, you can do some productive bass fishing. You'll need a long rod, but also remember, that bass are more frequently caught on a short cast. When they come in, they can come in, depending on the water, very close indeed.

→ Plenty of parking at The Wash. 52.8777, 0.2032 Free Beach Bass

32 MANOR FARM FISHING LAKE

A beautiful, peaceful farm carp pond. Great value for money. Also a good spot to try fly fishing for carp. YouTube has many videos telling you how to do it. If you hook a carp on a fly rod, you'll see why this sport is starting to attract so many followers.

→ Manorfarmrunctonholme.co.uk 52.661, 0.3977 £10 Fly, bait, spin, led Carp, roach, tench

33 TAVERHAM MILL

Generally regarded as not an easy water to fish, but you could run into a lot of tench. However, with application, you can do well here. The lake has plenty of gravel bars, weed, lilies, and silty patches for long and short-range fishing but don't ignore the margins.

→ Anglianwaterparks.co.uk 52.6775, 1.1929 £8 Fly, bait, spin, led Coarse

34 BLICKLING HALL

One end is shallow and quite weedy, where fishing can be tricky but rewarding. The other end, near the dam wall, is clearer and deeper at up to 10ft. has been known for years as a top bream fishery, with some topping 10lbs. It's a large lake of around 20 acres which has, apparently, carp to over 40lbs. Some large pike too.

→ Nationaltrust.org.uk 52.8129, 1.231 £8 Fly, bait, spin, led Bream, carp, pike

27

32

31

34

40

30

36

35 TRIMINGHAM BEACH

Bass are common here from spring to autumn, and you can also expect codling, whiting, pouting, dabs, and flounders. Trimingham was once a place of pilgrimage with medieval Christians coming from all over the country to see the alabaster head of St John the Baptist.

→ Beach car parks 52.8906, 1.4138
Free Beach Whiting, flounder, bass

36 NORFOLK BROADS

I've divided the Broads into Norfolk and Suffolk Broads. There are plenty of free places to fish and also plenty of places to pay too. The Broads are home to large pike and it's worthwhile to target them. In fact, its one of the premier pike fishing venues in the UK. Pike should only be fished for when the water is cool in the late autumn through to early spring. Warm water pike fishing in shallow venues is not good for pike's health due to low oxygen levels.

→ Norfolkbroads.com 52.6893, 1.6518
Free Fly, bait, spin, led Pike, coarse

SUFFOLK

37 SUFFOLK BROADS

If targeting pike on a fly, I find that tube flies are an excellent choice. They can have long bodies without too much material density. This makes them far easier to cast a decent distance, than heavier, more ungainly flies. Be aware that pike are tricky to handle and release back into the water unharmed. If you're not confident, there are plenty of other fish to target.

→ Norfolkbroads.com 52.4664, 1.6108
Free Fly, bait, spin, led Pike, coarse

38 KESSINGLAND BEACH

The village has been settled for a very long time, evidence shows it's been inhabited since Paleolithic times. Part of the reason will be the fishing that's available here. In the winter, it's primarily a cod fishery, but during the summer, it's good for sole.

→ Park right at the beach. 52.4155, 1.73
Free Beach Cod, sole

39 DUNWICH BEACH

A steep shingle beach which can be fished during all tides and be productive. Good bass fishing during the summer. With rays a possibility too. Dunwich has been described as the English Atlantis; it was once a thriving medieval port - all gone now. Silently disappeared under the waves.

→ Carpark at the beach. 52.2787, 1.6337
Free Beach Bass, rays

40 ALTON WATERS

It's a huge water and gets deep quickly, down to 20m. It has now matured into a very pleasant place to spend time with its bays and tree-lined banks. Highly regarded for bream fishing and tench too, but it's most famous for its roach fishing. Two pounders are not uncommon.

→ Anglianwaterparks.co.uk 51.9755, 1.1464
£8 Deadbait Roach, bream, carp

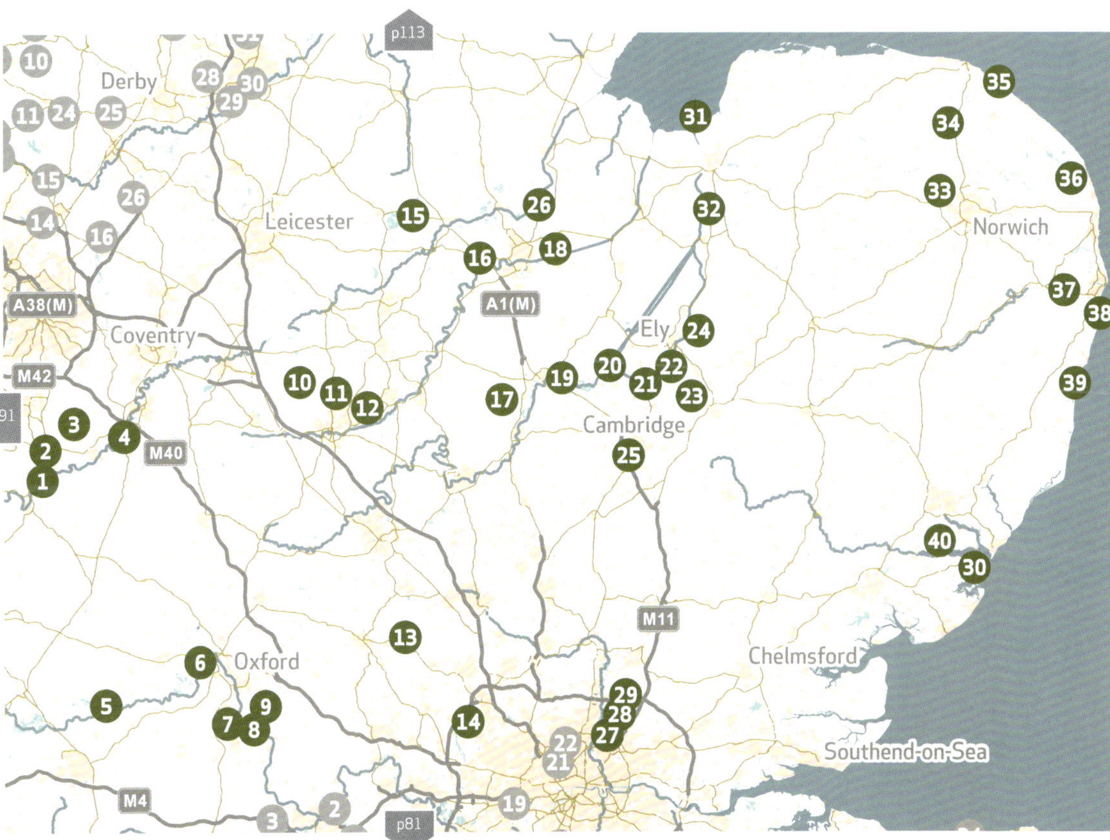

Peaks & Shires

Derbyshire is steeped in angling history. Izaak Walton, who wrote *The Compleat Angler* in 1653, would, with Charles Cotton, fish the River Dove in Derbyshire. The fish in the Dove have not changed since Walton's day. The modern-day piscator can still ply his pastime searching for the elusive barbel, chub, bream, roach, dace, carp, perch, pike, grayling, and trout along the river. All this angling history for a mere £6 a day, courtesy of the Peak Angling Passport. "Study to be quiet" was one of Walton's most quoted aphorisms – still highly relevant to this day and even more so when fishing for wild fish, who will scarper at the first whiff of an angler lumbering along the bank.

Cheshire has fewer rivers compared to other parts of the country. Its biggest and probably best-known angling river is the Dee, which offers excellent coarse and game fishing, including fishing for salmon. Probably equally well known is the River Mersey, which starts at the confluence of the Rivers Goyt and Tame in Stockport. Although water quality in the Mersey was severely affected by industrialisation, the river is now in better shape than at any time since the Industrial Revolution, with reports of salmon having been seen. However, of more relevance for wild fishermen, are the smaller rivers of the Cheshire Plain including the River Dane, the Goyt, Dean, Bollin, and the River Weaver. Here, for a few pounds, you can fish in solitary splendour with only a few sheep to critique your choice of flies or casting technique.

Nottinghamshire is famous for its proud coal mining heritage, Sherwood Forest, and the mighty River Trent, which is rapidly regaining its place as one of the top fishing rivers in the country. This is thanks to diligent work by the local angling clubs and improvements in water quality since the reorganisation of the water industry in the mid-1970s. Nowadays, catches of large barbel and chub are commonplace, while its main tributaries, the River Soar, Erewash, and Idle, continue to shine, particularly for coarse fishing.

2

CHESHIRE

1 HURELSTON RESERVOIR

The banks are fairly steep here, so care is required. A good year-round fishery with some very large fish recorded, including pike to 28lb and carp to 33lb. It's not the easiest of fishing, but if you're prepared to put in the hard yards, the results will be very gratifying.

→ Nantwichangling.com 53.0938, -2.5651 £20/year Fly, bait, spin, led Pike, carp, coarse

2 WEAVER RIVER

Meandering miles through the Cheshire countryside and into the River Mersey before entering the sea, the River Weaver is a great all-round coarse fishery. We're told the fish are quite bold here, so a 12/14 size hook is ideal. Specimen fish abound, and it's perhaps one of the keenest priced fisheries in England.

→ Northwichanglers.co.uk 53.2271, -2.5419 £5 Fly, bait, spin, led Coarse

3 DANE (URBAN FISHING)

Most UK freshwater fish can be found in these waters. We're told it's the cleanest river in Cheshire and a delight to fish.
You can try all styles of fishing, from ledgering through to fly fishing, even, one of my favourites, a solo, unweighted worm on a hook.

→ Northwichanglers.co.uk 53.2594, -2.5156 £5 Fly, bait, spin, led Coarse

4 WOORE FARM/LOWER POOL

Another new addition to the Fenton and District portfolio of waters. This pool is packed with features, and around the islands are large shoals of double-figure chub. Also, if you're minded, you can spend the day causing havoc to the plentiful silver fish population.

→ Fdasofficial.co.uk 52.9771, -2.3873 £23/year Fly, bait, spin, led Chub, coarse

STAFFORDSHIRE

5 STOUR/STOURTON CASTLE

This is a new fishery for the BAA. So, as yet, the facts are few and far between. That said, a new fishery that, perhaps, has not been fished heavily before needs a careful look. It's overlooked by Stourton Castle, believed to be a medieval hunting lodge dating from the reign of King William II.

→ Baa.uk.com 52.46, -2.2069 £40/year Fly, bait, spin, led Coarse

6 KNYPERSLEY RESERVOIR

Described on the Fenton and District website as an absolute beast of a water. It's certainly a spectacle. There are reputedly very large carp in here, but locating them will be daunting. Frankly, I'm not sure how you would start to go about it - the experts would, but they never tell me. Very large pike here too.

→ Fdasofficial.co.uk 53.0925, -2.1561 £23/year Fly, bait, spin, led Pike, carp, coarse

7 BLACK LAKE

One of Fenton and District's most picturesque lakes, it's lovely to behold. Giant perch lurk in these waters, up to three pounds. They've been taking them on lob worms. They describe it as a moody lake, but when it's on form, you can expect sensational days of fishing.

→ Fdasofficial.co.uk 52.946, -2.0886 £23/year Fly, bait, spin, led Perch, carp, coarse

8 DILHORNE LAKE

Set within the Dilhorne Estate and owned by the Buller family, who were, apparently, London lawyers. They obviously did well; it couldn't have only been conveyancing work, the estate must have cost a fortune. These

13

12

15

two lakes are big carp and pike waters.
→ Fdasofficial.co.uk 52.9904, -2.0452 £ £23/year Fly, bait, spin, led Pike, carp, coarse

9 HAMPS/REDMORLEE

Don't ignore the wet fly - sparsely dressed spider patterns can be useful if fish are showing but refusing the dry fly. Also, nymphs. This section of the Hamps is good for wading. As usual, wade with care, and even though it's easy wading, a wading staff is always helpful.
→ Peakanglingpassport.co.uk 53.0592, -1.9116 £ £12 Fly BT

10 CHURNET RIVER/RED ROAD

Coarse anglers have a great time here with a trotted maggot accounting for an array of species: roach, dace, perch, chub, and the odd bream. But the Churnet at this location is really about the mayfly hatch, which is significant - so, trout and grayling make up the majority of angling intentions here, certainly during the mayfly season.
→ Fdasofficial.co.uk 52.9871, -1.9075 £ £23/year Fly, bait, spin, led BT, Gr, coarse

11 BLITHE RIVER/LOXELY

I've always liked the sound of the Blithe River, it sounds so British. Edwardianly English. Yet another Fenton river with serious chub fishing potential. Again, good for the game anglers too, with both trout and grayling. Even, so we're told, a tiger trout, probably an escapee.
→ Fdasofficial.co.uk 52.8771, -1.9358 £ £23/year Fly, bait, spin, led Chub, BT, Gr, coarse

12 TRENT/WESTON

This stretch had a pollution incident many years ago and has been nursed back to health. The club describes fishing here as like jungle warfare because of this, it's rarely fished. So now's your chance to open up an innocent stretch of water. One angler did have a phenomenal haul of grayling here once.
→ Fdasofficial.co.uk 52.8403, -2.048 £ £23/year Fly, bait, spin, led Coarse

13 SOW RIVER/TIXALL

A new addition to Fenton and District's waters, the Sow river has some very large chub finning about at Tixall. There's also a large shoal of roach and some dace, perch, and barbel. It's the specimen chub that are of most interest to me. Catch a record on a fly, for example?
→ Fdasofficial.co.uk 52.7952, -2.0341 £ £23/year Fly, bait, spin, led Chub, barbel, coarse

14 COPPICE LANE FISHERY

Beautiful spot, very quiet with good quality fish. There are about one hundred double-figure carp in the pool, a mixture of commons, mirrors, ghost, and a single leather. There are some gorgeous heavy-plated mirrors, ghosties, and, of course, the single leather.
→ Coppicelanefishery.co.uk 52.6618, -1.8878 £ £8 Fly, bait, spin, led Carp, coarse

15 TRENT/HANDSACRE

This is generally regarded as a winter roach water. You can fish here during the summer months for barbel, chub, and bream, but it usually becomes heavily weeded, which can frustrate even the most dedicated angler. So, mark your calendars for the winter months and target the lovely roach.
→ Baa.uk.com 52.7477, -1.8669 £ £40/year Fly, bait, spin, led Roach, coarse

21

16

22

24

16 ANKER/BOLEHALL

Not Urban Fishing, but close to Tamworth. For a small river, it contains a good head of chub, roach, tench, barbel, and pike. The website suggests you can use the Bolehall Social Club; not sure if this is only for parking or if you can also venture inside. Perhaps pop your head in and ask?

→ Baa.uk.com 52.6326, -1.6843 £40/year Fly, bait, spin, led Pike, coarse

DERBYSHIRE

17 DOVECOTES LODGE

Slap bang in the middle of this pool is an island with a Grade 2 listed Victorian dovecote. Not a known hotspot for specimen fish, but it's got some bream and, I believe, the odd trout swimming about - doubtlessly admiring the dovecote too.

→ Dnmac.org.uk 53.3747, -2.037 £60/year Bait Bream

18 GOYT RIVER

This has been a polluted water previously, but it has been brought back to rude health by the club. The beats are in a mixture of urban and rural areas, allowing the angler to practise his, or her, urban fishing skills and then to retreat back to the usual fishing in peace and quiet that we all enjoy.

→ Dnmac.org.uk 53.37, -2.0313 £60/year Fly, bait BT, Gr

19 SETT RIVER

The River Sett is a tributary of the River Goyt. We're told that the ubiquitous Adams fly works well here, doubtless in sizes 14 and smaller. Of course, you should be fishing these small streams and brooks with a long leader. However, I much prefer a small leader. Light as possible but not too long. I need that for line control.

→ Dnmac.org.uk 53.3802, -1.9677 £60/year Fly, bait, spin, led BT

20 BIRCH VALE RESERVOIR

The Disley is a little more money than most clubs in the book, and they don't offer day tickets but, to my mind, it's still a bargain. Birch Vale Reservoir is set in the remarkable scenery of the High Peak. There are specimen pike, carp, and perch. I think of it as a pike water. The water is gin clear, so stealth is crucial to catch anything, even including the swarms of roach.

→ Dnmac.org.uk 53.3795, -1.9653 £60/year Fly, bait, spin, led Pike, Pe, coarse

21 LADYBOWER FISHERY

As almost everybody knows, this is the reservoir connected to the Dambusters. So, you can hum the tune as either a) you make your way to the water or b) as you first start fishing. To do both will create bad fishing luck. If you do it correctly, you can expect some serious trout fishing and even, an odd monster (20lbs). This is not the type of water we normally champion; it's not Wild Fishing. However, it's done well and if you fancy a go at large stocked trout, this is the place.

→ Ladybowerfisheries.co.uk 53.3687, -1.6994 £22 Fly BT, RT

22 MONYASH POND

Located in the centre of the pretty village of Monyash. The Domesday book lists the village as Maneis, which means "many springs or waters," which, I guess, refers to the pond you'll be fishing in almost a thousand years later. Small tench here can be caught in some numbers on a float.

→ Dnmac.org.uk 53.1947, -1.7767 £60/year Bait Tench

23 DOVE/MILL LANE

Small stream fishing again. Made famous by the immortal Izaak Walton and Charles Cotton. Small rods, long light leaders, and a stealthy demeanour should see you through. True of all waters but, perhaps, even more so of The Dove - you need to be in the right place at the right time.

→ Peakanglingpassport.co.uk 53.1401, -1.821 £6 Fly BT

24 DOVE/DOVERIDGE

Massive chub are here; some have been caught in excess of six pounds. Double-figure barbel too. This is a specimen hunter's patch. To finish it off, there's also plenty of free rising trout and grayling too, for the game angler. That said, it's the chub that interest me most here.

→ Fdasofficial.co.uk 52.8823, -1.8134 £23/year Fly, bait, spin, led Chub, barbel, BT, Gr

25 SUTTON BROOK

A small tributary of The Dove, which was stocked with brown trout in the past. At one time, it was only fished with a dry fly, presumably upstream, and anything else was sneered at. Thankfully, this southern snobbery has disappeared, allowing the paying angler to fish as he or she wishes (within the guidelines, of course). I'm partial to downstream nymphing, which is very common in the States. Another great spot to

30

29

target large chub and barbel on a fly.

→ Fdasofficial.co.uk 52.8729, -1.6428 £23/year Fly, bait, spin, led BT, Gr, chub, barbel

26 MEASE/NETHERSEAL

What a delight this stream is! It twists and turns and almost turns back on itself. It is varied in depth too, from deep pools to shallow speedy runs. Something for everybody, but it really suits the roving angler who will put the miles in scouring the river looking for fish. Specimen size pike and barbel are here.

→ Baa.uk.com 52.7119, -1.5743 £40/year Fly, bait, spin, led Pike, barbel, coarse

27 BUTTERSLEY RESERVOIR

It's really two reservoirs made of a larger one split in two by a railway. In summer months, the shallow areas are more productive, and in the winter months, the deeper sections come into their own. Many large carp of 30 lb plus.

→ Butterleyreservoir.co.uk 53.0581, -1.4313 £12 Fly, bait, spin, led Coarse

28 SOWBROOK LAKE

A former quarry that was not producing good fishing until, in 2001, the club completely transformed it with a great deal of work (essentially a two-year project to reduce the depth). Now, good catches of bream and roach are far more common. Tench too.

→ Nottinghamanglers.co.uk 52.9521, -1.3156 £55/year Fly, Bait Coarse

NOTTINGHAMSHIRE

29 ATTENBOROUGH NATURE RESERVE

Opened in 1966 by David Attenborough. I assume they named the reserve for him; it couldn't have been a coincidence, could it? To the west of the River Erewash, these three gravel pits can be fished year-round. Expect good catches if you can locate the fish. No spinning permitted on these waters.

→ Nottinghamanglers.co.uk 52.9011, -1.2336 £55/year Fly, bait Bream, coarse

30 TRENT/BEESTON

This is a well-run club, so some of its waters are included here even though it's more expensive than most in the book. It's still a bargain for an entire year's fishing and over a dozen waters to choose from. Fast and shallow water in this location where you can pick up both chub and barbel.

→ Nottinghamanglers.co.uk 52.9109, -1.2013 £55/year Fly, bait, spin, led Chub, barbel

31 BESTWOOD DUCK PONDS

Lovely heavily wooded environs, a very pleasant place to fish. Five ponds, each with their own character and fish. The club website will explain which is which. Number 5 pond, for example, has specimen carp; it's prone to weeding up in summer months, but you can always fish one of the banks throughout the year.

→ Nottinghamanglers.co.uk 53.0388, -1.1737 £55/year Fly, bait Coarse

32 MAUN RIVER

The club tells us that the Maun is a small, winding river but subject to weed, prohibiting fishing in parts. Ideally suited to the often forgotten art of trotting and requiring a minimal amount of tackle as searching out the fish often requires frequent moving.

→ Nottinghamanglers.co.uk 53.2075, -1.0169 £55/year Fly, bait Coarse

LINCOLNSHIRE

33 HARTSHOLME LAKE

This is a large body of water, and all the main species are present and, again, due to its size, the fish are variously sized, as you would expect. Bream to 11lb, tench to 7lb, carp to 32lb, with the predators here too, pike and perch.

→ Lincolnangling.org 53.2166, -0.5847 £10 Fly, bait, spin, led Carp, coarse

34 STEEPING RIVER (URBAN FISHING)

In Wainfleet, good free, semi-urban fishing. Narrow and weedy, it doesn't look like ideal water, but it is. Try a waggler and corn for bream. You can also hunt for pike in here. Probably gentle spinning with a Mepps would do the job.

→ Wainfleet.info 53.1038, 0.236 Free Fly, bait, spin, led Coarse, Pe, roach

35 MOGGS EYE BEACH

Moggs Eye, also known as Huttoft Beach, is a quiet, rural beach backed by grassy sand dunes. It has a wide strip of golden sand which slopes gently into the sea. Good for cod, we are reliably informed. Named by The Guardian as one of the best wild beach walks.

→ Car park at the beach 53.2704, 0.32 Free Beach Cod

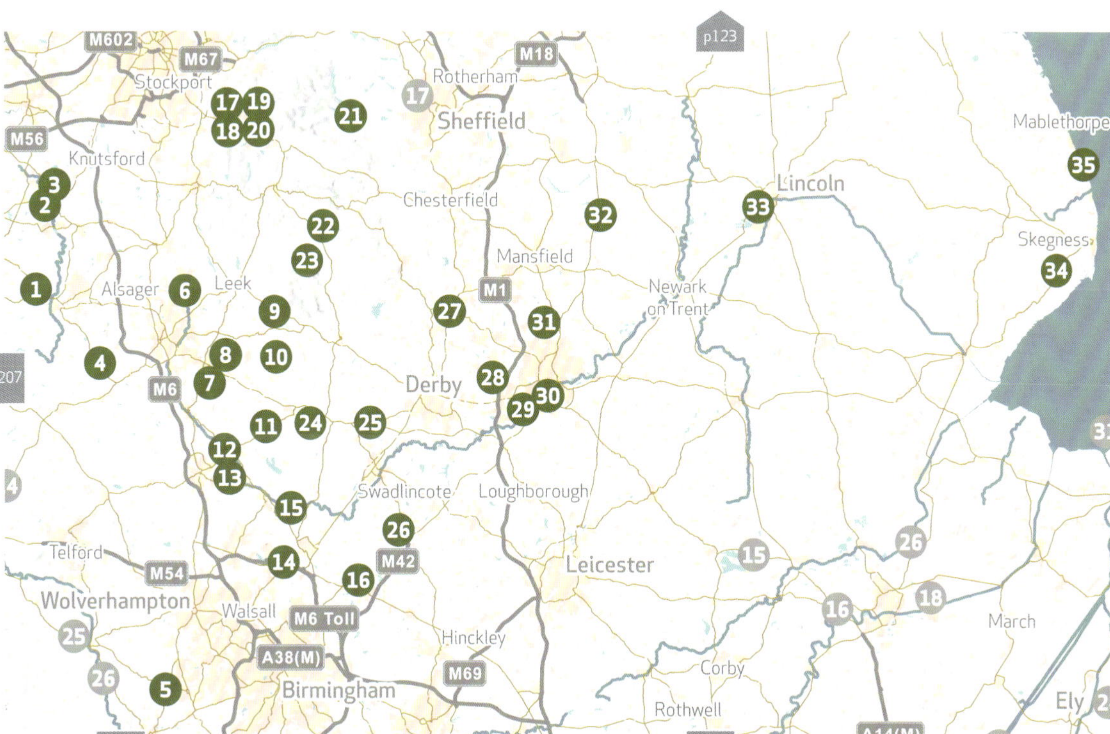

13

Lancashire & Yorkshire

I'm guessing L.S. Lowry is to blame for the perception that Lancashire is a county of cotton mills and factories spewing oily smoke. It's true that Lancashire incorporates Liverpool and grand old northern towns like Preston, Blackburn, and Burnley with their long industrial heritage. But the county is also where magnificent scenery can be enjoyed, including expansive moorlands, the foothills of the Pennines, the beautiful Forest of Bowland, and famous enchanting rivers like the Ribble, Lune, and Wyre, along with their tributaries the Calder, Darwen, Douglas, Hodder, and Yarrow.

The Ribble is safeguarded by the Ribble Trust, and they offer an angling passport to fish their rivers. This scheme, and others like it, notably the Wye/Usk Passport, is an innovative scheme that permits anglers, both local and visitors, to fish obscure beats, rivers, and brooks. This allows those who enjoy fishing off the beaten track to explore waters all over the country.

Yorkshire is famed for the Yorkshire Dales and the North York Moors, where the rivers include the Tees and the smaller Esk to the east; the River Ouse and its tributaries; the Derwent in the north; and the Swale, Nidd, and Aire in the centre of the county, whilst further south, there's the River Don. The Yorkshire Dales especially are known for their water purity, and the rivers are filled with trout from the Wharfe, the Ure, and the Ribble, to the more obscure Doe and Twiss. All will give you the complete Wild Fishing experience.

The modern version of fly fishing was developed on the tumbling, rocky rivers of this region and southern Scotland. T.E. Pritt wrote *Yorkshire Trout Flies* in 1885, but of course, the flies themselves had been around for centuries before. Simple to tie and cheap to buy, North Country Spider flies are austere, elegant, and highly effective. So much so, they have travelled around the world. In the US, they are called Soft Hackle flies, and a modern-day Pritt, Sylvester Nemes, wrote the most approachable series of books I have ever found on the subject called, with not much imagination, *The Soft Hackle Fly Addict*. He writes far better than he names books.

LANCASHIRE

1 FORMBY BEACH

This is a big sandy beach, so it fishes best a couple of hours either side of high and low tide. Researching this beach, I was reminded that when shore fishing, always look for gullies behind you. You don't want to get caught out on an incoming tide. Good chance of landing a bass, or two here.

→ Use Lifeboat Road car park 53.5466, -3.102 Free Beach Bass

2 LUNE RIVER

The LDAA has been going for 100 years and they have a five-mile stretch of the River Lune, sometimes called The Loyne, available on a day ticket with good salmon, sea trout, and brown trout fishing. Especially good for sea trout fishing with a fly at night.

→ Ldaa.fish 54.0734, -2.7335 £20 Fly, spin, worm BT, Sa, ST

3 LOUD, UPPER

It's a lowland-type river with a few tree-lined places. The fishability is quite good, however, still requires accurate casting with short rods. There are brown trout and every chance of grayling or even chub. Time to perfect your chub fly fishing and, of course, roll casting technique.

→ Ribbletrust.org.uk 53.8565, -2.5876 £5 Fly, spin, worm BT, Gr, chub

4 LOUD, LOWER

Mainly short rods are required because there are plenty of trees to catch the unwary. However, there are open sections if you're getting tired of unhooking flies from trees on your backcast. You'll expect to catch trout, chub, and even, if very lucky, a sea trout.

→ Ribbletrust.org.uk 53.8829, -2.5345 £5 Fly, spin, worm BT, ST, Gr, chub

5 BOTTOMS BECK

Deep within the Ginsburg Forest area, this beck offers a lot of variety and contains some excellent pools. You'll be fishing in a tranquil spot with little to disturb you. Small rods, no more than four weight, will be required to sensibly fish here.

→ Ribbletrust.org.uk 54.0019, -2.3929 £7.50 Fly BT

6 BASHALL BROOK/TWITTER LANE

Oystercatchers, grey wagtails, sand martins, and herons are frequently seen along Bashall Brook. You can expect both trout and chub here, but caution and stealth will yield the best results. With only the occasional tree to hide behind, it will make creeping up on the fish difficult, but as they face upriver, not impossible.

→ Ribbletrust.org.uk 53.8799, -2.43 £5 Fly BT

7 RIBBLE AND CALDER/MITTON

Fish in this stretch of the River Ribble includes chub, barbel, dace, eels, grayling, and dace, and, of course, trout and sea trout so there is plenty to fish for in this beautiful river. Ideal time to only bring a fly rod and see how many different fish you can target and catch in a day.

→ Ribbletrust.org.uk 53.8434, -2.4316 £15 Fly, spin, worm BT, ST, Sa, coarse

8 STOCK BECK/DEEP DALE

The beck offers a lot of variety and contains some excellent pools. With little bankside vegetation, the access and ease of casting are excellent. A beautiful beck surrounded by glacial drumlins that make it a scenic place to fish. It has an excellent population of trout up to surprising sizes and also offers the opportunity of grayling.

→ Ribbletrust.org.uk 53.9433, -2.2481 £5 Fly BT

9 FOULRIDGE RESERVOIR

Apparently a big bream water but, I also note, the club record is a carp of 34lb 6oz! Not large, you can walk around its entirety in ninety minutes. As ever for these types of waters, be mindful of the wind; the fish frequently follow it.

→ PendleburnleYdaa.co.uk 53.8677, -2.1627 £4 Fly, bait, spin, led Coarse, pike, carp

12

8

11

15

YORKSHIRE

10 TWISS & DOE

Both rivers start high up in the fells. This is delightful wild trout fishing. Arm yourself with a lightweight rod (2wt to 4wt), although I find a 2wt far too difficult if there is any wind at all. Then, get moving and check out all the pools. Great fun on a summer evening.

→ Ingletonanglingassociation.co.uk
54.1561, -2.4708 £10 Fly BT

11 BAIN/BAINBRIDGE

The River Bain is the shortest river in England, so beats for day tickets are scant. Not only is it small but it's narrow; best to fish a 7-foot, 4 wt rod. The trout are free-rising here and will merrily grab a dry fly. We're told they're always hungry, scant rations in the river so, perhaps, choice of fly is not that crucial.

→ Yorkshire-dales-flyfishing.com 54.31, -2.1023 £10 Fly BT

12 URE/BAINBRIDGE

Incredible scenery marks these fishing beats, all priced very keenly. Good head of native brown trout and lovely grayling. As it's near the headwaters, you'll find the fishing is best after a good rainfall. You can also get to fish the River Bain too on this day ticket.

→ Yorkshire-dales-flyfishing.com 54.3104, -2.1058 £10 Fly BT, Gr

13 MALHAM TARN

Arguably, one of the best UK wild trout fisheries. Not easy but high quality and large trout. Blank days are to be expected on these waters. The water doesn't seep into the ground; the impermeable slate just keeps it there within the tarn.

→ Nationaltrust.org.uk 54.1005, -2.1692 Free Fly BT

14 WHARFE/KILNSEY

The second oldest club in the country offers a lovely stretch of Wharfedale, but the beats are somewhat small and, perhaps, at the top end of our budget. Large, stocked trout on the lower beats but the upper beats provide an excellent wild fishing experience.

→ Kilnseyanglingclub.co.uk 54.1066, -2.0401 £35 Fly BT

15 WHARFE/BOLTON ABBEY

This river runs through the Bolton Abbey estate, so it can be tourist-heavy. Best avoided on the weekendws but usually fine on the weekdays- and well worth the extra effort. Both wild and stocked brown trout, with a good head of grayling.

→ Boltonabbey.com 53.9835, -1.8863 £23 Fly BT, Gr

16 HOLME/HUDDERSFIELD (URBAN)

There's enough invertebrates in the River Holme to support a decent head of grayling and trout. We're told small klinkhammer flies do the job (as they do in most cases). Float fishing with a maggot for roach and bream is highly recommended by the locals (and great fun).

→ All accessible spots through Huddersfield, Kirlees Council 53.6292, -1.7988 Free Fly, bait, spin, led BT, chub, barbel, dace

17 LOXLEY/SHEFFIELD (URBAN)

These waters can hold large trout- fish of a lb and a half are relatively common. Nymph fishing can be problematic due to subsurface impediments, relics of Sheffield's industrial past. Ideally fish on the surface, or at a pinch, wet flies. Otherwise, you could drag anything up.

→ All accessible spots through Sheffield, Sheffield Town Council 53.4002, -1.5149 Free Fly, bait, spin, led BT

20

27

19

22

18 NIDD/PATELEY BRIDGE

Yorkshire Bitter is commonly how the colour of this river is described; it's caused by the peat substrate. A good head of brown trout and grayling are to be had and both rise well to a dry fly throughout the season. Best flies are commonly held to be CDCs and Emergers and the ubiquitous Klinkhammer.

→ Nidderdaleac.co.uk 54.0849, -1.7612 £15 Fly BT, Gr

19 STOCK BECK, UPPER

Superb views to enjoy while stalking the resident wily brown trout. It feels much more like a stream. For me, it's ideal water to wade upstream flicking an Elk Hair Caddis as you go. The Elk Hair is a superb fly for these kinds of waters, hard to sink and the trout love 'em.

→ Ribbletrust.org.uk 54.1666, -1.7035 £5 Fly BT

20 LEIGHTON RESERVOIR

Leighton Reservoir is 105 acres with 90 acres fishable by bank anglers. 90ft deep when full but the level can vary through the year due to rainfall. In common with most upland waters, the reservoir carries a permanent peat stain and has its own fly life.

→ Bessybecktrout.co.uk 54.2015, -1.7591 £32 Fly BT, RT

21 COVER RIVER

When the conditions are right, the river Cover offers a knowledgeable angler excellent fly fishing. There can be some very large grayling and trout in here considering the size of the water. It is a gently meandering river with beaches leading to wooded, low banks.

→ Thecoverbridgeinn.co.uk 54.2789, -1.7794 £9 Fly BT, Gr

22 SWALE/RICHMOND

The Swale offers an excellent opportunity to target barbel on a fly. Challenging but a great feeling of accomplishment is yours with a barbel capture. Best flies? As they're bottom feeders, tungsten nymphs are your best bet. Probably with a strike indicator.

→ Richmondangling.org.uk 54.4008, -1.7345 £8 Fly BT, barbel

23 OUSE RIVER/BENNINGBROUGH

A bargain for £47 a year. All the main river fish are present with specimen pike having been caught around The Nidd mouth. Shoals of bream are living here year-round, making this a very attractive beat for the dedicated bream angler.

→ Ydaa.org.uk 54.0045, -1.1826 £47/year Fly, bait Pike, coarse

24 OUSE/YORK (URBAN)

The Ouse here is deep and sluggish, with depths of 15 to 20 ft in the middle. Best bet is float fishing. There can be lots of boats and, of course, you'll need to be prepared to answer the perennial question - have you caught anything yet? But it's free...

→ york.gov.uk 53.9675, -1.1037 Free Fly, bait, spin, led Coarse

25 BARTON HILL BECK

A joyous little stream, tiny and clear flowing, best fished in the spring and summer. Caution should be your watchword; there are a number of wild brown trout but they will scatter at the slightest provocation. Chub are also here in the deeper pools and are more tolerant of man.

→ Ydaa.org.uk 54.0683, -0.9134 £47/year Fly, bait BT

26 SEVEN RIVER

An opportunity for classic small stream fishing, containing all types of species,

33

30

32

from native brown trout to grayling, dace, chub, and pike. The fish may not be of record-breaking size but can be a challenge of rivercraft in such small a water. Ideal for trotting with a centerpin, light floats and maggots, but will also produce to the fly, or with dead baits for pike.

→ Ydaa.org.uk 54.1908, -0.8617 £47/year Fly, bait BT, pike, coarse

27 RYE RIVER

Most coarse fish are present and the river averages seven feet in places and responds well to running lines and stick floats used in conjunction with maggots or casters. Regular little and often feeding should draw the fish to the angler. Larger fish are caught using static ledgered baits, meat, cheese paste, or pellets.

→ Ydaa.org.uk 54.1735, -0.8527 £47/year Fly, bait Coarse

28 LOCKWOOD BECK RESERVOIR

An ex-trout fishery. We're told excessive cormorant predation made it very difficult to continue. So, it's now a coarse fishery. Tench are somewhat cormorant-proof but other fish? Time will tell...

→ Bookwhen.com/watersideparksnorth 54.5172, -0.9679 £7 Fly, bait, spin, led Roach, Pe, BT

29 SCALING DAM RESERVOIR

The pike respond well to lure fishing at Scaling Dam, but dead baits also work very well here. The coarse fish roam the lake in big shoals, so baiting a nice-sized area is a good idea. If the weather is decent, expect swimmers here too but, given the size of the reservoir, they can easily be avoided.

→ Bookwhen.com/watersideparksnorth 54.5036, -0.8563 £10 Fly, bait, spin, led Roach, pike, Pe

30 RUNSWICK BAY

Decent-sized cod can be caught here close in after poor weather. It stirs up the seabed and frees sources of food. The bay is made up of some sandy, clean ground with weed cover and much heavier rocky ground. It can get very kelpy.

→ Park at the beach but be quick, few spaces 54.5288, -0.7443 Free Beach Cod

31 CLOUGHTON BEACH

Bit of a snag pit but you needn't cast out far to be in the action. It's a fairly easy rope descent via the grass-filled cleft. Be wary of the incoming tide; people have been cut off. Big cod are here in the winter, which can make the rope descent seem worthwhile.

→ Park at the beach 54.3402, -0.4287 Free Beach Cod

32 CORNELIAN BAY

Cornelian Bay (love the name) has big cod, which come in close to shore after a big storm. Nearby Clayton Bay also offers large cod after a big storm too. It's dramatic after a storm here; the two mute pillboxes staring out to sea are your only company.

→ Short walk from the beach. 54.255, -0.3691 Free Beach Cod, whiting, coalfish

33 SPURN POINT

Spurn Head or Spurn Point, is a spit of land on the Humber Estuary. Three miles long and often only fifty metres wide. At low water go to the very tip for the best results. Good cod close in during the winter months. It's a long walk, but truly wild fishing. Best advice: travel light, otherwise you'll be too tired to fish.

→ £5 to park all day 53.5783, 0.1131 Free Beach Cod

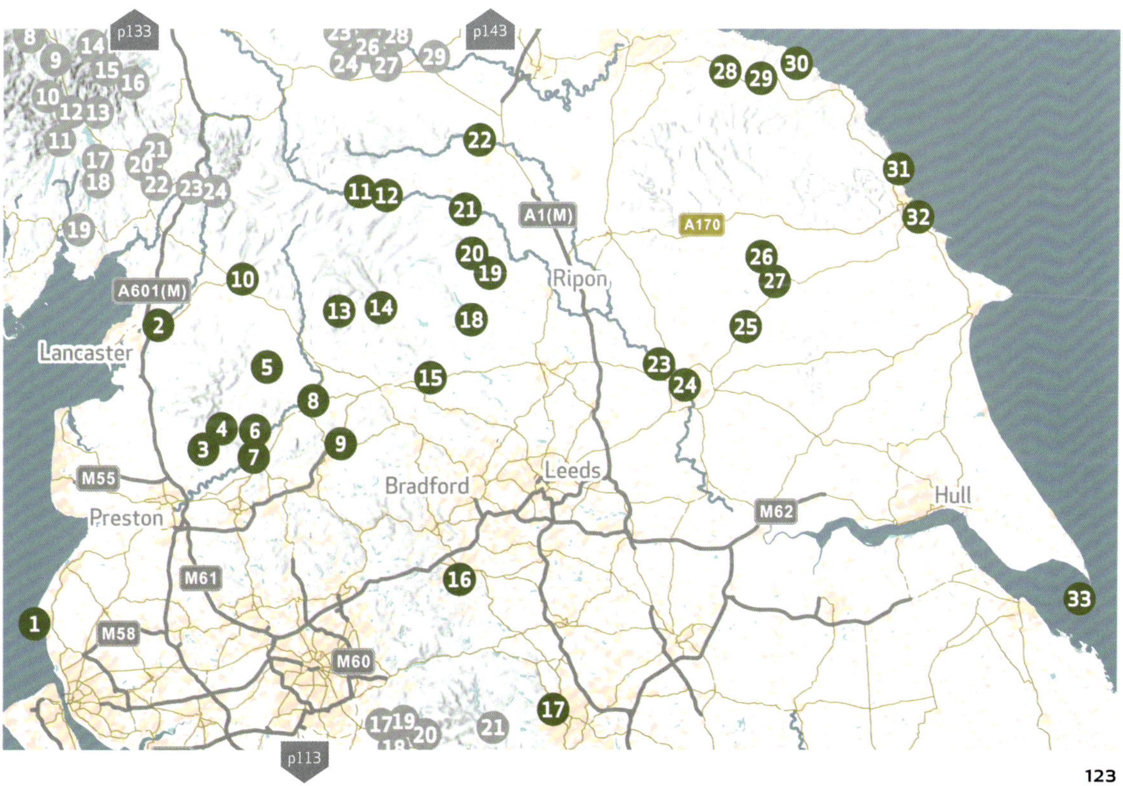

Cumbria

Peter Rabbit's father and Mr Fisher would spend many long summer afternoons in fruitless pursuit of their nemesis, Jack Sharp, the legendary and elusive giant trout who dwells somewhere in the depths of Esthwaite Water. These days, Beatrix Potter's characters would be spending their time chasing giant pike. The largest one hauled from Esthwaite Water was 46lbs, almost a British record. We anglers still have the same cock-eyed optimism as Mr Fisher, who described his house, which is at the bottom of Esthwaite Water, as having a "slight damp problem".

The rivers of Cumbria are some of the cleanest in England, as it's mostly an agricultural economy with very little industry. The farming of Cumbria involves sheep, over two million of them, scattered tastefully around the hills, quietly and diligently growing wool.

The Eden, with its many prolific tributaries, flows north and then turns west at Carlisle into the Solway. This is the biggest and best-known river in the area for its good runs of salmon, sea trout, resident wild brown trout, and grayling. The Eden Valley, most of it hidden from the road, has some stunning scenery. To the immediate south are the Howgill Fells with, I'm sure, the ghost of Wainwright still tramping around, scribbling in his notebook.

The smaller rivers, Border Esk and Derwent, are two other prolific fisheries which can be easily accessed and are perfect for the fly fisher, with good salmon and sea trout fishing. Then there are a host of minor rivers in Cumbria which have excellent trout and grayling fishing. It would take a lifetime to explore them all. Not to my mind a wasted life, if this is what you choose to do with your allotted span. You might, for example, try the Lyvennet. It's described as "technical" fishing, which to me means hard but also rewarding if you are fortunate. The trout are a delightful butter yellow colouring, and these are strong, healthy fish. It's a river that supports healthy hatches of olives and caddis but also Danica mayfly.

1 ST. BEES HEAD

Fishing below the sandstone cliffs of the North Heads gives access to deep water, providing the opportunity to catch better-quality fish. Crabs are best in the summer months for cod, bass, and pollack. Spin a jellyworm or sandeel in calm conditions for pollack and bass. A large mackerel bait fished close in tempts conger eels.

→ Free car park at the beach. 54.5149, -3.6398 Free Beach Pollock, bass

2 MARYPORT

The home of serious plaice anglers. It's where the River Ellon meets the Solway Firth, so the sea fishing is greatly influenced by the strong tides. Flounder and plaice will make up the bulk of catches and can be targeted twelve months of the year, with sport peaking between March and September.

→ Maryport South car park. 54.7199, -3.4978 Free Beach Flounder, plaice

3 LOWESWATER

A smaller lake often bypassed by Lake District visitors, making it a good place to fish in the high season. It's a place of refuge from the crowds. You can fish for brown trout with a bag limit of three. There is also coarse fishing with pike and perch here too.

→ Nationaltrust.org.uk 54.586, -3.3568 Free Fly BT, Pe

4 CRUMMOCK WATER

A magnificent setting with unparalleled views. There are opportunities for trout, char, pike, and perch fishing, with a bag limit of 20 char on the lake. There are also plenty of the yellowish trout too, but you have to search them out. It's not easy fishing.

→ Nationaltrust.org.uk 54.5617, -3.3048 Free Fly BT, ST, Sa

5 BUTTERMERE

Voted as having one of the country's favourite views. Trout, char, pike, and perch can all be found in Buttermere with a bag limit of 20 char. That's a lot of char. Thankfully, they've limited the number of boats permitted at any one time to ten, which, as they say, "keeps the lake's quiet character".

→ Nationaltrust.org.uk 54.5289, -3.2545 Free Fly BT, ST, Sa

6 WASTWATER

Due to its loneliness and surrounding scenery, Wastwater is much admired by photographers and artists and was one of the favourite lakes of Alfred Wainwright. Arctic Char and Trout are the main catches, it is understood that there are also Salmon during the spawning season plus eels and ferox trout. Fishing is from the shore only and, as in all of the other lakes, no live bait is allowed.

→ Honesty box car park at Overbeck. 54.4421, -3.3016 Free Fly, bait, spin, led Ch, BT

7 ESK RIVER

Made famous by Hugh Falkus, much of his writing and filming was centred on this river. Sadly, it has suffered in the past from acid rain but now appears to be making a comeback. Well worth fishing, for, at the very least, walking in a famous angler's footsteps. As a spate river, it always fishes better after heavy rain.

→ Millomanglers.co.uk 54.3844, -3.3128 £20 Fly, spin BT, ST, Sa

8 DERWENT WATER

Massive water, so large you might not see anybody for the entire day while you hunt for a specimen Rainbow Trout. Unlike most of the larger lakes, Derwent Water is

14

9

13

11

10

relatively shallow, having an average depth of just under twenty feet. In terms of fish production, this gives it a significant advantage and the lake carries a higher biomass than most of its counterparts in the region.

→ Bookwhen.com/watersideparksnorth 53.3972, -1.7403 £19 Fly RT

9 THIRLMERE

A large, scenic lake alongside the A591 between Grasmere and Keswick. Thirlmere holds brown trout, pike, perch, and char. Despite its size, this is not a rich lake, and the fish biomass of all species is comparatively small. This feeds through to the pike population, which although healthy, is present in nothing like the size or numbers found elsewhere in Cumbria.

→ There's a number of car parks around the lake 54.5365, -3.0642 Free Fly, bait, spin, led BT, pike, coarse

10 EASEDALE TARN

Thomas de Quincey described Easdale Tarn as a 'Chapel within a Cathedral'. About a two-mile walk from Grasmere, expect to find a lot of trout that will respond well to teams of flies: perhaps a diawl bach on point and a bushy, palmered wet fly on the dropper.

→ Thelakedistrict.org 54.4692, -3.0659 Free Fly BT, Pe

11 YEW TREE TARN

The tarn was formed when a local landowner dammed Yewdale Beck in the 1930s. Fly only and sweet, fat brown trout can be pursued. However, because the tarn is so photogenic, expect to be sharing it with tourists in the high season. Time your trip accordingly.

→ Day permits are available for non-members and can be purchased from the Coniston Tourist Information Centre. 54.3953, -3.0461 £30 Fly BT

12 GRASMERE LAKE

This small lake is one of the region's best natural coarse fisheries, holding prolific shoals of roach, quality perch, and big pike. The main problem with Grasmere is the lack of free parking, although this protects the fishery from overuse. There are two lay-bys on the main road taking three vehicles each.

→ Lakedistrictfishing.co.uk 54.4464, -3.0129 £15 Fly, bait, spin, led Pike, Pe, roach

13 RYDAL WATER

The pike, especially, are present in substantial numbers, averaging seven or eight pounds but with plenty of doubles and twenties to satisfy the specialist angler. A new fishery record was set in 2005 with a magnificent fish of 31lb.

→ Lakedistrictfishing.co.uk 54.4462, -2.9964 £15 Fly, bait, spin, led Coarse

14 ULLSWATER

Well known for brown trout. The best time to fish for them is from early spring through to early summer – March to June seems best. It can be busy, with a lot of various water-based activities being pursued, but you can walk away from most of it and fish in solitude.

→ Western-lakedistrict.co.uk 54.5625, -2.9493 Free Fly, spin BT, pike

15 ANGLE TARN

Lots of brown trout are here, but they are difficult to reach because of herds of small perch. Popular with the wild camping and the wild swimming brigade, so you'll have to work a little for your solitude, but if you time it right, you'll be fine.

→ Nationaltrust.org.uk 54.5206, -2.9032 Free Fly BT, Pe

16

15

17

16 HAWESWATER RESERVOIR

Free rising smallish brown trout up to half a pound. It's rarely fished, so you'll probably be there alone, which can make it all the more daunting. We were assured that they moved the bodies in the churchyard before they submerged the village of Mardale. Still, it gives the area a haunted air.

→ fisheryguide.co.uk 54.4989, -2.8214 Free Fly BT

17 WINDERMERE

Well known for its char, the preferred technique is metal lures dragged along the bottom from boats. The northern basin is often claimed to be the best spot; we also recommend fishing in secluded bays, particularly next to tree-lined banks. Also excellent for bream fishing from the bank, if done correctly you'll get large hauls.

→ Western-lakedistrict.co.uk 54.3618, -2.9272 Free Fly, spin BT, Sa, Pe, char

18 GHYLL HEAD

Trout move around here as the season develops, but early on, most will hold in the deeper holes and respond well to mini lures on sinking lines. Early April sees movement into the shallows, to take advantage of the huge daytime buzzer hatches. During May and June, fish can be all over the fishery but return to the deeps as the water temperatures rise in mid-summer.

→ Lakedistrictfishing.co.uk 54.3238, -2.9255 £28 Fly RT

19 OTTER TARN

The early season buzzer hatches provide exciting surface sport during April, usually followed by good hatches of olives from early May. Later in the year, trout rise freely to the big sedge hatches that occur on warm summer evenings.

→ Lakedistrictfishing.co.uk 54.2393, -2.9822 £28 Fly RT

20 RATHERHEATH TARN

Many anglers fish exclusively for Ratherheath's head of carp. These fish currently top out around the twenty-five pound mark, but there are large numbers in the low to mid-teens. During the warmer months, Ratherheath carp are invariably on the surface and stalking with floating baits is a favourite, and often very successful, tactic.

→ Lakedistrictfishing.co.uk 54.3552, -2.7931 £15 Fly, bait, spin, led Coarse

20

20

24

21

22

23

21 KENT RIVER

The River Kent flows out of Killington Reservoir, and a mile from the reservoir, it joins the River Mint and then becomes the River Kent proper. The river has many waterfalls and weirs which migratory fish have to negotiate. Excellent fishing in this fast-moving water but do be careful of your footing.

→ Kentangling.co.uk 54.3644, -2.7757
£30 Fly, bait, spin, led BT, Sa, ST

22 KENT/KENDALL (URBAN ANGLING)

An illustrious river for free fishing. The River Kent is a designated Salmon River by the EEC. This being so, the water quality is kept at the level acceptable to that governing body. Also, English Nature has designated the River as a Special Site of Scientific Interest as the River supports the habitat of the White Clawed Crayfish and White Pearl Mussel. The Kent is the only river in the country able to do this.

→ Nether Bridge to Victoria Bridge, Kendal Town Council. 54.3207, -2.7445 Free
Fly, bait, spin, led BT

23 KILLINGTON RESERVOIR

Best known for large 20lb pike that haunt these waters but also good fun can be had chasing the lively brown trout here too. Somewhat marred by its proximity to the M6, but you can soon scoot to the other side of the reservoir for peace and quiet.

→ Kentangling.co.uk 54.3149, -2.6341
£5 Fly, bait, spin, led BT, Pike

24 LUNE RIVER/SEDBERGH

The Lune at Sedbergh has a few sea trout and even some salmon for the catching amongst the sizable population of brown trout. All this makes for excellent fishing in the gorgeous countryside around Sedbergh. Lovely day out.

→ Sedberghanglers.org.uk 54.3113, -2.582
£20 Fly BT, ST, Sa

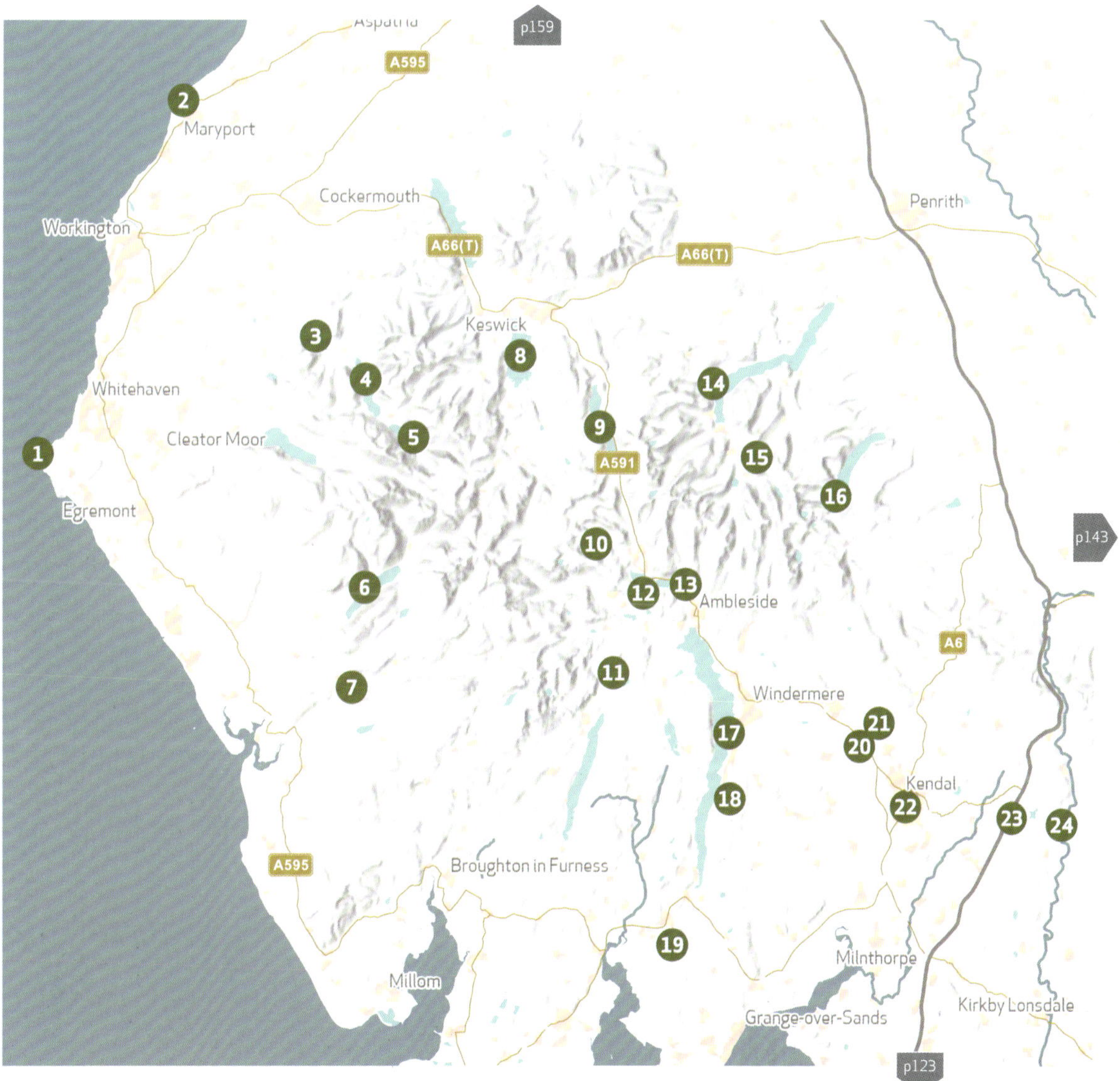

North East
England

Here flows the mighty Tweed and its sister, the Tyne, to the south. Serving these two beasts are the lesser but delightful wild fishing rivers of Coquet, Aln, Wansbeck, and Till. For southerners, the temptation is to pronounce Coquet as if it's some river in France; its actual pronunciation is refreshingly northern and straightforward – coke-utt. For £45 a day, you can hope for a sea trout, surely one of the more mysterious of our native fish. As is often the case, Ted Hughes, the unofficial Poet Laureate of Wild Fishing, captures the essence of the fish:

"Then a shattering
Of the river's hole, where something leaps out –..."

Still, it's Hugh Falkus who has written *the* guide on sea trout called, rather uninspiringly, *Sea Trout: A Practical Guide* (it sounds more like a self-help book which, I suppose, in a way it is). That said, he did not invent night fishing for sea trout as he claimed, but with all his failings, he writes in a beautiful, lucid prose, and his works have enriched angling literature.

Larger reservoirs, such as Kielder and Derwent (famous for grayling fishing in the autumn and winter), allow anglers to bait, spin, or fly fish. It's chilly fishing chasing grayling on a large expanse of water in the winter, but with the correct clothing, it's great fun.

The rich fishing grounds off the North East coast have drawn fishermen for years, and the abundance of fish in the River Tees has made it a popular spot for anglers. There are plenty of places to fish in County Durham, from the rocky shores of Hartlepool to the vast open waters of Teesdale. Cod are one of the most popular fish for the shore angler, and they can be caught off the North Eastern English coast throughout the year but with a couple of brief lulls in the spring. However, to give yourself the best chance, you should concentrate your fishing season from mid-September to early February.

NORTHUMBERLAND

1 NORTH TYNE/KIELDER BURN

You can practise the ancient art of worm fishing to trout on this beat until August. It's all in the retrieve, as slow as possible. You need to give the fish time to inspect your worm, which takes a little time. However, this river also has a good mayfly hatch to compete for your fishing hours. Perhaps worming through the day and dry flying in the late afternoon onwards?

→ Tyneriverstrust.org 55.2333, -2.5796
£8 Fly, worm BT

2 KIELDER WATER

Northumbrian Water's boat fishery, and with over 2,000 acres of water to explore, you can try a different spot every time you fish. It's Europe's largest man-made water. It can get noisy with the motorboats, but given the size, you can always find somewhere to fish.

→ Watersideparksuk.com 55.1772, -2.462
£19 Fly BT, RT

3 REDE/COTTONSHOPEBURN

If there's a particularly good run of sea trout, you could connect with one up here. However, best to concentrate on the brown trout. There's enough of them to keep you occupied, and if you chance across a sea trout or even salmon, change your tactics.

→ Tyneriverstrust.org 55.3045, -2.3519
£8 Fly BT, ST, Sa

4 REDE/STOBBS FARM

There are some overhanging trees along the beat to ensure that you keep your casting precise. One of the most highly regarded beats in the area, marvellous that it can be fished on a day ticket. Make the best of it.

→ Tyneriverstrust.org 55.2615, -2.2476
£8 Fly, worm,spin BT

5 NORTH TYNE/HESLEYSIDE EALS FARM

The North Tyne starts north of Kielder Water and flows through to the Tyne. It's well known as a salmon river, but it's got a very good head of native brown trout too. You can fish all the various fly methods, but it is strictly fly only. It's a bargain to fish the same water for trout that others are paying a great deal more for.

→ Tyneriverstrust.org 55.1431, -2.2633
£8 Fly BT

6 SOUTH TYNE/LAMBLEY

This beat is not often fished, and it's a mystery why not. It's a productive salmon and sea trout fishery. We're concentrating on the brown trout for our day ticket, and it's got a good head of them here.

→ Tyneriverstrust.org 54.9212, -2.5096
£8 Fly BT

7 DEVILS WATER/SWALLOWSHIP

Daring, exciting fishing, but our attention is drawn to a major hazard on the water which will be fully explained when you buy your ticket. This is a narrow, powerful river that featured in the War of the Roses way back in 1464. I guess this is where the name comes from.

→ Tyneriverstrust.org 54.9495, -2.0717
£8 Fly BT, ST, Sa

10

12

14

13

9

8 TYNE/WATERSMEET

Watersmeet is where the North and South Tyne converge. As in almost all fishing when two rivers meet, the fishing gets good. This is a highly regarded salmon river, but you can catch brown trout here too. However, you must give way to salmon fishers.

→ Tyneriverstrust.org 54.989, -2.1307
£8 Fly BT

9 NORTH TYNE/CHESTERS

There's a good number of native trout here, and the fishing is not too challenging. If you stick to your task diligently and fish intelligently, you should catch quite a few. The fishing on the North Tyne can be affected by releases from Kielder Reservoir. Occasionally, it can be rendered unfishable. Always worth checking before you venture out.

→ Tyneriverstrust.org 55.0259, -2.1322
£8 Fly BT

10 ERRING BURN/CHOLLERTON FARM

The Erring Burn has been heavily modified by industry in the past but is now a sweet little river. The landscape changes markedly as you fish down or up. Ideal fishing, deep pools interspersed with deep(ish) pools. No call for wading here.

→ Tyneriverstrust.org 55.0406, -2.1027
£8 Fly BT

11 ERRING BURN/BEAUMONT HOUSE

I've included sea trout and salmon in the description, but this is really a trout fishery. Most of the beat is within sight of Hadrian's Wall, which puts our fishing somewhat into perspective, especially if we have a blank day. It has some good deep pools to hold fish in.

→ Tyneriverstrust.org 55.0476, -2.0664
£8 Fly BT, ST, Sa

12 WHITTLE DENE RESERVOIR

This large bowl-shaped water is a bit like fishing wild Irish loughs with its rocky shoreline. We're told a waggle float works better when levels are low during summer and early autumn. When the reservoir is topped up, feeder tactics are preferred.

→ Watersideparksuk.com 55.0064, -1.9
£7 Fly, bait, spin, led Roach, Pe

13 FONTBURN RESERVOIR

The fly purists have been saying that the water is not as good as when it was fly only. Apparently, monster rainbows were caught before. Our view? Come one, come all. Easy

16

for us to say, however, because it's not our home water.

→ Watersideparksuk.com 55.236, -1.924 £7 Fly, bait, spin, led RT, coarse

14 TILL RIVER

The River Till is an important tributary of the Tweed. A very good head of grayling, but the Till is one of the best sea trout fisheries in the UK, and it is known for runs of large fish in the early season – April and May being the best months. Smaller fish are found in July and August.

→ Northumbrian-angler.co.uk 55.5704, -2.0029 £45 Fly ST, Gr

15 CRASTER

Craster means Crow's Earthwork in Anglo Saxon. No idea why. The harbour has lovely mackerel fishing in the summer, and really, there's not much better fun, at least to my mind. Spinning for mackerel is a delightful pastime, underrated in my book.

→ Craster is well served with car parks. 55.471, -1.5913 Free Beach Mackerel

16 CULLERNOSE POINT

Juts out into the North Sea and, most importantly, gives relatively easy access to deep water, invariably increasing the prospect of success. It can be dangerous when the sea is rough. Good cod fishery during the winter months, but the ground is hungry, so factor in equipment losses. Also good for pollock and wrasse.

→ National Trust car park just outside the village. 55.4611, -1.5901 Free Beach Cod

17 COQUET RIVER

The Coquet is a winding river which will appeal to those fishers who enjoy stalking wild fish in remote waters and are prepared to go "off-piste" searching for wild trout, sea trout, and the occasional salmon. What could be better?

→ Northumbrian-angler.co.uk 55.3481, -1.6273 £45 Fly BT, ST

18 DRURIDGE BAY

Coalfish are a common catch around this area and take a variety of baits fished on the bottom, as well as being caught on spinners and lures. Druridge Bay was thought of as a likely landing place for the German invasion, hence the pillboxes, and the area was mined out to sea.

→ Parking at the beach 55.2388, -1.5448 Free Beach Coalfish

15

18

23

24

25

TYNE & WEAR

19 MARSDEN BAY

Famous locally for its colourful history of wrecks and smugglers and a ghost called John the Jibber. All nonsense, I'm sure. Still, fishing this secluded bay at night can give one room for thought. Unfishable in big seas, but the cod will come in within casting distance in the winter.

→ Parking on the coast road and then a series of steep stairs 54.9808, -1.3813 £ Free Beach Cod

20 WHITBURN BEACH

A wide, flat, sand beach, which is usually best in winter for cod and whiting, but other species can turn up throughout the year, such as rockling, flounder, and dab. You could try kayaking here too in the summer months.

→ Park in Whitburn and walk over. 54.9593, -1.3556 £ Free Beach Flounder, dab

DURHAM

21 COW GREEN RESERVOIR

We're told the best flies here are: Foam Beetle, Black Hopper and a Claret Bumble. Best bait? Floated worm. Full of fighting fit, uniquely coloured trout, these natives have descended from the original upland brownies, which lived in the streams before the dams were built. Lightning quick and very hard fighting, these fish are a joy to catch.

→ Watersideparksuk.com 54.6729, -2.2967 £ £9 Fly, bait, spin, led BT

22 TEES RIVER

It's at the bottom of Cauldron Snout (what a name) that fly fishing on the Tees begins. Excellent brown trout fishing and perfect small stream fishing too. Best fished with North Country Spiders and dry flies.

→ Yorkshire-dales-flyfishing.com 54.6516, -2.2901 £ Free Fly BT

23 SELSET RESERVOIR

Full of excellent brownies that are descendants of the river fish that were here before the dam was built. This is excellent reservoir fishing and as natural as one could expect. The price reflects catch and release only. Note that they allow any fishing method, which really frees you up to experiment.

→ Watersideparksuk.com 54.5866, -2.1349 £ £9 Fly, bait, spin, led BT

29

24 BALDERHEAD RESERVOIR

Just like Balderhead's neighbours, these uniquely coloured trout have descended from the original upland brownies, which lived in the streams before the dams were built. They will respond well to a dry fly and, especially, small black flies such as black ants.

→ Watersideparksuk.com 54.5554, -2.1147 £9 Fly, bait, spin, led BT

25 GRASSHOLME RESERVOIR

The deep water ensures that Grassholme fishes consistently even during the warm summer months. During the early season, as the spring air warms the water, the shallows and the stream mouths are the places to fish. As the summer heats up, you need to start looking at Grassholme's depths.

→ Watersideparksuk.com 54.5982, -2.0818 £7 Fly, bait, spin, led RT

26 BLACKTON RESERVOIR

Wild brown trout, again you'll be fishing from the original upland strain before the dam was built. Just like in Cow Green Reservoir and the others, this gives the fishing a little history, and it's heartening that the original strain has not been replaced, nor have they had to revert to stocking rainbows.

→ Watersideparksuk.com 54.5643, -2.0841 £9 Fly BT

27 HURY RESERVOIR

Another of the Victorian reservoirs built in the area. Stocked from their own farm. We've been told the following flies are considered effective: Diawl Bachs, Black Buzzer, Black Boobies, Cats Whiskers, and Dawson's Olive. We're told that roaming is the way to fish here: the middle reaches and where the water flows in from the Selset tunnel on the north shore seem to be best.

→ Watersideparksuk.com 54.5683, -2.0532 £19 Fly RT

28 BALDER RIVER

A stonking little river, running off Hury Reservoir. They call it a gem, and for once, that's not a misnomer. It's not easy fishing, but it's a wonderful mixed water with small deep pools. The fish are unlikely to have seen a fly, spinner, or worm (with a hook in); it's great fun.

→ Fishingpassport.co.uk 54.5746, -2.0159 £5 Fly, bait, spin, led BT, Sa, ST, Gr

29 TEES & GRETA RIVERS/ BARNARD CASTLE

For the £15 ticket, you can fish the Tees around Barnard Castle, but to my mind at least, even better is the quiet unknown river Greta – a real wild fishing experience. Both rivers are well worth fishing, and if you get your skates on, you can do both in a day.

→ Fishingpassport.co.uk 54.5453, -1.9299 £15 Fly BT, Ga, Sa

30 DERWENT/LINTZFORD

Lovely spot with a charming village. Excellent unstocked water, with a good head of grayling and brown trout. The bulk of fish will be below 12oz, with fish over 1.5lb from the better, and more difficult to fish, lies.

→ Tyneriverstrust.org 54.9085, -1.7636 £8 Fly BT, Gr

31 DERWENT/ROWLANDS GILL

This is a lovely stretch of water through relatively built-up areas. While resting between chasing elusive trout, you can see the Gibside Folly, which now has plays set in it. It's about four young people who conduct a seance with all kinds of consequences raining down on their heads.

→ Tyneriverstrust.org 54.9333, -1.748 £8 Fly BT, Gr

32 RYHOPE BEACH

Fishing is done here primarily from the cliffs during high water. The ground is snaggy, and

be aware that many of the low water marks can get cut off by the incoming tide. Ryhope was a colliery town during the 19th century and expanded quickly, but the colliery closed in 1966.

→ Ryhope Road by the village green and walk over. 54.8583, -1.3468 Free Beach Codling, bass, coalfish

33 CHEMICAL BEACH

Love this name, which came from a chemical factory housed here that closed in the 1800s. It's a steep climb to gain access to the beach. Fishing around the huge rock on the beach (known locally as the Stack) is seen as one of the best places to fish.

→ Park at Nose's Point and walk over. 54.8264, -1.3226 Free Beach Bass, cod, whiting

34 HORDEN BEACH

Horden was a mining village until 1987. The spoil used to be tipped onto the beach but now is entirely cleaned up. Generally seen as a high tide fishing beach, there are a number of gullies that can be fished into – winter will produce cod and whiting.

→ Park at the beach. 54.7603, -1.2931 Free Beach Cod, whiting

Scotland South

Of course, the south of Scotland is best known for salmon fishing, but nevertheless, it has some fine hidden trout fishing too. For example, there is excellent trout and grayling fishing in the Rivers Clyde, Nith, Annan, Tweed, and Teviot, as well as many smaller streams, and, in addition, some good loch fishing in the Pentland Hills and the hills of Ayrshire, Renfrewshire, and Galloway. Also, most salmon rivers hold sea trout too. This is one of the most beautiful and even mystical fish to be caught in the UK. Usually done at night, the intrepid angler comes armed with a torch, and until you have fished a river in the dead of night, when your senses are sharpened in the darkness, you don't appreciate how alive the river is. Not just the murmuring of the water as it rushes past you, but nocturnal animals crashing through the bushes as they go about their business.

Scotland has year-round trout fishing, but the spring and summer seasons are the most productive. Brown trout start to spawn between April and June, which makes them more active and more straightforward to catch. Getting trout to take your fly during the summer is easier because they are more active in the warmer waters.

Anglers braving the rugged west coast will find everything from cod and halibut to beagle sharks. The warm waters of the Gulf Stream even create reasonable conditions for sea bass. As a shore angler up here, you can get catches that would be difficult with a boat elsewhere in Britain. Take pollock on a fly, for instance – in Scotland, a 6lb pollack caught from the rocks is very realistic. This is unheard of elsewhere. You'll need a 9 or 10 weight rod and a large arbour reel, as pollock are tenacious fighters, known for jagged, powerful runs. If you're tempted to try lighter equipment, don't – you stand a good chance of being broken into bits. These are strong fish.

Oh, and one final word on fishing in Scotland, don't get caught out – in many places, it is not permissible to fish for trout on the Sabbath. It is frowned upon in some parts as an affront to Christianity, and in others, it is prohibited in the name of conservation. Beware.

DUMFRIES & GALLOWAY

1 SANDEEL BAY

A beautiful little cove with a waterfall and caves. A sand and shingle beach—straight out of a children's book. A treasure. In amongst all this beauty, you should/could catch some codling.

→ Free parking at the beach. 54.8509, -5.1298 Free Beach Codling

2 DINDINNIE RESERVOIR

A small reservoir of thirty acres or so, stocked with rainbows and with a head of native trout. Excellent spot and good fishing. The road to get there is rough, so, if like us, you drive a smaller car without much clearance, beware. It's 4x4 territory.

→ Stranraerfishing.com 54.901, -5.0866 £20 Fly RT, BT

3 PORT LOGAN BAY

The long sweeping Port Logan Harbour Bay boasts a lighthouse, marine life centre, and exotic botanical gardens. The main species to target include dogfish, coalfish, pollack, codling, wrasse, rockling, conger, flatfish, occasional huss, and maybe even a bass or two. We're told that Ardwell tackle shop will sell you an ordnance survey map with all the fishing marks highlighted.

→ Daytime car park at the beach 54.7267, -4.9569 Free Beach Wrasse, codling, flatfish

4 SOULSEAT LOCH

A large loch close to Stranraer, which is why we suggest starting in the late afternoon. It's highly recommended to fly fish this loch in the evening. As it gets dark, things begin to move under the surface... While you're there, have a go at coarse fish using a fly; you could tempt some of the resident roach and perch, along with the trout.

→ Stranraerfishing.com 54.8883, -4.9659 £20 Fly, bait, spin, led BT, RT, Roach, Pe

5 PENWHIRN RESERVOIR

A large hill reservoir with dark peaty water. No lunkers here but a good head of native brown trout. It was built in the 1950s to provide water for the local area and has since had its capacity increased quite markedly. Not sure if this changed the fishing or not.

→ Stranraerfishing.com 54.983, -4.9254 £20 Fly BT

6 FYNTALLOCH LOCH

A small loch which lies immediately to the southwest of Loch Ochiltree, into which it drains through a small channel. An ideal opportunity to practise targeting coarse fish on a fly, certainly perch—the small greedy ones are easier, but the larger ones? A different story and you'll need stealth.

→ Nsdaa.co.uk 55.032, -4.6411 £20 Fly BT, RT, Pe, pike

7 LOCH OCHILTREE

The loch is stocked regularly with rainbow trout up to 7lbs, although larger fish are caught each season. Bait fishing is permitted on a part of the west bank. You can ask exactly where when you're there to ensure you're not falling foul of the rules.

→ Nsdaa.co.uk 55.0378, -4.6331 £20 Fly, bait, spin, led RT

11

10

14

8 KIRRIEREOCH LOCH

This is a fairly shallow loch with a good head of native brown trout. It's delightful and found deep within the Glentool Forest. It would be an ideal setting for a watercolour, if only our artistic skills were good enough to do it justice. I'll stick to fishing; I have enough trouble with that.

→ Nsdaa.co.uk 55.1469, -4.5669 £20 Fly BT

9 LOCH ENOCH

The nearest parking is at Loch Trool, and from there, it is a hike to Loch Enoch. When you're there, it's hard fishing too. However, we're told that the Galloway Rivers Trust would like you to record what you catch and let them know. They're looking for location, fish, time of day, etc. It would be nice to help them out.

→ Lets.fish 55.1348, -4.4397 Free Fly BT

10 LOCH NELDRICKEN

Again, the nearest parking is at Loch Trool, and you hike in to fish Loch Neldricken. Once there and getting your breath back (it's a stiff one-hour walk which always seems uphill), you might try mixing up hairy loch-style flies with a nymph. The theory is that the attractor fly pulls the curious fish in and then the nymph does the catching.

→ Lets.fish 55.1171, -4.436 Free Fly BT

11 LOCH DEE

The loch is filled by water running from the surrounding Galloway hills and a marshy area to the north known as the Silver Flow. A good head of brown trout which, we're told, are not easy to catch, but it's rewarding just being in this scenery, and a trout or two are a bonus.

→ Nsdaa.co.uk 55.0817, -4.4011 £20 Fly BT

12 CREE RIVER

The beat begins at the tidal part of the Cree, which can be very productive even in low water. Spring salmon are caught each year, and there is a run of summer salmon in May/June, with good runs of grilse entering the river in July. If you are keen to fish in the evening, the Association's water is the most productive sea trout beat on the river, and good night fishing can be had from early June.

→ Nsdaa.co.uk 54.9606, -4.4821 £20 Fly BT

13 WEE GLENAMOUR

Can get very weedy on occasion, always check the website page before you make the trip. It's really not worth the travel if it's unfishable, and this can be the case here, especially, I believe, in the summer months. But, when this loch is on song, it's a great day's fishing.

→ Nsdaa.co.uk 54.9765, -4.4281 £20 Fly BT

14 LOCH KEN

Renowned for its fishing qualities, producing large nets of pike, perch, roach, dace, and bream. James Murray caught a 72 lb pike here, and it was seven feet long. There are good-sized wild brown trout in the river and the loch, now that the leviathan pike was caught.

→ There are a number of car parks around the loch. 55.0056, -4.044 Free Fly, bait, spin, led BT, coarse

15 ROCKCLIFFE

Rockcliffe is considered one of Scotland's most scenic coastlines. At high tide, the sea can be almost in touching distance of the sloping sea wall, but at low tide, it can be the best part of a mile away. Cod, eel, whiting, and flounder are the main catches, all on lugworm bait.

→ Short stay car park at the beach. 54.8651, -3.7966 Free Beach Cod, eel, whiting, flounder

16 MILL LOCH

A small loch and a former reservoir, there is fine brown trout fishing on Mill Loch. Fish up to two lb or so. Apparently, quite free-rising, so the best idea might be dry flies and/or dapping, especially if there's a bit of a breeze.

→ Park in Lochmaben and walk over. 55.1338, -3.4477 Free Fly, bait, spin, led BT, Sa, ST

17 ESK/LANGHOLM

On the Esk, and I'm quoting from the Border Esk AC, "...a 12ft or 13ft rod will do in low-water, and a 14 or 15 footer is best when it's high. You should note the water height—there is a white marker on Canonbie Bridge (painted on the downstream side of the pillar nearest the playing field). If the water is on or above the mark at 9am, you can spin or worm. Providing the water is not carrying too much colour, the fly can be very successful."

→ Bordereskfishing.co.uk 55.1411, -2.9885 £30 Fly BT

9

13

15

16

21

18

23

19

18 LOWER LIDDEL

The trout average 3/4lb, and fish of 1 1/2lb are not uncommon. Both the Esk and Liddel flow through picturesque countryside typical of the Border area, and much of the bankside is wooded with indigenous hardwoods. The rivers are generally fast-flowing and with beds of rock outcrop or pebble shingle with no natural weed growth.

→ Borderes kfishing.co.uk 55.0954, -2.8818 £25 Fly BT

19 LIDDEL/NEWCASTLETON

Fishing is best from July to September, with September being the best month. The salmon season runs from the 1st. The best fishing can be found after June where, with good water levels, fish start to run into the Lower Liddel. Good size catches can be made with salmon and sea trout bagged at over 10lbs over each season.

→ Bordereskfishing.co.uk 55.1785, -2.8099 £25 Fly BT, Sa, ST

AYRSHIRE

20 LOCH BRECBOWIE

This, like most high-up lochs, can be very breezy. However, while a tad uncomfortable for the angler, a good breeze can conceal a multitude of the angler's sins. The fish's visibility is curtailed, making for more impetuous strikes. I suspect that the fish here are relatively unscathed from angler attention, but the remains of an old boat are there.

→ Lets.fish 55.2338, -4.4665 Free Fly BT

21 LOCH DOON

In WW1, this loch was used to train pilots and aircrews; remains of this activity are still visible to this day. The loch has a large head of wild brown trout averaging about 8oz, though 12oz-16oz fish are not uncommon, and some are much larger.

→ There's a car park at the castle with a well-marked trail. 55.2607, -4.3636 Free Fly BT

22 MAIDENS BEACH

Beside the lovely little coastal village of Maidens and the evocative statue is this long sandy beach with grassy foreshore. It's a wonderful place to try your luck. The most caught fish here are ling, flounder, garfish, and haddock. Across the water lies Ailsa Craig and sometimes the Mull of Kintyre can be seen. To the south of the beach, there is a small harbour, traditionally used for fishing but no more.

→ Daytime parking at the beach. 55.3382, -4.8109 Free Beach Ling, garfish, haddock

23 IRVINE RIVER

The Irvine has been messed about with in times past by the landed estates in the area, changing the course, adding weirs, and who knows what else. The estates have now calmed down, leaving a lovely little river. The grayling population, which was introduced in the 1850s, is thought to have died out. The salmon catches are thought to be about one hundred a year through the Irvine. Spinning is the most common method here.

→ Dreghornangling.com 55.6052, -4.6064 £25/year Fly ST, BT, Sa

24 ANNICK RIVER

Gorgeous, crystal clear water. While crystal clear is aesthetically pleasing, it also means the trout can see you very easily; caution should be your watchword. Good dry fly water (with long leaders and small flies), but also upstream nymphing and spiders work well too.

→ Dreghornangling.com 55.6312, -4.6224 £25/year Fly BT

LANARKSHIRE

25 DUNEATON WATER

Another significant tributary to the mighty Clyde. You should expect to encounter wary trout here. While you can catch and eat them, most people are now catching and releasing. If you intend to release your fish, barbless hooks always make it easier. You can also pinch down the barbs on normal hooks with a pair of pincers.

→ Ucapaltd.com 55.516, -3.690 £12 Fly, spinner BT, Gr

26 DOUGLAS WATER

The Douglas Water is a small river, no more than 12 miles long, which flows swiftly into Loch Fyne between Furnace and Inveraray. It has a rocky channel with an abundance of waterfalls and rocky pools. The river has been unfished for some years, and a new fishery is being established.

→ Ucapaltd.com 55.608, -3.793 £12 Fly, spinner BT, Gr

27 MOUSE WATER

This river flows into the Clyde at Lanark and is popular with canoeists, so it's best to pick times when they won't be there (if you can). Good grayling water. I feel the grayling is still somewhat underrated in comparison

20

22

25

27

28

37

30

39

to the brown trout, and I'm not sure why—it's a gorgeous fish.

→ Ucapaltd.com 55.6782, -3.799 £12 Fly, spinner BT, Gr

28 CLYDE RIVER

The Clyde is graced with a significant population of wild brown trout, plus salmon and sea trout. It was marred with decades of heavy industry spewing who-only-knows-what into the water, but it's far better now and certainly worth a trip.

→ Ucapaltd.com 55.6541, -3.7269 £12 Fly, spinner Sa, ST, BT, Gr

29 MEDWIN

Fishing here at the correct time of the year, coming to the end of the trout season, you'll witness enormous flights of geese in the Flying V formation that they've made their own. Good spinning water with a size 3 Mepps.

→ Ucapaltd.com 55.679, -3.6223 £12 Fly, spinner BT, Gr

LOTHIAN

30 AVON

Excellent fishing just after a rain. Seven miles of different pools, runs, gorge, and open farmland in this beat, and then there are two other beats shared with the other clubs that include incredible sea trout fishing down near the estuary. Dry flies and emergers are a great option in the upper farmland.

→ Fishforth.org 55.9357, -3.7418 £10 Fly, bait, spin, led BT, ST

31 WATER OF LEITH/EDINBURGH (URBAN ANGLING)

We're told that 4lb trout have been caught in these waters. Exciting, if true. In the lower reaches, grayling of up to half a pound have been recorded. Antony Gormley's sculpture of 6 Times is in and around these waters. The river is home to thousands of brown trout, the wild stock being supplemented each year with over a thousand stocked fish. Grayling have appeared in the last 10 years and have spread throughout the lower river. A few rainbow trout can escape from Harlaw Reservoir to join them. There are also eels, minnows, stickleback, stone loach, bullhead, and lampreys.

→ No cost permit at visitor centre 55.9529, -3.2145 Free Fly, bait, spin, led BT, Gr

32 TYNE WATER

One of the best brown trout fisheries to be found anywhere. It's challenging (or can be), but the slow-moving and characterful river is surely what fishing is all about. It will, over time, put you in a reverie, bringing out your inner poet. Quite seasonal: April to September are fantastic, and then that's your lot.

→ Fishforth.org 55.9111, -2.8943 £10 Fly, bait, spin, led BT, Sa, ST, Gr

33 WHITEADDER WATER

Czech nymphing works well and, we're told, in the last five years, there has been a rapid rise in grayling numbers. Perhaps the loveliest of all game fish, even though it's technically a coarse fish. It smells of thyme. Called the Lady of the Stream, she also makes very good eating, but don't do it—they're too precious to eat. By the way, there's no Sunday fishing here and in a number of other places in Scotland, so always check.

→ Whiteadderanglingassociation.jigsy.com 55.8269, -2.3532 Free Fly BT, Gr

ARGYLL & BUTE

34 CARRADALE BEACH

In the 17th and 18th centuries, there were small communities of crofters and fishermen working in and around Carradale. Carradale Point, at the eastern end of the beach, is a nature reserve where there are feral goats, but we've never seen them. The river Carradale is known for both salmon and sea trout.

→ Parking at the beach 55.5799, -5.4795 Free Beach Pollock, Sea Trout

35 LOCH QUIEN

Catch and release. Best fishing is early morning or the late evening, with traditional flies and nymphs, but large black flies can also work. The fish are easily spooked, so be cautious. Further flies to try are; Greenwells, Dunkeld, Blue Zulu, Olive Woolly Worm, Pheasant Tail Nymph, and Hoppers in Orange or Black.

→ Lochfad.co.uk 55.7876, -5.0886 £10 Fly, bait, spin, led BT, Pike

36 LOCH FAD

Surrounded by wooded hills (this was the site of the first Douglas Fir plantations way back in the 1840s). This long loch is filled with rainbow trout and a good head of brown trout. Loch Fad's 175 acres sit directly on the Highland fault line and so is deep (50 feet in places). Here you can watch ospreys showing you how to fish successfully.

→ Facebook.com/kylesanglingclub 55.8056, -5.0743 £20 Fly RT, BT

33

34

37 LOCH ASGOG

Excellent water to try your hand at fly fishing for pike. The pike, due to their aggression, will hit larger flies than you think, given their size. So, large muddler minnows and clousers are well suited for the task. You'll also find a good amount of rainbow trout and a few overwintered brown trout here too.

→ Facebook.com/kylesanglingclub 55.8255, -5.0395 £20 Fly Pike

38 LOCH FYNE

Loch Fyne is mainly known for its mackerel fishing, but there are also sea trout and salmon present. Rays and flatfish can be caught too. No permit is required for sea fishing, but salmon and trout fishing will require a permit.

→ There are a number of car parks around the loch. 56.0662, -5.2846 Free Fly, bait, spin, led ST, Sa, mackerel

39 RUEL RIVER

The Ruel is fly only, and for the most part, the water is very peaty, even in low water. Patterns such as the Cascade and Ally's Shrimp can do well given good conditions. Patterns of this nature in small doubles or singles will work well in lower water too.

→ Dunoonangling.com 56.0196, -5.2112 £15 Fly BT, ST, Sa

38

43

40 LOCH TARSAN

Even on the Dunoon website, Loch Tarsan is described as a cold, bleak place in the early season, but later on, it can be a joy. From June onwards, great evening fishing can be had, with fish coming close into shore to feed on sedges, moths, and small fry.

→ Dunoonangling.com 56.0094, -5.0834
£20 Fly BT

41 MASSON RIVER

The river provides a variety of pools, glides, broken water, gorges, and falls for the angler. There is a healthy population of brown trout present. Salmon and sea trout are also in the system from June onwards during spate conditions.

→ Dunoonangling.com 56.0346, -5.0195
£15 Fly, spin, worm BT, Sa, ST

42 LOCH LOSKIN

A six-acre loch where you can hone your dry fly skills when the conditions are right—the trout will respond. Note: fly fishing is via boat only, and three boats are available. A well-written and researched website will tell you all you need to know for each part of the season.

→ Dunoonangling.com 55.9656, -4.9332
£20 Fly BT, ST

43 LOCH LONG

You can fish with bait or with spinners from the shore or on a boat, as long as you return any migratory fish which, in this case, are salmon and sea trout. This still leaves you with cod, whiting, plaice, mackerel, skate, wrasse, pollack, spurdog, and many other species—enough to be going on with.

→ Trossachs.co.uk 56.0344, -4.8856
Free Fly BT

44 FINART RIVER

You'll need to be on your toes fishing here and armed with a small brook rod. The overhanging vegetation will snatch and keep all the errantly cast flies. As we know, there is little more frustrating in all of fishing than bushes and trees attriting your flies and/or terminal tackle. However, if you can cast your fly so it actually lands on the water, you can do well here.

→ Dunoonangling.com 56.0582, -4.9213
£15 Fly, spin, worm BT, Sa, ST

45 CUR RIVER

The midges can be out in force here, so a midge net is a must. A single-handed 7/8 rated rod is more than adequate, or, if possible, go lighter. Spinning and worming is also allowed on the Cur, and good sport can be had using a light spinning rod with a small Mepps. If worming, let the worm drift downstream close to the bank, or if the flow is too fast, put a small weight on and let the worm bounce along the bottom.

→ Dunoonangling.com 56.1265, -5.0153
£20 Fly, Spin, Worm BT, Sa, ST

46 LOCH GOIL

You can find mackerel, cod, and pollock depending on the time of year, while the River Goil has both salmon and sea trout runs from mid-March to October (permit required). The locals point us to popular fishing spots off the shoreline at the village, as well as the rocky shore by the pier at Carrick Castle.

→ Trossachs.co.uk 56.132, -4.8923
Free Bait, spinner BT

47 LOCH A' PHEARSAIN

Fish are found all around the loch, some quite close in, so it pays to fish along the bank as well as out in front of you. If you are fishing from a boat, then a good drift into the large weed bed halfway down the right bank will see you set.

→ Glenbegfishing.com 56.2683, -5.4654
£10 Fly BT, Char

48 LOCH AN LOSGAINN BEAG

There are a large number of lily beds around the edge of the loch which can make fishing difficult in the latter part of the year, but it is around them that the large fish of this loch live. That's where you need to be fishing, as difficult as it is.

→ Glenbegfishing.com 56.2576, -5.4562
£10 Fly BT

49 LOCH NA CURRAIGH

There's a boggy area which you should not fish; it's not worth getting caught up in it. Smaller fish are plentiful around the footpath, and the larger fish are on the other side, where you have to deal with the steep hillside. Who said remote loch fishing was easy?

→ Glenbegfishing.com 56.2617, -5.4504
£10 Fly BT

50 LOCH A' MHINN

When you first come over the hill to this loch, the most productive places to fish are from the shore in front of you. The loch contains brown trout, char, and rainbow trout (the rainbows here are particularly hard-charging fish). None are straightforward to catch but worth a bit of perseverance.

→ Glenbegfishing.com 56.2596, -5.4478
£10 Fly BT, RT, char

40

42

46

47

51

54

55

58

51 LOCH AN LOSGAINN MOR

There was talk on various fly fishing forums that some of these lochs have been stocked with rainbow trout. I must say I don't know, but there are certainly some in Loch a' Mhinn, the close neighbour of this loch. It seems that nobody has caught a rainbow at Losgainn Mor.

→ Glenbegfishing.com 56.2523, -5.4467
£10 Fly BT

52 LOCH NAM BAN

Like all Glenbeg fishing, it pays to roam around the various lochs until you hit the fish who are in an obliging mood. The mobile angler catches far more than a stationary angler. You should certainly include this loch in your tour.

→ Glenbegfishing.com 56.2572, -5.4377
£10 Fly BT

53 UPPER FEINN LOCH

This loch is smaller than Feinn Loch and is called by the locals Wee Feinn. Fish can be discovered all around the loch, but casting can be difficult because of the steep hillside. We're told that there are larger trout here, up to 2lb.

→ Glenbegfishing.com 56.2775, -5.4430
£10 Fly BT

54 FEINN LOCH

The casting is relatively easy on the south side where the ground is flat, but as you move round the loch, the hills move in and casting becomes that bit more interesting. Fish are all around the loch and can be close into the shore in places where the water is deep.

→ Glenbegfishing.com 56.2748, -5.4391
£10 Fly BT

55 IASG LOCH

Typical of the Glenbeg Lochs, very clear water and small flies are almost always the most productive. In fact, go as small as you can and still see the fly. Or, in my case, if you can't see the fly, at least see the swirl and then strike.

→ Glenbegfishing.com 56.2804, -5.4358
£10 Fly BT

56 LOCH CHEIGEIN

This is fly fishing of the highest order. The fish aren't easy to catch, but the surroundings are magnificent. Perhaps fish a team of flies instead of just a single; try a double, or even a triple. It increases your chances, I feel. Casting can get more difficult with a triple on, especially in wind, but it's a trade-off.

→ Glenbegfishing.com 56.2706, -5.4321
£10 Fly BT

57 LOCH NA SAILM

Many of these Loch na Sailm fish, and this holds true for all the Glenbeg lochs, will never have seen an artificial fly in their lives. This is what wild fishing is all about. Untrammelled waters. Far off the beaten track.

→ Glenbegfishing.com 56.2758, -5.4291
£10 Fly BT

58 LOCH A' CHAORAINN

The casting is pretty easy on this loch as the banks aren't quite as steep as some of the other lochs in the area. Fishing can be slow, but hit it at the right time, and fish will be rising all around the banks. They're not large but are generally between 8-12oz and, if they were in a taking mood, would merrily take
a dry fly, wet fly, or nymph.

→ Glenbegfishing.com 56.2678, -5.4208
£10 Fly BT

59 LOCH A' CHREACHAIN

The lochs of this area, indeed all the lochs of The Glenbeg, were a favourite of Colonel Oatts, and his experiences of the fishing here formed much of the basis for his book on "Loch Trout," published in 1958. His book is still relevant today, especially because the entire area is devoid of hard-pressed angling pressure, which can cause changes in fish behaviour.

→ Glenbegfishing.com 56.2716, -5.4139
£10 Fly BT

60 LOCH DUBH MOR

A well-regarded and popular loch to fish. It's deep in the middle but very pleasant to wade around the edges. Typically, the fish are lined up in the drop-off. Best flies: most of the standard wets, plus a selection of Olives. Size 10-14 should be about right.

→ Obanandlorn-anglingclub.co.uk
56.2793, -5.4064 £10 Fly BT

61 LOCH SEIL

This is a heavily weeded loch but that shouldn't deter you. Lots of smaller brown trout with, apparently, some sea trout at the back end. Usual flies in about the 12 to 14 size range are the most productive. Apparently, there is an artificial island here, mainly submerged.

→ Obanandlorn-anglingclub.co.uk
56.3247, -5.5519 £10 Fly BT

58

59

60

61

67

64

62 LOCH NELL

A 2-mile loch, known for great catches of arctic char, sea trout, salmon, and brown trout. It's a pleasant little spot that's close to towns and is easily accessible. The loch sports a small island to the south, an enjoyable place to perch whilst you fish.

→ Plenty of free parking around the loch area. 56.3915, -5.423 Free Fly, bait, spin, led Ch, ST, Sa

63 AWE RIVER

Firstly, please keep all the rainbow trout you catch. The club is trying to winkle them out of the river system. The rocks can be slippery here, and the current strong, so care is required when wading. There's even a chance of a salmon here in the season. The best flies are all the usual suspects, plus Ally's Shrimp, which is especially favoured by the local experts.

→ Obanandlorn-anglingclub.co.uk
56.4444, -5.2246 £10 Fly BT

64 LOCH NANT

Another very popular loch with the local anglers and with good reason. This is a loch for fishing on warm summer evenings when loch fishing becomes sublime. Spalding Gray, the American raconteur, was fond of seeking out the "perfect moment". You can find it here.

→ Obanandlorn-anglingclub.co.uk
56.3657, -5.2392 £10 Fly BT

65 LOCH AIRIGH SHAMRIGH

A pleasant little loch with tons of features, everything from reed beds to boulders. Fishes well all season, and the trout are delightfully speckled, even on the tail which is quite rare. Mini Muddler flies do well here. An hour from the road, but it can seem like a very long hour.

→ Obanandlorn-anglingclub.co.uk
56.3668, -5.2046 £10 Fly BT

66 LOCH AWE

It's charming and picturesque and right by the road. And Loch Awe holds a lot of trout. If you're up here for the mayfly hatches, you'll be well rewarded. The hatch is voluminous, and you can be fishing in the middle of a trout feeding frenzy which you will never forget.

→ Lochawe.net 56.3430 -5.1408 £7.50 Fly BT

67 LOCH TULLA

Home to a good head of wild brown trout and a few pike. The pike have been historically troublesome. In 1892, the Fishery Board noted that Loch Tulla was unsurpassed in its trout fishing but was subsequently ruined by Lord Breadalbane, who introduced pike, with predictable results. Not sure how true this is, but there are pike in the loch.

→ Park at the Viewpoint car park. 56.5499, -4.7557 Free Fly BT, Pike

68 LOCH SUNART

The clear waters of Loch Sunart house some massive skate of around 200lbs, along with thornback rays and spurdog. Beware of the midges — you have been warned. Local legend has it that the absence of resident swans in Loch Sunart results from a doomed love affair between a Celtic chieftain and a local girl.

→ There's a number of parking sites at the loch. 56.6766, -5.9147 Free Beach Skate, rays

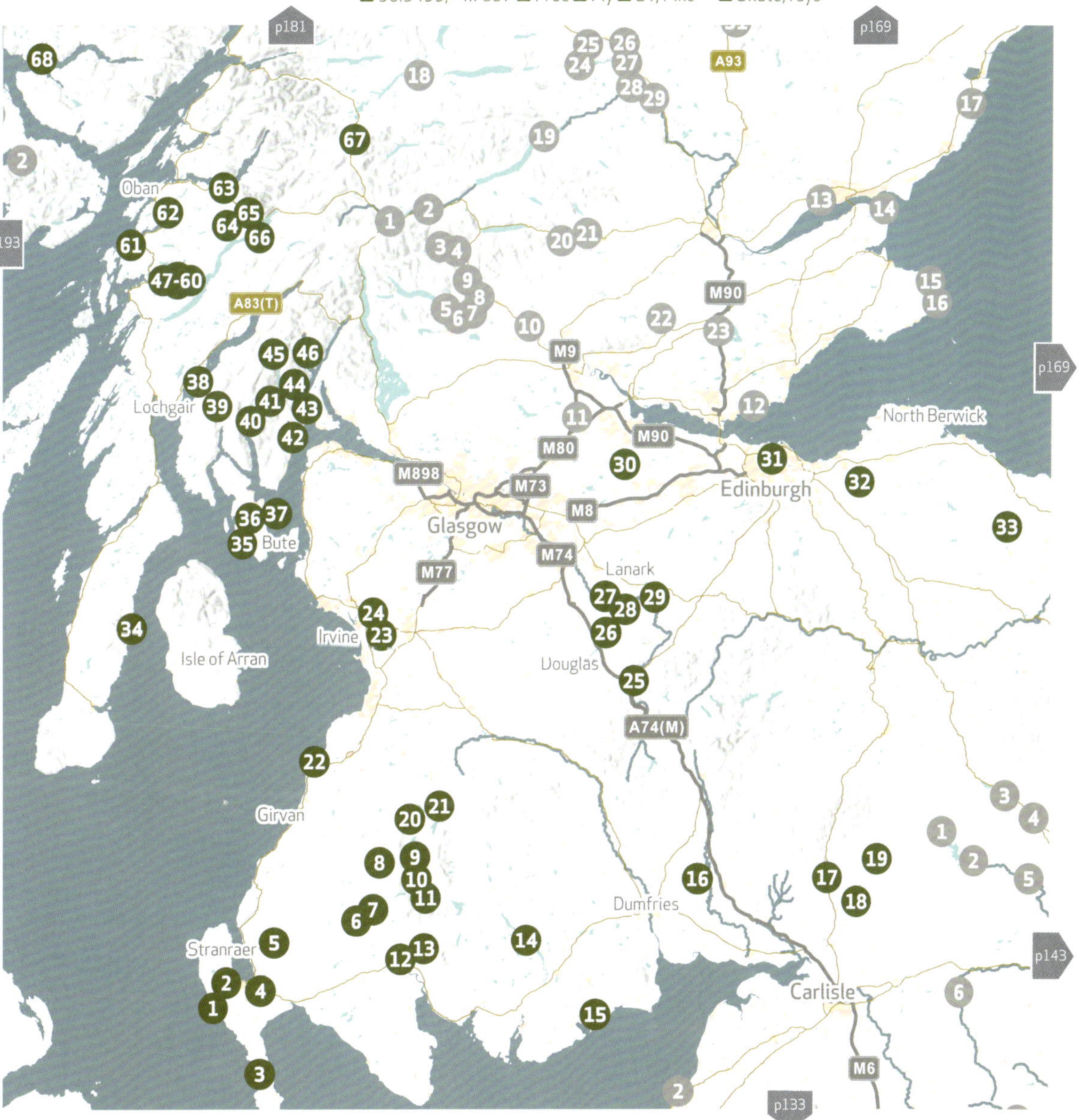

Central Scotland

1

3

4

Georgina Ballantine's epic two-hour struggle with a salmon that was over half her own weight happened on 7 October 1922. Eventually, when the great fish was on the bank, it weighed in at 64lb, the largest ever taken from a British river on rod and line. The salmon, known as the Great Tay Salmon, is unbeaten to this day. We try to keep the costs down in this book, so salmon fishing isn't featured prominently, but Ms Ballantine's achievement couldn't go unmentioned when discussing wild fishing in Mid Scotland.

Mid Scotland is also known for its soaring mountains, heather moors, and wooded glens, its peaty moorland lochs, high corrie lochans (smaller lochs), and long glacial lochs, all of which offer fine fly fishing for truly wild brown trout, from both boat and bank. Here we have such famous brown trout fisheries as Loch Leven and Carron Valley, the beautiful lochs of the Trossachs, and we mustn't forget the renowned river trout fishing on the Don, Tay, and Tummel.

Loch Leven is worth a special mention. One of the most expensive fishing spots mentioned in our book, it is still a bargain at £30 for an evening's fishing. Why? Well, they only allow boat fishing in the loch, so part of the cost is the boat, but the rest? The experience. People have been fishing for trout in the loch for over one hundred years, and these are special trout. The loch is famous for its unique strain of brown trout, Salmo Levensis, which has been used to stock rivers, lakes, and lochs not only in this country but also all over the world. Why are they regarded as special? They have a striking dark colouring and pink flesh with a graceful form, but they're famed for their sporting qualities. Yes, we don't necessarily always approve of stocking in this book, preferring our fishing to be the native species of that waterway, but this does speak to the specialness of these particular fish and, of course, you would be fishing for the native fish in Loch Leven.

STERLINGSHIRE

1 FILLAN RIVER

Worth investing in some Skin So Soft (which really works), the insects can be very troublesome here. A good fly combination would be a gold-ribbed hare's ear and, perhaps, a black spider as a dropper. The wise angler usually fishes upstream of the viaduct, but really the entire length of The Fillan is good but challenging fishing. Fishing fine and far off should be your maxim here.

→ Crianlarichstore.co.uk 56.394, -4.616 £10 Fly, bait, spin, led BT, Sa, char

2 DOCHART RIVER

We are told there are salmon, brown trout, and arctic char; also, eels, pike, and perch all present, very similar to its close neighbour Loch Lubhair. The River Dochart is the route used by most of the Loch Tay salmon. So, perhaps that might tempt you to give it a go?

→ Trossachs.co.uk 56.42, -4.4787 £8 Fly, bait, spin, led BT, Sa, ST

3 LOCH VOIL

You get your permit from the farmhouse, very old school fishing. Brown trout, arctic char are here and some salmon and sea trout later in the season. Loch Voil has a rich history extending back to the Celts, who considered this area a 'thin place' – where the boundaries between Earth and Heaven are particularly narrow. I'll leave you to judge if they're correct. Fishing success, I suspect, will increase your agreement with the Celts.

→ Trossachs.co.uk 56.3482, -4.4301 £8 Fly, bait, spin, led BT, Sa, ferox, char

4 BALVAIG RIVER

This is a short river, some five miles long, and it has some of the best salmon and sea trout fishing in Scotland. Or anywhere else, for that matter. It's a bit of a secret (now blown). You can do very well here when the conditions are correct.

→ Trossachs.co.uk 56.3411, -4.3708 £10 Fly, bait, spin, led BT, ST, Sa

5 LOCH ACHRAY

Very similar to its larger sibling Loch Venachar. Mackerel is the best bait, but also casting Mepps and spoons can work. Framed by Ben Venue with, we're told, the likelihood of incredible sunsets. In the summer, wading the margins with large muddler minnows and the like can be great fun.

→ Fishforth.org 56.2273, -4.4027 £12 Fly, Spinning BT, Pe, Pi

6 LOCH DRUNKIE

You can only fish on the roadside, but it's worth it: a lovely brown trout fishery. Only catch and release here, please. It's been a renowned brown trout and pike fishery since the eighteenth century. Small worms work well, and Mepps. As for flies: Hares Ear, Pheasant Tail, Kate McLaren, Daddies, Mayflies, and Sedge. And, of course, any worm flies you have in your box.

→ Fishforth.org 56.2101, -4.3574 £10 Fly, bait, spin, led BT

7 LOCH VENACHAR

This is big pike water: the record on the loch was 43lb. By far and away the best baits are mackerel and lamprey eel. At its western end, long uninterrupted drifts may be achieved, casting into a depth of 6 to 8

9

11

8

10

feet – great conditions for brown trout. There's an abundance of invertebrate life which fattens the fish up, making for even larger pike. The circle of life.

→ Fishforth.org 56.2209, -4.3059 £20 Fly, spinning Pi, BT

8 LENY RIVER

Mainly a salmon river, but both sea trout and brown trout can also be found. A spate is required for running fish, and the Leni slows the salmon down long enough for the lucky fly anglers on that day to have a chance.

→ Trossachs.co.uk 56.2523, -4.2802 £6 Fly, Spinner BT, Pe

9 LOCH LUBNAIG

Permits are available at The Cabin at Loch Lubnaig. There have been some large salmon caught here in times past. You'll be sharing the water with wild swimmers, but there's plenty of room for everybody. The main angling fish are perch and brown trout, however char can often be caught averaging 6-9", and there are salmon passing through from the River Leny to the River Balvaig throughout the season. The perch get large here and reportedly the Scottish record was held on Lubnaig for some time.

→ Incallander.co.uk 56.2671, -4.2851 £12 Fly, spinner BT, Sa, ST, Char, Pe

10 TEITH (BLUE BANKS)

This is the lowest beat of the River Teith. Plenty of visible fish and at its best from July onwards. Dry flies and emergers are a great option in the slower farmland areas downstream for brown trout. Swinging small traditional wets is very popular with trout and sea trout anglers.

→ Fishforth.org 56.1993, -4.0981 £20-£35 Fly, bait, spin, led BT, Sa, ST, Gr

11 CARRON RIVER

Those with a love for any style of river fishing can find what they want on the Carron. Fish for trout and sea trout at the same time. Often sea trout will be picked up whilst trout fishing with the fly/spinner and vice versa. The Carron was hopelessly polluted and devoid of fish even as recently as twenty years ago due to the heavy industrial era and its aftermath. Now, with the devoted actions of the angling club and many other community organisations, the River Carron is a beautiful river that runs clean and holds a great head of game fish.

→ Fishforth.org 56.0252, -3.9165 £9 Fly, bait, spin, led BT, Sa, ST, Gr

FIFE & ANGUS

12 SILVER SANDS

This area was known as the "Jewel Of The Fife Riviera". Silver Sands is a small, sandy beach with good views of the Islands of Inchmickery and Inchcolm. Backed by woodland, the beach has a very tranquil feel. Lots of seals which could make the fishing challenging. It's primarily a flatfishing area.

→ Silver Sands car park. 56.0559, -3.285 Free Beach Flatfish

13 TAY ESTUARY

Best fished by boat, provided you know what you're doing. Expect to catch good runs of sea trout, typically in the two-pound range, but you might get lucky and collar a five-pounder or two. Definitely wear a life vest. There's a large population of seals here too.

→ Dundeecity.gov.uk 56.4581, -3.0532 £22.50 Estuary ST, Sa

14 TENTSMUIR SANDS

Look out for grey and common seals, both of which are frequently spotted basking on the sandbanks. There is also a variety of birdlife to be spotted, including eider ducks and oystercatchers. The forest is home to red squirrels. Primarily flatfishing here.

→ Cheap all day car park at the beach. 56.4429, -2.8202 Free Beach Flatfish

15 KINGSBARNS BEACH

We're told the most frequently caught fish here are the common skate, mackerel, John Dory, and red bream. Apparently, the name came from the barns used to store grain here prior to transport to the Royal Castle at Crail and the Palace at Falkland, which now makes sense of the name.

→ Parking at the beach. 56.3034, -2.6448 Free Beach Skate, mackerel, John Dory

16 ROOME BAY (CRAIL)

The bay is south-facing and combines a cove of sand and rock pools, with natural peace and quiet. There is an old disused swimming pool at one end of the beach that is now a haven for wildlife. The setting has been used many times for films and by artists. It's a good cod fishery.

→ Small car park at the beach, so get there early. 56.2615, -2.6195 Free Beach Cod

12

15

16

17

23

24

17 LUNAN BAY/TAYSIDE

This east-facing beach is backed by sand dunes and framed by low cliffs to the north and south. It's primarily a cod fishery. The 12th-century ruin, originally built for King William of Scotland, contributes mightily to the ambiance while you're fishing. You can also look at the way traditional fishing is done here, trapping fish when the tide recedes.

→ The carpark is on the north side of the bay. 56.6494, -2.5029 Free Beach Cod

PERTHSHIRE

18 LOCH EIGHEACH

The loch is typically highland in character with its boulder-strewn banks, which are mainly peat and heather clad. It contains lots of native brown trout, averaging around three to the pound, but there are much larger fish and, in recent years, trout in excess of 2lbs have been landed.

→ Pitlochryanglingclub.com 56.6795, -4.5299 £8 Fly BT

19 EAST LOCH TAY

More of a brown trout fishery but, like Loch Tummel, perch and pike are here in relatively significant numbers. Perhaps target the trout first and then swing into action on the perch, followed by the big boys – pike.

→ Pitlochryanglingclub.com 56.569, -4.0669 £8 Fly BT, Pi, Pe

20 THE WATER OF RUCHILL

A surprisingly large river compared to most of Scotland's spate burns and has a very alpine feel to it. Essentially, it is one large rapid. Alongside the sea trout and native brown trout are some rainbow escapees. The club asks that you take these out and kill them when caught. While we are big fans of the catch and release ethos, in this case, take 'em home and eat 'em. Delicious – and you're doing your part for the ecosystem.

→ Ruchil.co.uk 56.3673, -3.9916 £15 Fly BT, Gr, ST, Sa

21 EARN RIVER

The Earn has a late salmon run, mainly in September and October. Sea trout are worth pursuing from May onwards, but the numbers appear to be going down year on year. However, The Earn has always been a river with trout too. The River Earn Improvement Association, a voluntary organisation composed of fishing rights holders and local angling clubs, works well to improve fish stocks in the river. We need groups like this on all our UK fisheries.

→ Ruchil.co.uk 56.3722, -3.9549 £15 Fly BT, Gr, ST, Sa

22 DEVON RIVER

This river divides into three sections; in the upper, stealth should be your watchword. Remember to keep a low silhouette, hide behind bushes, and beware of casting a shadow over the water. I've seen anglers gradually crawl up on unsuspecting trout – a bit too energetic for me. In the middle section, fish April/May when the sea trout and grilse start to run, and at the lower section at the Wharry Burn, you'll find exceptional fly fishing.

→ Fishforth.org 56.2212, -3.6245 £8 Fly, bait, spin, led BT, Sa, ST, Gr

23 LOCH LEVEN

Both nationally and internationally known as a brown trout fishery of very long standing – over a hundred years. It has a unique strain of brown trout, Salmo Levensis, which has been used to stock rivers, lakes, and lochs not only in this country but across the world. After trials of stocking both brown trout and rainbow trout during the latter half of the 20th century, Loch Leven has reverted to once more being a natural brown trout fishery.

→ Fishlochleven.co.uk 56.1997, -3.4158 £30 Fly BT

24 LOCH TUMMEL

This is one of the lochs up here where you can brush up on your skills in catching coarse fish on a fly. Both pike and perch are present in some numbers. While the greedy perch should be (relatively) easy pickings, to catch a pike on a fly is a sterling achievement.

→ Pitlochryanglingclub.com 56.7098, -3.9451 £8 Fly BT, Pi, Pe

25 LOCH BHAC

This loch has been stocked with rainbow trout, but there are still some natives lurking amongst the bully boys from America. Standard wet flies will often be successful but, if conditions are right, buzzers and dries can be deadly, especially in the late afternoon and evening.

→ Pitlochryanglingclub.com 56.7378, -3.9256 £18 Fly BT

26 GARRY RIVER/RUAN RUARIE

There are at least twelve holding pools spread along the length of the beat, with ample water suitable for both fly and spinning. For fly fishing, a single-handed rod can be used when the water is low. However, in most conditions, a double-handed rod of between 12 and 14 feet gives an advantage. For spinning, Devon minnows and Toby spoons are the weapons of choice.

→ Pitlochryanglingclub.com 56.7352, -3.7725 £20 Fly, Spinning Sa

27 UPPER TUMMEL RIVER

The Upper Tummel is far more lightly fished than downstream. It's a riot of a river. It holds lots of small, free-rising trout. Fly fishing here is best done poking around the riffles and stalking out the deep pools. Be aware of sharp fluctuations in the water level; don't get caught out.

→ Pitlochryanglingclub.com 56.7167, -3.7723 £3 Fly BT

28 PITLOCHRY DAM

There are good runs of summer salmon and grilse, and in some years, given favourable conditions, good catches can be made in July and August. Generally, larger flies (4s and 6s) and tube flies are popular early in the season or when the water is high, and smaller flies (8s and 10s) when the water is warmer and lower.

→ Pitlochryanglingclub.com 56.6998, -3.7389 £20 Fly Sa

29 TUMMEL RIVER

You might have to explain to your partner, so perhaps show this entry: invariably it is better to fish The Tummel deep into a summer's night because that is when the river comes alive with the larger, cautious fish moving out of cover to gorge on the very prolific Olives hatch.

→ Pitlochryanglingclub.com 56.649, -3.6705 £10 Fly BT, Gr

30 LOCH NAN EUN

This small loch deep within the Cairngorms National Park is a hike to reach, but once there, you will find small brown trout in abundance. You'll be asking yourself how so many trout got to such a remote loch. The fish are in the half-pound range; a three-quarter-pounder is a decent catch. Some larger fish lurk deep within the loch too. Flies of choice are: Kate McLaren, Mallard and Green, Mallard and Claret.

→ Cairngormpark.co.uk 56.8858, -3.5358 £10 Fly BT

31 LOCH BEANIE

A brisk forty-five minute walk brings you to this small, shallow loch. Depending on the weather, it can be challenging fishing, but if the Gods are with you, it can be memorable. This loch has a boat which can be reserved by telephoning Mrs Young, Invereddrie Farm, Glenshee, tel: 01250 885241.

→ Invercauld.estate 56.8017, -3.3766 £10 Fly BT

MORAY & ABERDEENSHIRE

32 AVON BEATS 1, 2 AND 3

The salmon in May tend to run to the top of the Avon in early season, but they do stop to rest in various pools on the way up, which is where these silver, fresh-run fish can be caught. In June, July, August, and September, the salmon are still making their way upstream, and from May, sea trout are in the beats and can be caught on fly in the white water in daylight and at night in the pools.

→ Riveravonfishingassociation.weebly.com 57.2499, -3.3932 £30-£60 Fly Sa, ST

33 DON RIVER

Trout are abundant here, with some over 5lb. Expect sea trout to turn up from June onwards. There are thirteen named salmon pools as well. The middle reaches of the beat are perhaps better known for their brown trout fishing, but as you will find, the brownies are well spread out across the entire river.

→ Fishingthefly.co.uk 57.2454, -2.7006 £10 Fly BT, Sa, ST

34 YTHAN RIVER

The upper section of this water (near Gight Castle) only fishes well with a spinner; you need to really cover a lot of this water. Also, worming is encouraged. This beat is at its best during spells of high water. You needn't bring your fly rod to fish this water well.

→ Sites.google.com/view/haddohouseanglingclub 57.4412, -2.2901 £15-£30 Spinner, worm Sa, ST, BT

30

34

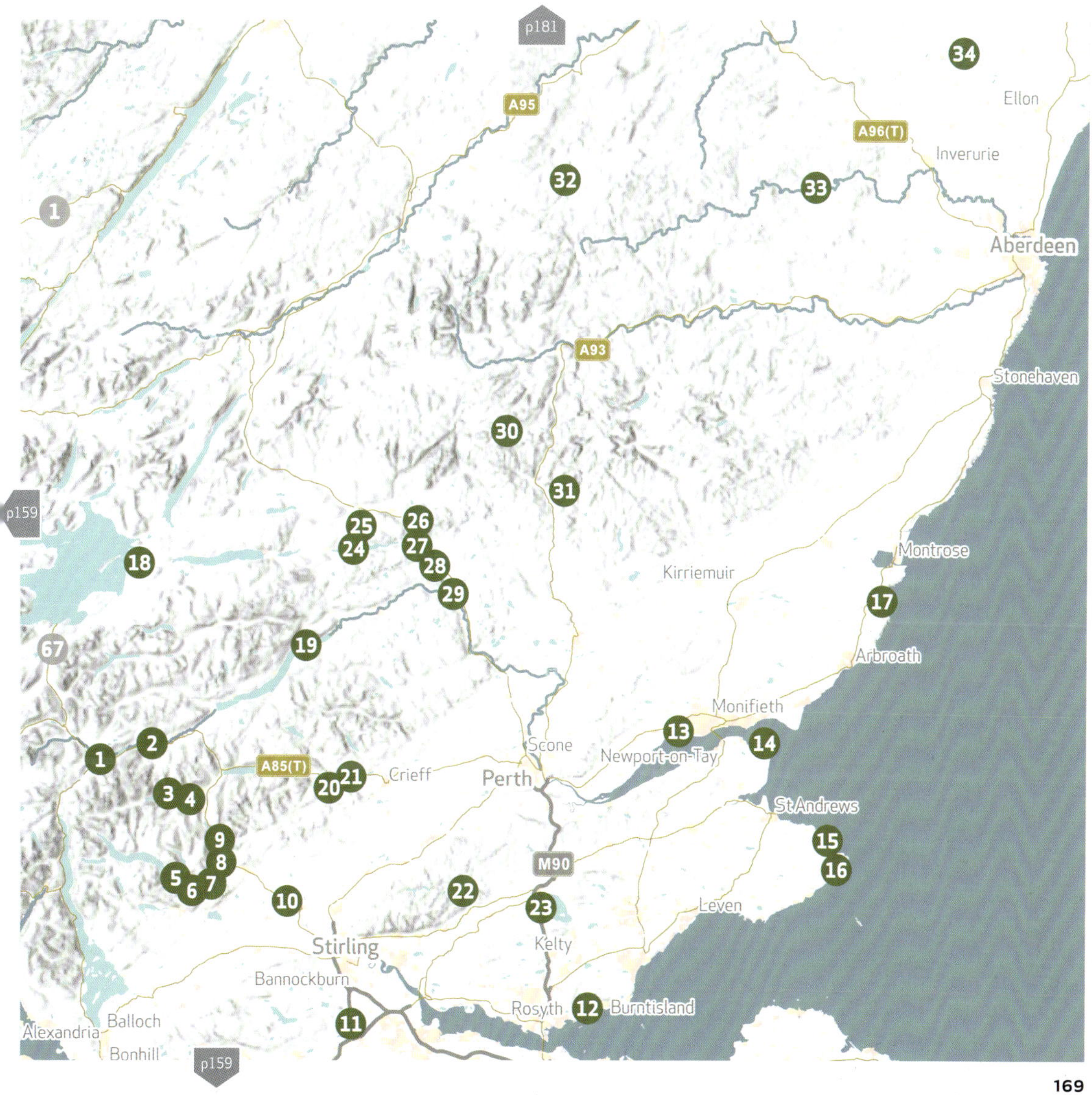
p181
p159
p159
A95
A96(T)
A93
A85(T)
M90
Ellon
Inverurie
Aberdeen
Stonehaven
Montrose
Kirriemuir
Arbroath
Monifieth
Newport-on-Tay
Scone
Perth
Crieff
St Andrews
Leven
Kelty
Stirling
Bannockburn
Rosyth
Burntisland
Balloch
Alexandria
Bonhill
1
67
1
2
3
4
5
6
7
8
9
10
11
12
13
14
15
16
17
18
19
20
21
22
23
24
25
26
27
28
29
30
31
32
33
34

1

Scottish Highlands

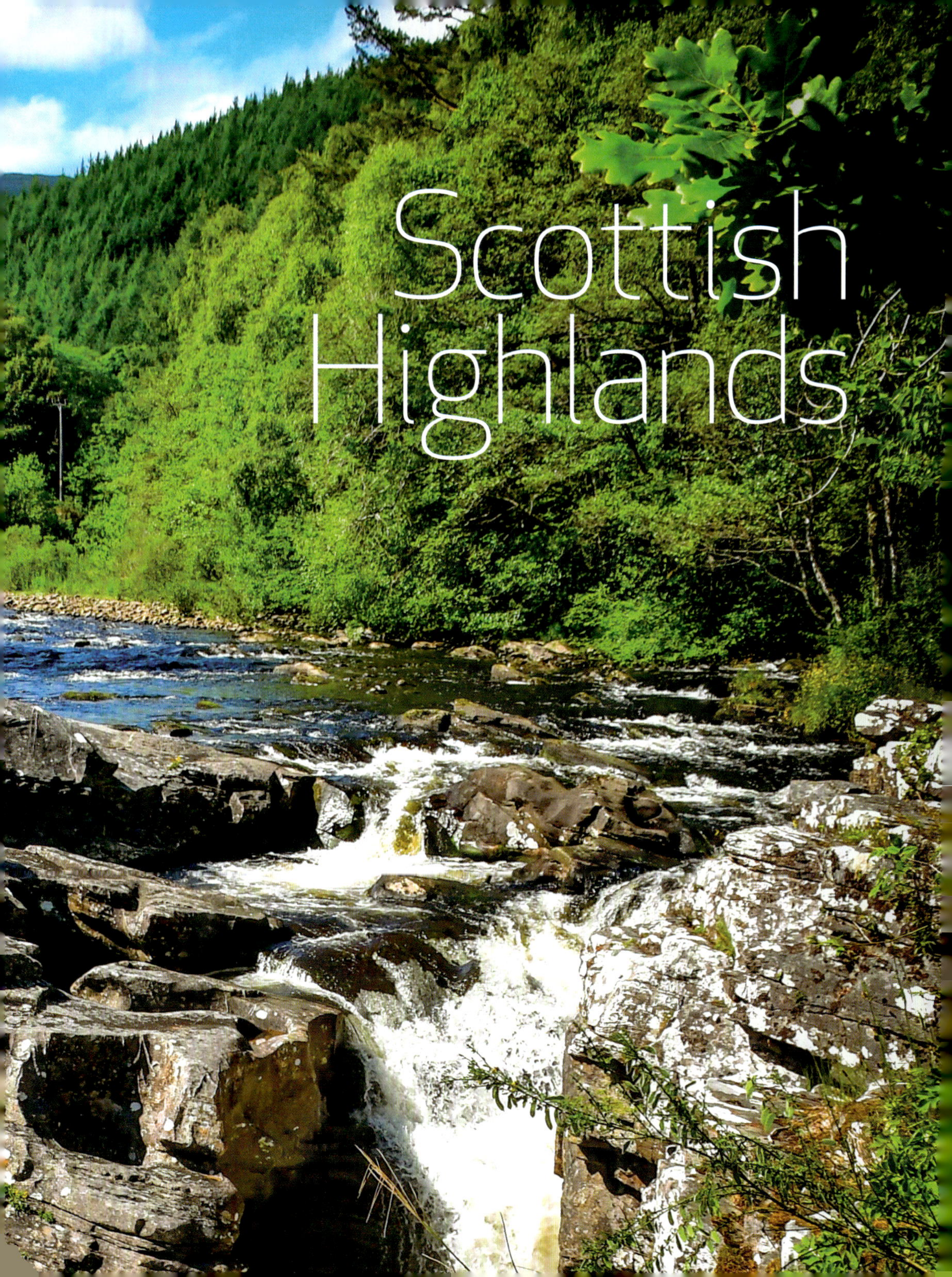

Fishing in the Highlands is all about hiking and wind. Mastering the wind is about positioning yourself in the correct place. Do it correctly and you'll have enough wind assistance to make even the worst of your casting carry the fly soaring out deep into the loch. There are hundreds of lochs to explore, some so isolated that the trout will not have seen a fisherman or a trout fly in many years, if ever. All that you require to reach them is a mobile phone and your GPS, or, as is often the case due to a lack of signal, a compass and an Ordnance Survey map. You'll also need a stout pair of boots, a fly rod and reel, a box of flies… and midge repellent and a mask. Whatever you do, don't forget the latter two items.

Success in loch fishing is dependent on the weather. May and June are considered the best times to head north and explore the wilder waters of the Highlands. Broadly, the larger the waves on the loch, the bushier the fly. Ideal conditions would be a slight breeze to gently ruffle the waters to mask you and your intentions and, as importantly, your fly and leader. All this is more difficult to do in the height of summer with the flat, calm conditions, where your every move can be scrutinised by the wary, wild brown trout.

The Assynt, a sparsely populated area in the south-west of Sutherland, neatly encapsulates the experience of wild fishing in the Highlands. The wild terrain of Assynt and the almost complete lack of 'proper' trails or paths mean that accessing the fishing, sometimes even just a short distance from the road, can be a very strenuous undertaking. This, I suggest, is the point: we come here to cast a fly over fish that are not often, or ever, fished to. To ensure this, we need to go further and perhaps suffer more than the more casual angler.

The Assynt will reward the angler who makes the effort with large catches of fish, typically weighing 2 or 3 to the pound. However, lurking amongst the smaller fish are a number of fish above a pound. There are even a few four-pound fish caught each year by the lucky or skilful angler. A number of lochs also have Arctic char and ferox brown trout.

INVERNESS

1 MORISTON RIVER

This major tributary runs into Loch Ness and holds very large trout. Undoubtedly better known as a salmon river, the trout here seem to grow exceptionally large for some reason. You can have an excellent day here by eschewing salmon and concentrating solely on trout.

→ Glenbegfishing.com 57.1809, -4.7979 £35 Fly, spinning BT, ST, Sa

ROSS

2 MELLON UDRIGLE BEACH

Beautiful views of Highland mountains backed by dunes and framed by rocky promontories make Mellon Udrigle one of the most attractive pieces of coastline in Wester Ross. It's an excellent pollock fishery and you can't get a more lovely spot to chase them.

→ Parking at the beach. 57.9016, -5.5578 Free Beach Pollock

3 LOCH MAREE

Noted for its enormous catches of sea trout, with fish of ten pounds not uncommon. The best sea trout taken from the loch weighed almost twenty pounds, and the record salmon exceeded thirty pounds. Unfortunately, with the decline in sea trout stocks, catches have dropped dramatically. However, the scenic splendour and the chance of connecting with a few of these splendid fish make Loch Maree well worth a visit. Also known for its otters and black-throated divers.

→ Kinlochewe Angling Club 57.7105, -5.5306 £10 Fly BT, ST, Sa

4 LOCH GARBHAIG

Though some fish enter the loch in July, the majority stay within the estuary, running later in the season. This system offers possibly the best estuary fishing for salmon and sea trout in the Hebrides, with more than 95% of salmon and sea trout being caught in the sea, along with some large estuary trout.

→ fideachangling.co.uk 57.6672, -5.5271 £15 Fly, Spinning Sa, ST

5 LOCH COULIN

About a mile and a half long and good for salmon and trout fishing. All along the West Ross-shire coast are a number of small spate salmon rivers including the Polly, Kanaird, Ullapool, Broom, Dundonell, Gruinard & Little Gruinard, Kerry, Badachro, Torridon, Balgy, Applecross & Carron, as well as the larger River Ewe, which flows out from Loch Maree.

→ Kinlochewe Angling Club 57.543, -5.318 £10 Fly BT, Sa

6 LOCH SGEIREACH

I don't think it's worth fishing this loch for the entire day due to its relatively small size. It's described as a deep, thin, and clear loch. A morning or afternoon will suffice. Apparently, trout here can grow to large sizes; we've been told over 7lb, which is massive for such a small loch.

→ Assyntanglinginfo.org.uk 57.7143, -4.968 £7.50 Fly BT

7 LOCH ACHONACHIE

The brown trout are typically up to a pound or so, but we're told there are also some very large ones. Two huge brown trout of 6½lbs and 5½lbs were caught by a club member, Alan Macdonald, in 2007. Recommended flies include Black Pennel, Greenwell's Glory, Bibio, Dunkeld, Claret Bumble, Kehe, Kamasunary Killer, and Teal & Green.

→ Highlandfishing.net 57.555, -4.625 £10 Fly BT, Sa

8

10

11

SUTHERLAND & ASSYNT

8 ACHMELVICH BEACH

This gorgeous, sheltered beach looks across the bay to the coastal village of Lochinver with the islands of Lewis and Harris just offshore. It can be crowded in the summer months, but cod, haddock, whiting, pollack, saithe, and mackerel are all waiting in the bay. By autumn, it starts to get quieter.

→ Parking at the beach. 58.1704, -5.3066 £ Free Beach Cod, haddock, whiting

9 LOCH CROACACH

A marvellous setting, thirty minutes from Rhicarn. Croacach is a large, irregularly-shaped loch, with many bays and islands to tempt the angler. Fast-rising fish, rocketing from the depths to snatch your fly, make for intriguing and exciting fishing.

→ Assynt Crofters Trust assyntflyfishing 58.1831, -5.2445 £ £10 Fly BT

10 LOCH CULAG

The English translation is the 'School Loch', so named, I'm sure, from the school on the promontory. Good trout fishing; you can catch many in a session. We've seen a fly called the Clan Chief, a bushy fly, recommended. From June onwards, you can also pursue both salmon and sea trout.

→ Assyntanglinginfo.org.uk 58.1431, -5.2347 £ £7.50 Fly BT, ST, Sa

11 LOCH A CHOIN

Easy to reach from the road with high-quality trout in clear water, but there's not a high amount of fish. They're hard to tempt because the water is so clear. So, as usual in clear water, you need to be very delicate in your fishing. That said, it gets easier with a wind to ruffle the water.

→ Assyntanglinginfo.org.uk 58.1147, -5.2542 £ £7.50 Fly BT

12 LOCH DRUIM SUARDALAIN (THE GLEN LOCH)

Expect salmon and sea trout to arrive from July onwards, and before that, the trout here are typically in the half to full pound range. You can do well here with Daddy Long Legs flies when the naturals start to get blown onto the water. No fishing on Sundays, and they're strict about it.

→ Assyntanglinginfo.org.uk 58.1448, -5.2043 £ £7.50 Fly BT, ST, Sa

13 LOCH FIONN

Set in spectacular scenery at the foot of Suilven and at the top of the River Kirkaig, this 3.5km long loch holds a superb head of brown trout with pink flesh; arctic char are here in some numbers. A plentiful supply of larger-than-average trout are taken, with a few real lunkers amongst them, each season.

→ Ledmoreestate.com 58.1094, -5.1824 £8 Fly BT

14 LOCH BEANNACH

Beannach is a small V-shaped loch, an easy 25-minute walk from the road. It has a large population of wild brown trout, but also arctic char and a few salmon and sea trout, although neither of the latter have been reported caught in recent years.

→ Assyntanglinginfo.org.uk 58.1878, -5.1673 £7.50 Fly BT, char, Sa, ST

15 LOCH AN RUIGHEIN

Gorgeous, small lake with fine silvery trout. All typically under a pound, but with diligence, larger fish can be brought to the bank. The best bank is held to be the southern bank. Like many of these lochs, if you catch them on the right day, you can catch large numbers of fish in a single afternoon.

→ Assyntanglinginfo.org.uk 58.1913, -5.1404 £7.50 Fly BT

16 ABHAINN GLEANN LEIREAG

Not too far away from the famous Bone Caves at Creag nan Uamh, 'the crag of the caves', in Inchnadamph, where significant discoveries were made of prehistoric bear bones. Perhaps prehistoric bears fished where you are fishing? Gin-clear waters mean that if you're quick, you can see the fish with your polaroids.

→ assyntflyfishing.com 58.2286, -5.1413 £7.50 Fly BT

17 LOCH BEALACH CORNAIDH

Bealach a' Chornaidh separates the northern peak from the eastern ridge of Quinaig, set in the valley floor. Sometimes dour, it has silvery fish of good average size, with much better fish being taken from time to time.

→ Assyntanglinginfo.org.uk 58.206, -5.0515 £7.50 Fly BT

18 LOCH ASSYNT

A large, brooding water with, we're told, a 14lb trout hauled to shore within living memory. It's the largest loch in the area. This place can be dangerous in high winds. Check the weather forecast and don't bother going if it's

21

18

19

23

20

too windy. However, it is easily accessible by the road.

→ Assyntanglinginfo.org.uk 58.1755, -5.0505 £7.50 Fly BT, ferox, char, ST, Sa

19 LOCH NA BEINNE REDHE

Nice fat trout in the one-pound range. Typically, they're blessed with large black and red spots. They're quite striking. Gold head nymphs and deer hair sedges should work. It's a hill loch so it can catch the sun. Don't forget your factor fifty, especially those of us with less hair than we would like.

→ Obanandlorn-anglingclub.co.uk 58.1472, -5.037 £7.50 Fly BT

20 UIDH FHEARNA RIVER

Lovely broad (but short) river with a number of native trout over one pound. It's a bit of a deep wade, so care must be taken, but if you time it right, it can be glorious. Due to its short size, you can cover the entire water in a morning and then perhaps revert to the nearby lochs.

→ Ledmoreestate.com 58.0927, -5.141 £7.50 Fly BT

21 LOCH VEYATIE

Excellent trout fishing and also renowned for ferox trout, as mentioned in Ron Greer's book, *Ferox Trout*. The loch is over 4.5 miles long and over 150ft deep in places. It also has shoals of char amongst the ferox – with char giants swimming amongst them.

→ Ledmoreestate.com 58.0785, -5.0964 £7.50 Fly BT

22 CAM LOCH

Later in the season, weed can be a problem, but you'll find the fish liberally spread throughout the loch and very willing. We're told it fishes very well in May and then again in September. Best flies are considered to be Kate McLarens and Black Pennells.

→ Assyntanglinginfo.org.uk 58.0743, -5.0368 £7.50 Fly BT, Ferox, Char.

23 LOCHAN FADA

A long, but, weather permitting, perfectly pleasant walk in past Loch Cam. Medium-sized fish are common, though there are tales of far larger ones being brought to bank. Relatively easy fishing offsets the hour-plus walk to get there. It feels and is remote, enhancing the fishing experience.

→ Assyntanglinginfo.org.uk 57.6782, -5.2867 £7.50 Fly BT

24 LOCH URAGIL

Set at the heart of the Ledmore Estate, teeming with trout and the perfect place to introduce beginners to fishing. It's helpful that they get the 'feel' of fishing. Once you have that, you have the confidence to carry you through the many blank days that will come. It's a shallow loch but, as well as a generous head of fish, some are reported to be large.

→ Ledmoreestate.com 58.0491, -4.9962 £8 Fly Ferox trout

25 RED CORRIE LOCH

A steep, one-hour hike to get here. Known locally as Red Corrie Loch, its official title is Loch a Choire Dheirg. No particular hotspots, the lovely Red Chorrie trout can be taken almost anywhere on the loch. Close to Green Corrie Loch, well worth the visit if you have the time (and you've got your breath back).

→ Assyntanglinginfo.org.uk 58.1998, -4.9743 £7.50 Fly BT

26 LOCH FLEODACH COIRE

This can be a very productive loch if you time it right, but remember to bring the midge repellent. Long shank nymphs and the ubiquitous gold ribbed hare's ear should work

26

well. But, let's be honest, when doesn't the GRHE work?

→ Assynt Angling Association East Zone 58.1777, -4.9364 £7.50 Fly BT

27 LOCH GILAROO (LOCH MHOALACH-COIRE)

Apparently named for the type of trout that inhabit the loch, which came, we're told, from Ireland. They exclusively feed on molluscs and crustaceans, which give them their almost barrel-like shape. Local hotels in the area have large, five-pound-plus fish displayed in their glass cases, so you can live in hope.

→ Assyntanglinginfo.org.uk 58.1308, -4.9261 £7.50 Fly BT

28 LOCH AILSH

A shallow loch that is at its angling best in the middle and end of June. When the trout turn sulky, the sea trout and salmon turn up, extending the loch's fishing season. Apparently, you can hear the stags bellowing in the autumn evenings. Magical.

→ Oykelbridgehotel.com 58.056, -4.8572 £7.50 Fly BT, ST, Sa

29 LOCH SHIN

A large loch of some seventeen miles. Trout in this loch average 1/2 to 3/4 lb, although there are some very large fish lurking in the depths, and double-figure trout are caught relatively regularly. We're told that a good day at Loch Shin is two rods catching fifty fish between them.

→ Lairg-angling-club.co.uk 58.1468, -4.614 £30/year Fly, bait, spin, led BT, Sa

30 LOCH LARO

A beautiful sight to stumble across, and that is just what you do on the way into it. The view alone is well worth the trip. It is a chance to look down onto a hill loch, a pleasant change from climbing into one. For flies, small and black are the best.

→ Dornochangling.co.uk 57.9645, -4.36 £10 Fly BT

31 LOCH CRACAIL MOR

Cracail Mor can provide you with some spectacular sport: hard fighting, beautifully marked wild brown trout of a good size. If you get such a day, you will have earned it. This is a truly magnificent Highland loch set in rolling Sutherland hills, at the end of a long, soft trek.

→ Dornochangling.co.uk 57.9889, -4.3225 £10 Fly BT

29

30

34

32 LOCH CRAIGGIE

The jewel of the Lairg AC lochs is Craiggie, which lies in the hills to the north of Lairg village. Note: the boat is only available to club members. A magical place when the Mayfly hatch is on, with fish averaging 1lb+. This loch fishing is very special to both the locals and the fishing club. A very good fishing loch and lovely to fish from the bank. (So you don't need their boat).

→ Lairg-angling-club.co.uk 58.0301, -4.321
£30/year Fly BT

33 LOCH AN LAGAIN

Good quality brown trout are available on Loch Buidhe with smaller fish on Loch Lagain, both lochs enjoying fine scenery and good sport. A delightful, easily accessible loch with brown trout averaging 8oz and the occasional salmon and sea trout late in the season.

→ Dornochangling.co.uk 57.9293, -4.2669
£10 Fly BT

34 KYLE OF DURNESS

An unspoilt section of coast with lovely beaches, good views, and a remote feel. At low tide, the end of the River Dionard threads a winding route through an enormous expanse of immaculate sand. Superb sea trout fishing when the tide is low.

→ The overnight car park here has spectacular views. 58.5736, -4.7985
Free Beach ST

35 LOCH CROCACH

Crocach is generally regarded as one of the club's most attractive lochs, hence its inclusion. Set within a remote moorland location. A good head of fish here, most below a pound. Many interesting bays to cast within, which makes for absorbing fishing.

→ Forsinardflyfishers.co.uk 58.5007, -4.3306 £40/season Fly BT

36 LOCH BRORA

Both the loch and river are renowned for sea trout, providing good sport in July. The first runs of sea trout arrive in May but generally run quickly into the upper river. There is a tidal stretch of half a mile which can be fished by visitors from May until the end of the season.

→ Dornochangling.co.uk 58.047, -3.9397
£10 Fly BT

37 BIGHOUSE LOCH

This is the loch for breaking out the

33

35

terrestrial flies from the fly box. With lots of small bays to poke around in, you'll be catching fish of circa a pound with the odd specimen of two pounds a possibility. My favourite loch up here, and that's saying a lot.

→ Forsinardflyfishers.co.uk 58.5564, -3.8848 £40/season Fly BT

38 LOCH EARACHA

It's suggested that you fish the shallows from the bank as much as reasonably possible before you start wading out into the depths. Primarily this is due to undisturbed trout who will often hold tight to the bank and are eminently catchable because they are confident and relaxed.

→ Forsinardflyfishers.co.uk 58.5206, -3.8917 £40/season Fly BT

39 LOCH SAINN

Two for the price of one, you can comfortably fish both Sainn and her sister Saird in a day. However, you'll need to tie up your hiking boots; it's a stiff walk but more than adequately compensated by magnificent scenery. Good hard-fighting fish in both lochs, and they will rise to a well-presented dry fly too.

→ Forsinardflyfishers.co.uk 58.4414, -3.8069 £40/season Fly BT

40 LOCH LEIR

A productive early and late season loch, but you should avoid the mid-season algae which makes fishing difficult, to nigh on impossible, and frankly, don't waste your time here then. It's not like you don't have dozens of other lochs to choose from for your £40. That said, you'll have the loch to yourself then, and the trout will not have been casted over – a dilemma. Counterintuitive.

→ Forsinardflyfishers.co.uk 58.3875, -3.7866 £40/season Fly BT

41 LOCHAN NAM BREAC

Sheltered to the east by forestry but open to the north and west, Nam Breac is a shallow loch with comfortable wading from the southern and eastern banks. Expect nothing giant in here, but they say it's good for restoring confidence if you get skunked by Skyline.

→ Forsinardflyfishers.co.uk 58.4062, -3.7099 £40/season Fly BT

42 LOCH SKYLINE

You need to be even more cautious on Skyline than you would on other lochs, and that means very cautious. The fish are frequently lying tight to the bank, so cast before you are anywhere near the water. Ideally, your fly should just plop over the bank with you off in the distance.

→ Forsinardflyfishers.co.uk 58.4088, -3.6948 £40/season Fly BT

43 LOCH CAOL ALTNABREC

A small tear-drop shaped loch located in the Flow Country of Caithness. The shallow end is least productive, but good hard-fighting fish are found everywhere else. It is regarded as a loch best fished from a boat. Trout of up to 2lb have frequently been caught.

→ Forsinardflyfishers.co.uk 58.4134, -3.6691 £40/season Fly BT

44 LOCH GRASSIE

A fantastic little loch to visit and combine with either of the nearby lochs for added variation to the day. Grassie holds a smaller head of fish than neighbouring Garbh or Caise but trumps them both on size and quality, with fish of over a pound often encountered.

→ Forsinardflyfishers.co.uk 58.3995, -3.6602 £40/season Fly BT

CAITHNESS

45 DUNNET BEACH

Good beach fishing can be experienced from both Dunnet and Murkle Beaches. Fishing from the rocks all around this part of the coast can prove effective, but care regarding tide and weather conditions should be exercised. Boat angling is available from Scrabster Harbour near Thurso. The area produced a world record Halibut and Porbeagle Shark in addition to many huge skate.

→ The beach has its own car park. 58.6069, -3.3507 Free Beach Skate, halibut

46 LOCH OF YARROWS

This loch is well-stocked with brown trout and permits are available on a daily or longer basis. This is a great loch for a beginner or a lazy older person. Easy access and obliging fish, sometimes that's all you want. Who says you have to suffer for your art?

→ Thrumster.co.uk 58.3735, -3.1829 £8 Fly BT

47 LOCH SARCLET

Approaching the loch can be a task as several roads lead to houses and not to the loch itself. But it does not take long to find the correct one, and the locals are friendly and will happily direct you, as they have done many times in the past. The trout make the trip worthwhile, averaging a pound each, with monsters above five pounds not uncommon.

→ Thrumster.co.uk 58.372, -3.1265 £8 Fly BT

40

45

46

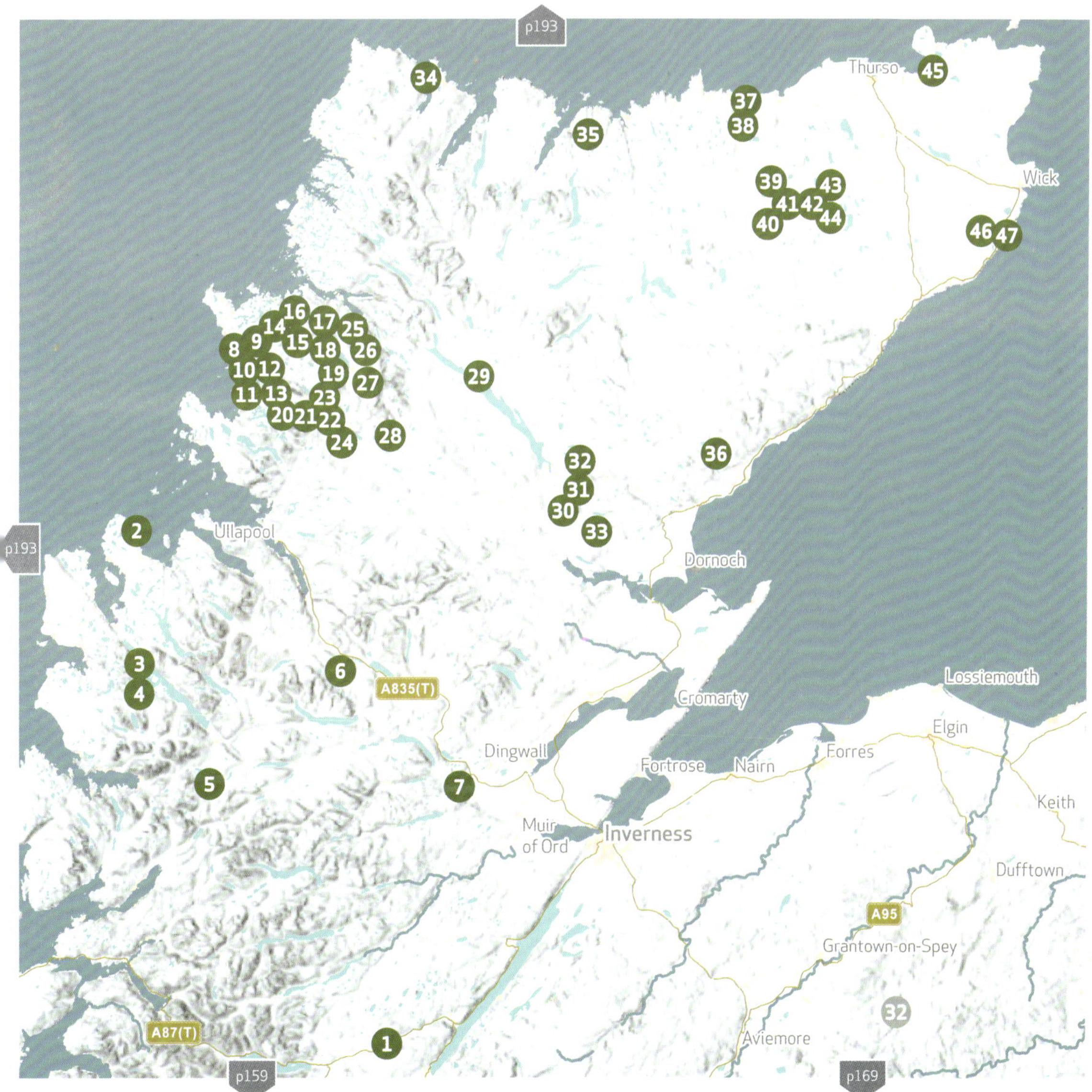
p193
Thurso
Wick
Ullapool
Dornoch
Cromarty
Lossiemouth
Elgin
Dingwall
Fortrose
Nairn
Forres
Keith
Muir of Ord
Inverness
Dufftown
A835(T)
A95
Grantown-on-Spey
A87(T)
Aviemore
p159
p169
1
2
3
4
5
6
7
8
9
10
11
12
13
14
15
16
17
18
19
20
21
22
23
24
25
26
27
28
29
30
31
32
33
34
35
36
37
38
39
40
41
42
43
44
45
46
47

Scottish Islands

3

4

5

Scotland is blessed with lochs. There are more than 31,000 freshwater lochs and lochans, with more than 7,500 located in the Western Isles alone. Many have populations of Arctic char as well as the large ferox trout that hunt them. To fulfil the incessant demand for fly fishing for trout in Scotland, especially in the highly populated areas, a number of man-made fisheries are being opened, many of them stocked artificially with rainbow trout bred specifically for that purpose. We're concentrating primarily on our native species, the wild brown trout.

The problem with writing about trout fishing in the Scottish Islands is not sourcing the places to fish; it's editing it down to a manageable amount. The Scottish Islands contain hundreds, perhaps thousands, of trout lochs and streams, providing a unique angling experience like no other available on the planet. There are the countless wild lochs of Lewis and Harris, the remote lochs of Shetland, and the fertile waters of Orkney. Most of the fishing is accessible to the visiting angler for under ten pounds, and often it's free.

Let's use Orkney as an example – but it could just as easily be any other group of Scottish Islands – trout fishing in Orkney is embedded in the local culture, and visiting anglers are warmly welcomed as a vital part of their economy. The Orkneys are fifteen miles from Caithness, which is a five-hour drive from Inverness or a quick hop by plane. For a mere £20 a year, you can join the Orkney Trout Fishing Association (OTFA), which manages all the fishing waters. Membership allows you to use all the facilities, including car parking, launches, shelters, and toilets. Surely one of the great bargains in fishing.

We should also mention the Machair lochs of Uist. These lochs produce some of the finest wild brown trout in Britain, mainly due to the rich alkaline environment caused by the high calcium carbonate shell content, which creates an environment in which flora and fauna thrive. The shells also increase the length of the island. The standard fishing technique (called Loch Style Fishing) is done from a drifting boat, ideally with somebody other than you on the oars, thereby allowing you to concentrate on the fishing.

2

MULL

1 LOCH FRISA

The largest trout caught in Loch Frisa weighed 15lbs. We're told that you can frequently catch fish here in the 4lb to 6lb range. All this, plus salmon and sea trout from July onwards, makes for a lovely setting with the trifecta of loch, hill, and forest views.

→ The loch has its own car park. 56.5626 -6.0936 £ Free Fly BT, ST, Sa

2 LOCH BA

A "Flying Barn Door" is how the local sea eagles are described by the locals. You needn't be so rude; after all, you're here for the fishing, just like the sea eagle. This loch can get crowded, so hike as far as you can. Top flies are the Hill Loch nymph size 12 to 14.

→ Loch Ba viewing point car park. 56.4774 -5.9668 £ Free Fly BT, ST, Sa

3 FIDDEN BEACH

A shallow, sandy bay with pink granite outcrops. Fish off the rocks and the sandy beach here for pollock and mackerel. The locals recommend silver lures, ideally a Dexter Wedge. This is another place to add midge repellent to your bag.

→ Best parking place to try would be the campsite. 56.3089 -6.3656 £ Free Beach Pollock, mackerel

SOUTH UIST

4 LOCH DRUIDIBEG

This is a good loch to try one of the classic three fly combos: traditional cast of a #12 claret bumble on the bob, #12 golden olive bumble middle dropper, and #12 mallard and claret point. The loch and the surrounding areas are managed by the RSPB. When fishing is slow, take a look about you, there's over 200 species of flowering plants and the area is also rich in birdlife such as redshank, dunlin, lapwing, and greylag geese.

→ Southuistanglingclub.co.uk 57.3154, -7.3295 £ £10 Fly BT

5 LOCH BI/MACHAIR

Besides being excellent for fishing, the area is important for the diverse species of birds it supports, including corncrake, little tern, and sanderling. The site also contains the rare slender naiad - no, I'd never heard of it either. Apparently, it's an annual aquatic plant. The unique shell sand alkaline of the machair lochs forms ideal growing conditions for quality brown and sea trout, making some of the best fishing for these species anywhere.

→ Southuistanglingclub.co.uk 57.3727 -7.366 £ £10 Fly BT, ST

BENBECULA

6 NORTH FORD SEA POOLS

There are both North and South Sea Pools on the club permit. Watch out for quicksand and the tides, but both are excellent sea trout fisheries. Bring a heavier rod than you normally would; a seven weight will do the trick for most situations encountered here. I might go traditional in my choice of flies here: Dunkeld, Mallard & Claret, Silver Doctor, Grouse & Claret, Pheasant & Yellow, Blae & Blue, and Blae & Black.

→ Southuistanglingclub.co.uk 57.4569, -7.2834 £ £10 Fly ST

18

NORTH UIST

7 LOCH STEPHAINN

You can fish Lochs Vausary and Stephainn in a day if you get your skates on; they're quite close to each other. Loch Vausary is quite shallow and fishes well from the bank. Loch Stephainn should produce fish around the burns in and out and along the shoreline.

→ Nuac.co.uk 57.5872, -7.4389 £8 Fly BT

8 LOCH BHIORAIN

This loch is to the immediate west of Vausary and Stephainn. It's got a decent head of average-sized trout, so you've a good chance of catching a few. Also present are both sea trout and salmon, but both species must be returned unharmed as soon as caught. The club does not retain the rights to them. Trout, however, can be taken for the pot if you want.

→ Nuac.co.uk 57.6042, -7.4963 £8 Fly BT

9 LOCH SCOLPAIG

Both these lochs can be waded, but take care around the boggy ground by the weed beds. Consult the website for exactly where you can fish here. The area was proposed by the Scottish government to be the site of a spaceport a few years ago, since rejected. The old film Local Hero bubbled up into my mind when I heard about the spaceport.

→ Nuac.co.uk 57.6238, -7.4847 £8 Fly BT

10 GEIREANN MILL LOCH

The hills surrounding the loch teem with life, including deer, golden eagles, and whirring snipe, making this a perfect spot. The shallower water round the shore is worth investigating, as is the deeper water in the main loch, particularly around the many skerries and islands. Zulus and Shrimps are apparently the fly of choice for the sea trout encountered here, but be prepared; you can see them ignore the vast majority of your attempts.

→ Nuac.co.uk 57.6427, -7.3759 £8 Fly BT, ST

11 LOCH AN AONGAIS

This loch lies to the north of the previous loch, Geireann Mill. There's an ancient fort at the site and the loch is known to hold good fish. Best flies, true for most of these lochs, are Bumbles, Zulus, Bibios, Kate McLaren, Invictas, and Black Pennell, which are some of the locals' favorites. A couple of flashier flies wouldn't hurt either.

→ Nuac.co.uk 57.6447, -7.27 £8 Fly BT

12 LOCH RUNAVAT

Fish up to two pounds are not remarkable here, although the average is smaller. If the conditions are right and the wind not too gusty, you could try a dry fly here with success, although it has to be acknowledged that all these lochs are really wet fly waters.

→ Nuac.co.uk 57.6385, -7.1994 £8 Fly BT

13 LOCH AN DUIN

This loch is brackish, which promotes good growth in the fish. You may also run across some sea fish to bring variety to your catch. We're told the sea fish will mainly be pollack and coalfish, but best of all, you might chance upon a sea trout.

→ Nuac.co.uk 57.6319, -7.1235 £8 Fly ST, BT, Pol.

HARRIS

14 SCARISTA BEACH

A wide and sandy beach with views in all directions. Flounder and turbot will be your

21

19

15

most likely quarries. The white-sand expanse of Scarista is one of the world's finest beaches, and the outcrops at Horgabost make it a great rock-pooling destination.

→ Park along the road in Scarista. 57.8266, -7.0482 Free Beach Flounder, turbot

15 BORVE BEACH

Gorgeous aquamarine waters contrast vividly with the red-hued rocks. Endless views of the Atlantic Ocean complete the picture. A dramatic fishing spot with small reefs and a little pool. You can catch a sea trout here that you will carry in your memory to the end of your days.

→ Access to beach via car park. 57.8387, -7.0172 Free Beach ST

16 LUSKENTYRE BEACH

One of the largest and most spectacular beaches on Harris. The most likely fish encountered here will be flounder, turbot, and dab. Tried and tested baits are mackerel slivers cut to resemble a sand eel or frozen sand eel. The ideal rod would be a light carp rod teamed with a 20lb braid and either a 1 or 2 hook.

→ Free car park at beach. 57.889, -6.9605 Free Beach Flounder, turbot, dab

17 HUISINIS BEACH

A sandy beach where you'll likely encounter a mix of flounder, turbot, and dab. Ideally, your tackle would be a light carp rod or similar, which will register a flatfish bite, 20 lb braid, three size 1 or 2 hooks well spread out on as long a trace as you can reasonably cast.

→ Ample parking. 57.9949, -7.0907 Free Beach Flounder, turbot, dab

18 LOCH NA CLEABHAIG

The loch is purported to hold large trout, but recent reports suggest otherwise. However, of course, it only takes one monster caught to completely change the picture. Meanwhile, there are reports of White-Tailed (Sea) Eagles around the crags above Loch na Cleabhaig. What are they feeding on, I wonder?

→ Outerhebridesfisheriestrust.org.uk
58.0107, -7.0735 Free Fly BT

19 LOCH A' GHLINNE

This loch in the south of Skye is known for its hard-fighting and vividly marked trout. It's excellent for stalking, but with gin-clear waters, extreme stealth is advised. They're opportunistic, so the choice of fly is not crucial, but local favorites are Kate McClaren, Blue Zulu, Bibio, and Clan Chief on a floating line.

→ Outerhebridesfisheriestrust.org.uk
58.0017, -7.0337 Free Fly BT

20 LOCH NA CRAOBHAIG

A 33-acre loch trout in which fish can be taken all over the loch in varying weather conditions. Trout average 10-12oz, with a full day's fishing yielding 8-15 fish (with luck). Dabblers, Bumbles, Clan Chief, Ombudsman, and Peter Ross will all produce fish.

→ Outerhebridesfisheriestrust.org.uk
58.1511, -6.917 Free Fly BT

21 LOCH NAN EILEAN

While writing 1984, George Orwell lived at Barnhill and fished this loch. In a letter to a friend, he described the loch as having plenty of fish but said he hadn't caught anything larger than half a pound. We're told there are considerably larger fish being caught, up to 4lbs. Stick to the writing Mr. Blair.

→ Outerhebridesfisheriestrust.org.uk
58.1817, -6.5385 Free Fly BT

24

27

25

27

28

LEWIS

22 RIVER LAXDALE

Laxdale River is approximately 5 miles long, running east from the Barvas hills. Along its route, there are several fishing pools for brown trout, sea trout, and salmon. Fish numbers are dependent on the river being in spate, allowing fish to move freely into the system. Fishing is available from the bank.

→ Fideachangling.co.uk 58.2252, -6.3785 £15 Fly, spinning BT

23 STEINISH POOL

Steinish Pool and tidal water are approximately 0.5 miles long and 60 feet wide. The pool is tidal, with depths varying depending on tidal conditions. Access and fishing are available from the south shore for sea trout and salmon. Lovely spot with a new path constructed.

→ Fideachangling.co.uk 58.2224, -6.3613 £15 Fly, spinning Sa, ST

SKYE

24 LOCH CORUISK

Fishing here would also include fishing Loch na Creitheach, Loch na Creritheach, Loch an Altham above, and the connecting river, but EXCLUDING the outflow from Loch na Creitheach to the sea. These lochs have a reputation for very large sea trout, which I would target here. They're also known for their salmon.

→ Portreeanglingassociation.wildapricot.org 57.2041, -6.1631 £15 Fly ST, Sa

25 LOCH DUAGRICH

You've got a chance of both salmon and sea trout from the bank here, and of course, brown trout too. Incidentally, it's called "Breacan" in Gaelic, meaning speckled. The surrounding land is used for deer stalking too, so keep your head down in season.

→ Portreeanglingassociation.wildapricot.org 57.3766, -6.3202 £15 Fly ST, Sa, BT

26 LOCH CONNAN

A productive hill loch that can be fished by boat and from the bank, all for the cost of £15 - bargain! You will do better by boat; the ground can be rough and treacherously boggy. Unless you want to spend the day retrieving Wellingtons from the bog after they've been sucked in, use the boat, I suggest.

→ Portreeanglingassociation.wildapricot.org 57.4024, -6.3489 £15 Fly BT

27 SNIZORT RIVER

This is the daddy of Skye's salmon rivers. You will struggle to find salmon fishing elsewhere in Scotland so generously priced. You can only fish the upper reaches on this permit, but you have a real chance of catching a salmon here. There is also an excellent run of sea trout.

→ Portreeanglingassociation.wildapricot.org 57.4567, -6.3233 £15 Fly Sa, ST, BT

28 LOCH LEATHAN

Loch Leathan trout are traditionally minded fish, favoring old-fashioned wet flies such as Invicta, Black Pennell, Grouse series, Soldier Palmer, and various sedge imitations. There is a prolific mayfly hatch, usually around the first half of June, when the usual mayfly imitations work well.

→ Portreeanglingassociation.wildapricot.org 57.4839, -6.1745 £20 Fly BT

29 LOCH CORGASCIL

These three lochs can all be productive given the correct conditions. As in all the hill lochs of the Portree, these lochs offer

34

32

39

the lone angler perfect seclusion. Surely, the most ideal way to fish? Or should it be with mates?

→ Portreeanglingassociation.wildapricot.org
57.5958, -6.2651 £15 Fly BT

30 BROGAIG RIVER

A diminutive spate river with a good run of sea trout and the occasional salmon. As with all spate rivers, you need to keep a careful eye on the weather. If you're travelling from far away, ideally, you will have an acquaintance in the area who can tell you how the river is fishing on any given day or week.

→ Portreeanglingassociation.wildapricot.org
57.6329, -6.2326 £15 Fly, bait, spin, led Sa, ST, BT

31 STAFFIN BAY

Located on the northeast corner of Skye, you'll be fishing while looking at fossilised dinosaur footprints, which are visible at low tide. All this and pollock, mackerel, and wrasse too. The midges can be an issue when the wind drops. A float-fished sand eel seems to be the preferred method in these waters.

→ Park at Staffin Bay. 57.6345, -6.2209
Free Beach Pollock, mackerel, wrasse

32 KILMARTIN RIVER

To encourage more young people to fish, the Portree Angling Association issues permits for all legal means of fishing.
Very public-spirited of them, and I wish other angling bodies would take note.
The Kilmartin fishes well with numerous holding pools.

→ Portreeanglingassociation.wildapricot.org
57.6056, -6.2044 £15 Fly, bait, spin, led BT

33 LOCH MEALT

No brown trout here, only char, oddly. No one appears to know why this is. Still, going after the Arctic char is fun in itself - wary and timid, it can often be found close to the bank. Use a small trout fly or nymph for the best results. They should do the trick.

→ Portreeanglingassociation.wildapricot.org
57.6048, -6.1798 £15 Fly Char

34 RIVER LEALT

Of course, you can fish with a fly here, but really, for best results, get spinning or use the worm. The steep cliffs discourage fly fishing. The locals use small toby-type spinners, spoons, or Devon minnows. Worm fishing is recommended. The Lealt Falls

are a popular stop on any road trip around Skye's Trotternish peninsula.

→ Portreeanglingassociation.wildapricot.org 57.5652, -6.1557 £15 Fly, bait, spin, led Sa, ST, BT

ORKNEY

35 HELDALE WATER

This is a very deep loch. It responds best to big bushy patterns, typical for a loch that depends for most fishing success on wind-blown terrestrial flies. With Arctic char being reintroduced in autumn 2002, the future for this loch could be very interesting.

→ Orkneytroutfishing.co.uk 58.8108, -3.2884 Free Fly BT, char?

36 LOCH OF CLUMLY

Fish grow large in this tiny loch, probably because of the abundant sticklebacks and Corixa. With heavy fishing pressure and due to its diminutive size, the fish can retreat under the reeds and will therefore be uncatchable. Recommended dries: Hoppers, Emergers, and Halfhogs.

→ Orkneytroutfishing.co.uk 59.027, -3.3023 Free Fly BT

37 LOCH OF BOARDHOUSE

The favourite, we're told, of visiting anglers. The fish can be found feeding right in the surface layers in overcast conditions, but in brighter conditions, the daphnia recede to the depths and so do the fish. So, this requires a change to a sinking line to locate the feeding trout. Recommended dries: Hedgehogs and Halfhogs, especially in claret, orange, olive, and Bibio, Foreman's favourite, hoppers, emergers, Daddies, and Shipmans.

→ Orkneytroutfishing.co.uk 59.1136, -3.2796 Free Fly BT

38 LOCH OF HUNDLAND

Somewhat peat-stained and with a lot of boat pressure, but fun can be found with the trout responding to wind-blown terrestrials. Intriguingly, we're told that it fishes well in bright sunshine. Is this due to the peaty water, and does this hold true for all stained water? Recommended flies: cowdungs and daddies.

→ Orkneytroutfishing.co.uk 59.1177, -3.2343 Free Fly BT

39 LOCH OF SWANNAY

This is a peaty loch that holds some of the best trout around. It's a moody water though: some days great sport, other days not, but when it's good, it's very good. Recommended wet flies: Zulu, Dabblers, Bibio, Sooty Olive, Stick Fly, Green Peter, and Bumbles.

→ Orkneytroutfishing.co.uk 59.135, -3.2047 Free Fly BT

40 LOCH OF HARRAY

Widely regarded as the jewel in the Orkney trout fishing crown and is their most famous fishery. As the season progresses and the water temperature increases, the fish move out into deeper, cooler water, which is when boat fishing comes into its own. The hard-fighting Harray trout average between 10-12oz, but fish in the 1-2lb range are not that rare.

→ Orkneytroutfishing.co.uk 59.0301, -3.2228 Free Fly BT

41 LOCH OF STENNESS

The Loch of Stenness is best fished from the shore as fish can be found in shallow water, sometimes barely enough to cover their backs. Fish hide here because they are safe from seals in the shallows! August and September are the best times to fish the Loch of Stenness when the sea trout come in to spawn.

→ Orkneytroutfishing.co.uk 58.9975, -3.2505 Free Fly BT, ST

43

45

47

42 STENNESS

Its unique semi-marine environment dictates that it is very much affected by the state and height of the tides, causing wide fluctuations in water height and salinity in the loch, both of which have a marked effect on the resident trout population. Best to fish when the loch is at its lowest.

→ Orkneytroutfishing.co.uk 58.9642, -3.2309 Free Fly BT

43 LOCH OF KIRBISTER

This is regarded as an excellent loch for those new to the sport due to the fact that the trout are so responsive in even the most unsuitable conditions. Wading is easy and large baskets can be taken from the first day of the season to the last. It's also good for jaded old fishermen who need their fishing batteries recharged.

→ Orkneytroutfishing.co.uk 58.9603, -3.1109 Free Fly BT

44 INGANESS BAY AND DEER SOUND

Just a stone's throw from Kirkwall, the first thing you'll see when heading down the steep hill to the bay below is the rusting wreck of the Juniata, a former WWII block ship at the Churchill Barriers, which was towed ashore during a salvage operation. You would expect to catch a mixed bag of flounder, dab, and turbot here.

→ Orkneytroutfishing.co.uk 58.963, -2.913 Free Beach Flounder, dab, turbot

SHETLAND

45 LOCH SPIGGIE

This shallow loch was formed when a fjord was cut off by the formation of a sand bar. It is very popular with swans, ducks, and geese. Consequently, it's an RSPB nature reserve. Spiggie trout are silvery in colour and fight strongly. The average weight is about 10oz, but there are larger trout up to two pounds. And, if you caught a two-pounder here, you would know about it.

→ Shetlandtrout.co.uk 59.9355, -1.3421 £30/year Fly BT

46 ST NINIAN'S BEACH

This beach is a long spit of sand that connects St. Ninian's to Shetland. Very picturesque. We're told it was (is?) good for bass. If you decide to fish it, you'll be boulder-hopping; it's full of them. Given that bass tend to not hit smaller metal lures, I would look at fishing a long-bodied metal lure or pencil. This will cast a long way, so you can search the water quickly for fish, even in the wind. They're highly satisfying to cast and make you look like a very accomplished angler.

→ Car park with beach access. 59.9711, -1.3319 Free Beach Bass

47 TINGWALL LOCH

Tingwall is one of the most popular lochs in Shetland and is good for bank and boat fishing. The trout average about 10 ounces, and the loch has regularly been stocked with fingerling fish. The north end of the loch contains the bulk of the shallow water, and drifts can be productive in any wind direction.

→ Shetlandtrout.co.uk 60.1698, -1.2522 £30/year Fly, spinning RT

48 PUNDS WATER

This is a roadside loch with easy access. The SAA hire boat is pulled up in a berth at the beach at the north end. The loch is good for both bank and boat fishing, and the trout average about 10 oz. The loch has been stocked with sea trout, and your catch is therefore likely to consist of a mix of brownies and sea trout. It is worth concentrating on the shallows on all sides of the roadside island.

→ Shetlandtrout.co.uk 60.4672, -1.4068 £30/year Fly, spinning BT, ST

49 GOSSA WATER

A small, shallow water that is reached after a stiff 20-minute walk over the hill west of the Sandy Loch. A slightly easier walk can be had from the road end on the top of Shurton Hill. Wading is fairly safe, and fish of over two pounds have been caught here. The loch is stocked on a regular basis by the SAA.

→ Shetlandtrout.co.uk 60.5453, -1.1588 £30/year Fly, spinning BT, ST

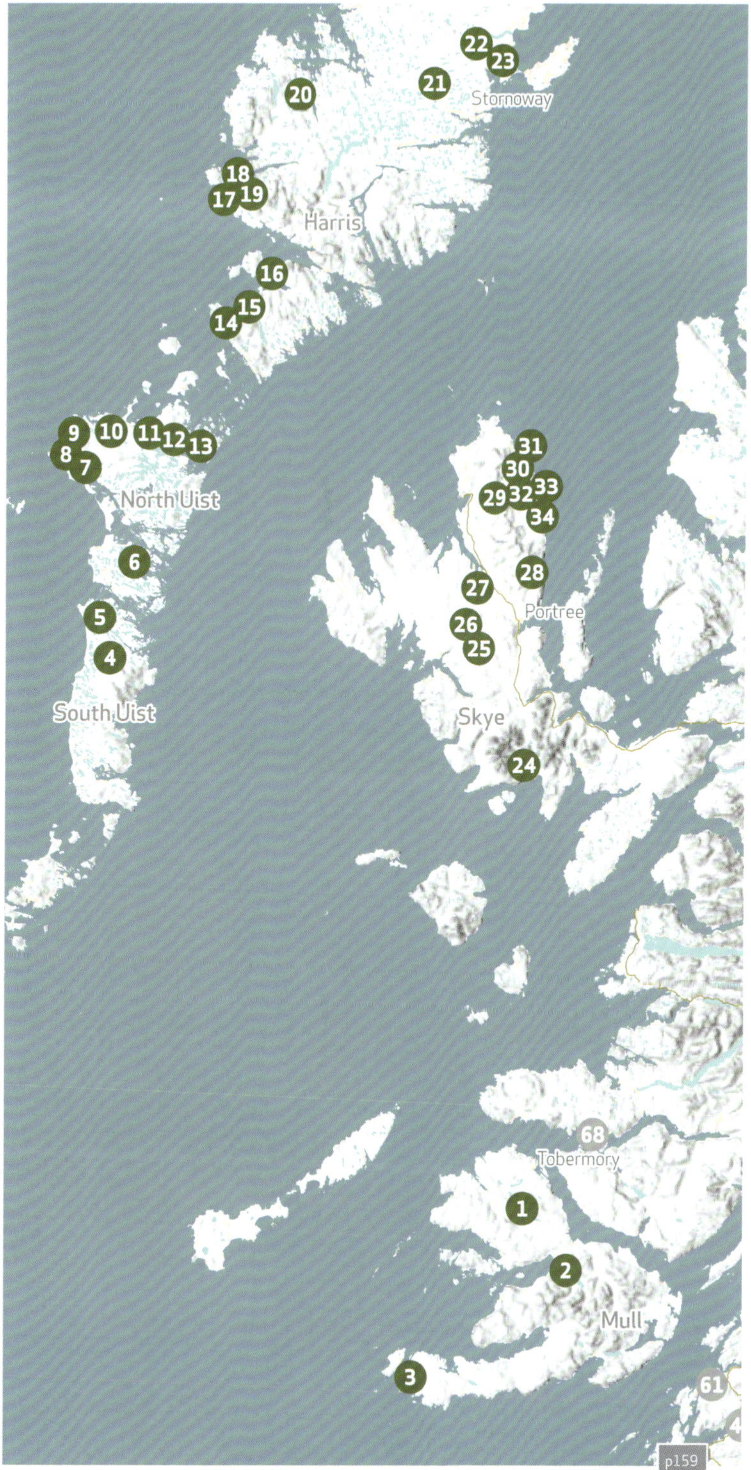
22
23
21
Stornoway
20
18
17
19
Harris
16
15
14
9
10
11
12
13
8
7
North Uist
6
5
4
South Uist
31
30
33
29
32
34
28
27
Portree
26
25
Skye
24
68
Tobermory
1
2
Mull
3
61
p159

49
48
Shetland
47
Lerwick
Scalloway
46
45

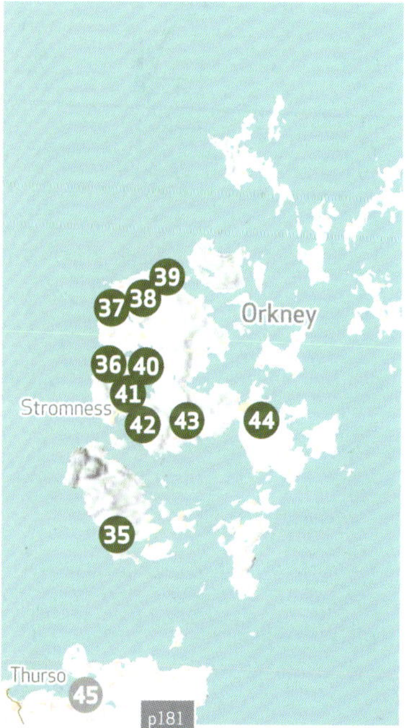
39
37
38
Orkney
36
40
41
Stromness
42
43
44
35
Thurso
45
p181

North Wales

North Wales and game fishing, one of the mainstays of Wild Fishing, are perfectly suited. The region's cold-water habitat creates ideal conditions for salmonids to thrive. There are five hundred llyns (Welsh lakes), most of which are perfect for wild brown trout to flourish in. However, you frequently have to earn your fish in North Wales. The hike in (and up) can be a lung-busting, hamstring-wrenching experience. Other llyns in this book, you'll be glad to know, are a mere two-minute saunter, rod in hand, and you're fishing. Grayling are common in the rivers, allowing you to extend your fishing throughout the winter months. Grayling fishing, with ice forming on your rod ferrules, is one of the most beautiful forms of fishing you can do in these Isles. Some of the grayling encountered in North Wales can exceed three pounds – specimen fish.

Some places you love because you've been fishing there since you were a child; some you love at first sight. Such was the case with me and Llyn Clywedog. Its solitude and deep sense of peace thrilled me immediately. It is one of those quiet places, like fishing in a church. We fished from the bank, but as we were leaving, I looked back and saw a few boats with two anglers in each. It struck me as a wonderful thing – what could be better than fishing with a mate, bobbing in the water, surrounded by steep hillsides, and with a chance of a fish or two?

As for Wild Sea Fishing, Anglesey leads the pack: a litany of fish awaits you; bass, bull huss, coalfish, cod, conger eel, dogfish, flounder, ling, pollack, and whiting. Sea bass are the game fish of the sea; you can devote your entire angling life to solely pursuing them and still not completely master the art. Dicentrarchus labrax can be caught throughout the year in Wales, with the peak months being May through November, when larger bass make an appearance around the shores. Bass are extremely slow-growing; a 10lb bass could be twenty years old. So, even though they are delicious, I would suggest returning all you catch. Or, at most, perhaps keeping just one for the pot.

6

ANGLESEY

1 PORTH PADRIG BEACH

The beach is named after St. Patrick because, apparently, the saint took shelter in a nearby cave after being shipwrecked. There is another man-made cave on the beach - the remnants of an old iron ore mine. It can be quite snaggy, so best fished with either a float or spinners; avoid the bottom altogether. Discretion is the better part of valor.

→ Park at Traeth Mawr and then walk 2 miles to the bay. 53.4215, -4.4455 Free Beach Wrasse

2 PORTH DAFARCH

A small bay on the west side of Holy Island. It's popular with canoeists and divers, so best to select a time that does not fit in with their schedules. Beware of big swells and do not fish in these conditions. Fish caught include huss, pollack, conger, dogfish, and whiting. I'm told you can also catch turbot on strips of mackerel here too.

→ Parking alongside the bay and toilets. 53.2878, -4.6511 Free Beach Dogfish, whiting, turbot

3 LLANFAELOG/PORTH NOBLA BEACH

This quiet rural beach is an attractive crescent shape. Porth Nobla is bordered to the south by cliffs and a headland which is home to the ancient burial chamber of Barclodiad y Gawr. Good for mackerel and bass during the summer months.

→ Roadside parking just south of the beach. 53.2118, -4.5016 Free Beach Mackerel, bass

4 TRAETH MAWR

Created in the late 18th century to reclaim land from the tidal estuary of Afon Glaslyn. It's mainly sandy, which means you'll probably be leaving for home with the same amount of tackle as when you started. You'll be fishing for dogfish, bass, and flounder, and you might also chance upon some whiting and dabs.

→ Park in Aberffraw and walk, it's not far. 53.1801, -4.4592 Free Beach Dogfish, bass, flounder

5 LLANDDONA BEACH

Reputed to have a famous family of witches with their powers being passed from mother to daughter. It's a sandy beach, fishing onto a predominantly sandy bottom. It can get crowded in the summer, so time your trip. Fish include dogfish, bass, codling, whiting, and flounders.

→ Parking available at the beach. 53.3036, -4.1519 Free Beach Dogfish, bass, flounder

6 PENMON POINT

Has a number of rock marks, fishing onto a rough bottom. Fish include mackerel, pollack, whiting, codling, bass, flatties, dogfish, dabs, and wrasse. Especially mackerel in the summer. What can be more delightful than fishing for them with feathers? Use either mackerel feathers or Sabiki feathers. Great place to see dolphins, porpoises, and seals too.

→ Parking available at the beach. 53.311, -4.0408 Free Beach Mackerel

GWYNEDD

7 TRAETH PENNLLECH

Set at the very northern tip of the beautiful Llyn Peninsula is Traeth Penllech. A sandy beach, it's framed at either end by rock pools, and behind are sloping grass-covered cliffs. You'll be fishing on sand but with a view of larger rocks jutting out – ideal places for fish to hide behind or around. Fish include pollack, dabs, dogfish, rays, bass, rockling, and whiting. Dawn and dusk are the best times to target the bass, especially around the rocks that are jutting out. Also, just behind the breaking waves.

→ Just around the western edge is a small cove, Porth Colmon, with parking 52.8819, -4.6657 Free Beach Bass, whiting, dabs

8 MORFA NEFYN BEACH

Nefyn's two-mile-long sweep of sands lines a sheltered bay and natural harbor on the Llyn Heritage Coast. Try feathering for mackerel here; there are usually plenty around in summer. If you don't pick any up, you will usually get a few pollack to this method. Whiting, codling, mackerel, dogfish, and bullhuss are here too.

→ This beach has a National Trust car park with its fees. 52.938, -4.5557 Free Beach Mackerel, Pollock

9 PORTH NEIGWL

In English, "Hell's Mouth" is a broad three-mile-wide bay on the south coast of the Llyn Peninsula.

→ Porth Neigwl has its own car park a brief walk from the beach 52.8069, -4.5469 Free Beach Bass, rays, dogfish

10 GWYRFAI

If you can find a copy of *A Snowdon Stream And How To Fish It* by W.H. Canaway, you will be schooled in fishing this wild river. However, finding the book is not so difficult, but the cost? It often changes hands for over £100, as it has long been out of print. This river has been left in its natural state, which means this fishing will be harder, especially fly fishing and spinning. Perhaps it's time to try your hand at worm fishing, a noble art. If you arrive at this river when the conditions are right, you will be well rewarded.

→ Sgll.co.uk 53.1117, -4.2297 £20 Fly, bait, spin, led BT, ST

11 NANTLLE LAKE

There is a ghost lake, Lower Nantlle Lake,

12

which was drained to protect a slate works. Nantlle Lake is in the foreground of the famous Welsh landscape painter Richard Wilson's painting "Snowdon from Llyn Nantlle," which is in the National Museum, Liverpool. It's considered one of the best lakes in Wales for wild brown trout. It is also one of a handful of Welsh lakes that have a run of sea trout. Boat fishing only.

→ Sgll.co.uk 53.0541, -4.2177 £20 Fly BT, Sa, ST

12 LLYN CWM SILYN

Lightly fished and overlooked by the brooding Craig Cwm Silyn, the lower lake is generally regarded as the more productive of the two. Don't wade; it's an uneven bottom, or if you do, use a staff to feel your way. Expect fish of half a pound or so, with larger ones lurking.

→ Park'n'hike. Probably Nantlle is the best bet for parking. 53.0312, -4.2159 £20 Fly BT

13 DWYFOR RIVER

The association has six different beats to fish on the river Dwyfor. Mainly a sea trout fishery, but also some brown trout and a salmon sometimes turn up. The sea trout runs usually start in June. The association also holds fishing rights on stretches of the rivers Dwyfach and Henwy too.

→ Fishingwales.net 52.9632, -4.2247 £10 Fly ST, BT, Sa

14 LLYN PADARN

This glacially formed lake is set amidst the spectacular scenery of Snowdonia. Llyn Padarn is named after Padarn, an early 6th-century saint who has a church dedicated to him in Llanberis. Brown trout fishing is well rewarded, and there are char in the deeper water, but you'll need a boat from the Cwellyn Arms. Park in the lay-by just after the bridge and walk over to the far quieter north shore.

→ Sgll.co.uk 53.1382, -4.1546 £20 Fly, bait, spin, led BT, Ch

15 LLYN CWM DWYTHWCH & CWM SILYN NEBO

Both lakes are in wild, remote areas, so be prepared to hike in. We're told that they're only really accessible by a 4x4, and then it's a mile walk to the lakes. Both lakes are gin clear and weeded. Neither are heavily populated with fish. Any fish you catch, you will have earned.

→ Sgll.co.uk 53.0998, -4.1375 £20 Fly BT

13

14

17

16

19

23

16 LLYN CWELLYN

A large lake of some 220 acres with excellent fishing to free-rising fish. It is also one of a handful of lakes with Arctic Char within. You can also fish Llyn Padarn (it too has resident Char) and Cwm Silyn (infrequently fished – it's a mile hike from the road, but worth the effort) on the same day.

→ Fishingpassport.co.uk 53.0722, -4.1507 £20 Fly BT, Ch

17 CWMYSTRADLLYN RESERVOIR

Regarded as one of the most beautiful lakes in Wales. H. M. Gallichan described Cwmystradllyn as a "lake charmingly situated in a green oasis among savage hills." We're told that the most productive flies are Hawthorn, Heather, Peter Ross, Dunkeld, Invicta, Haul a Gwynt, Mallard & Claret, and Black Pennell.

→ Pwllheliangling.co.uk 52.9786, -4.1412 £18 Fly, bait, spin, led BT, RT

18 OGWEN, LOWER SECTION

The lower section begins at the Pont y Twr. As you progress down, you will be amongst slow dark pools. We're now in sea trout territory. Dusk and darkness will be the time to tempt them. We're told that spinning for salmon can also work.

→ Fishingpassport.co.uk 53.1681, -4.0568 £20 Fly/Spin BT, Sa, ST

19 OGWEN, UPPER SECTION

The upper section is the sole preserve of wild brown trout. The rest of the Ogwen has salmon and sea trout to support too. But up here, amongst the waterfalls and pools, is wild brown trout water. And all the better for it, too, because the only anglers up here are after the trout.

→ Fishingpassport.co.uk 53.1601, -4.0454 £20 Fly BT

20 LLYN IDWAL

A small lake named after Prince Idwal Foel, a grandson of Rhodri Mawr, one of the ancient Kings of Wales. Apparently, and sadly, he was drowned in this lake. It's a hike up Idwal, but you should be there in twenty minutes, longer if you stop to take in the spectacular surroundings. Be careful wading; the lake bed falls away in places. While remote, this lake is popular with the fitter tourists.

→ Fishingpassport.co.uk 53.1149, -4.026 £10 Fly BT

21 LLAFAR RIVER

This is a collection of smaller streams: the Llafar, Lliw, Twrch, and Dee Bach. They all hold trout and are absorbing to fish, to puzzle them out. You'll probably have the place to yourself as you ponder how to bring the trout to the bank. The precise directions for each stream are on the Bala website.

→ Balaangling.co.uk 53.1658, -4.016 £17.50 Fly, spin, worm BT, Gr

22 LLYN FFYNNON LLOER

Ffynnon Lloer is a lake in the Carneddau range of mountains in Snowdon. It's a hike to reach, about an hour's walk. The remains of two wartime aircraft, which crashed in 1942 and 1943, lie on the slopes around the lake. Due to its smaller size, only fly fishing is permitted. Be aware that at these heights (the lake is 673 meters above sea level), the temperature can change drastically and quickly, so dress appropriately. Lots of layers.

→ Fishingpassport.co.uk 53.1392, -4.0006 £10 Fly BT

23 LLYN OGWEN

This is the site where King Arthur threw Excalibur into the lake, where it was caught by The Lady of the Lake and subsumed into the depths. In fact, Llyn Ogwen is quite a shallow lake, no more than three

23

27

meters deep. It's regularly stocked with Rainbow Trout (up to 12lb!) and also holds a good amount of native brown trout. If, while fishing, you happen upon Excalibur, you'll have something to bring to the next Antiques Roadshow. Popular with hikers and close to the road.

→ Fishingpassport.co.uk 53.1236, -4.0071 £20 Fly, bait, spin, led BT, RT

24 LLYN BOCHLWYD

The name translates as "Lady of the Greycheek." Local legend states that a grey stag escaped a hunter by leaping from a great height into the water and then holding its grey cheeks above the water in order to breathe. It's a hike to reach the lake, but no more than 45 minutes. You'll probably have to fish around the weeds, but clear patches abound, and in them, you can catch hard-fighting wild brown trout up to half a pound.

→ Fishingpassport.co.uk 53.113, -4.0106 £10 Fly BT

25 LLYN YR ADAR

A two-hour hike from Tan y Grisiau, but it's well worth it. The Hare's Ear is the most successful fly up here, with trout up to two lb being reported. All this and breathtaking scenery. The lake can be fished all the way around, and because it's in a shallow bowl, the water can be reasonably protected, but not enough to stop a good ripple from forming on the water in a moderate wind.

→ Fishingpassport.co.uk 53.0103, -4.0628 £16 Fly/Spin BT

26 LLYN LLAGI

Bit of a stroll of about forty-five minutes, or so. Has lovely clear water and the trout are easy to spot in the shallows. If the fly is well presented, with a minimum of splash and bother, you'll catch them. We're told the better fish are caught on dark patterns near the deeper drop-offs.

→ Cambrianangling.com 53.0143, -4.0148 £20 Fly BT

27 LLYNNAU'R CWN

Another long hike, ninety minutes depending on your stride and fitness level. When you get here, it's three small pools with plentiful native trout. It's also a further hour to the mysterious Llyn Edno. No one knows who owns the fishing rights to Edno; perhaps nobody does?

→ Cambrianangling.com 53.0197, -3.9974 £20 Fly BT

28 LLYN CWM CORSIOG

Sixty-minute hike to get here, but you'll be rewarded with a good head of native trout. Real Wild Fishing, and thank you Cambrian AA for keeping it all going. We're told they'll take any fly - perhaps experiment and see what you can get away with or perhaps develop your own Corsiog fly.

→ Cambrianangling.com 53.004, -3.9929 £20 Fly BT

29 LLYN CONGLOG

High in a remote upland plateau setting above Blaenau Ffestiniog at over 2000 feet altitude. Llyn Conglog has larger than average trout, which is a testament to the hard work of Cambrian Angling. All the native trout were believed to have perished in the severe frost of 1947, but judicious stocking through the 1990s has restored the fishery to rude health. In fact, it's possible, with skill and luck, to catch a specimen. Rich in fly life, including the famous sepia dun. A two-hour walk is required here, but you can fish two other llyns (Cwmorthin and Cwm Corsiog) on the way up. Fish can be caught on spinner or fly, with the old favorites for wild fish, Hare's Ear nymph, Diawl Bach, etc., working well.

→ Cambrianangling.com 53.0067, -3.9778 £20 Fly BT

30 LLYN CWMORTHIN

Lovely 30-minute walk to get here with a waterfall at the start. It used to be a slate quarry, which presumably was once a natural lake. Not the best fishing in Gwynedd, the trout being small and, without being too rude, stunted. However, the walk makes the trip worthwhile, and the fishing is the bonus.

→ Cambrianangling.com 52.9976, -3.9737 £20 Fly BT

31 LLYN GAMALLT FAWR

These trout will appreciate your bushy bob flies and/or sedges. A pleasant half an hour's walk will get you here. It's peaty (which I always like) and is actually quite shallow. These lakes were affected by acid rain but appear to be in rude health now, thank goodness.

→ Cambrianangling.com 53.0172, -3.9237 £20 Fly BT

32 LLYN Y MANOD

Lake of the Fallen Snow in English gives this charming llyn a romantic air. If you're lucky, you'll see peregrine falcons and the odd raven. It's easy enough to catch here, but the fish are somewhat stunted, perhaps

a good place to take a beginner? It's close to here that many of the nation's treasures were secreted away during WW2.

→ Cambrianangling.com 52.9842, -3.9114 £20 Fly BT

33 LLYN GAMALLT

Both Gamallt Lakes are in the western part of the Migneint Mountain. It's an easy half an hour stroll from the car park, and you'll be rewarded by one of the finest wild brown fisheries in Wales. Try to find the Ffestiniog Fly or tie it yourself for the best results.

→ Cambrianangling.com 52.9798, -3.8661 £20 Fly BT

34 LLYN DYWARCHEN

A mysterious lake. We're told tales of floating islands here, which are common enough in Welsh folklore. This floating island was swum out to by the astronomer Edmund Halley in 1698. He described it as "broad-spreading with fungous roots on its sides." The fishing is more tangible. Stocked rainbow trout will provide excellent sport, especially with a boat.

→ Sgll.co.uk 52.9612, -3.8435 £20 Fly RT

35 LLYN CWMPRYSOR

A small llyn twelve miles out of Bala. Beware of the midges; take a net and midge cream on warmer evenings. But provided you are prepared, what could be more pleasant on a warm summer's evening than casting for small wild brown trout on this delightful and solitary small lake.

→ Balaangling.co.uk 52.931, -3.8055 £17.50 Fly, worm BT

36 PRYSOR RIVER

You won't need to wade this river; it's too small, but the overhanging trees make it challenging. So, be armed correctly; a six or seven-foot rod is all you need. Also, accept that you'll spend some time retrieving flies from bushes and branches. Better to fish every pocket you can and accept this fact, then skip over the places where the trout will lie.

→ Fishingpassport.co.uk 52.9095, -3.8645 £10 Fly BT

37 LLYN TRAWSFYNYDD

Set in the heart of Snowdonia, Traws Lake is fed by the Prysor River, which also contributes to the marshland of Gors Goch, once known for peat cutting. Resident brown trout top the 1lb mark, steeply rising to a few 7lbers that have been caught. The rainbows are frequently in the 4lb to 7lb range.

→ Trawslake.com 52.9182, -3.9368 £25 Fly, bait, spin, led BT, RT, Pi, Pe

38 EDEN, LOWER

This spate river is famous for its freshwater pearl mussels, so no wading is allowed. The upper beat runs through a peat bog, which imparts a tea-coloured hue to the water. Excellent glides and pools hold fine brown trout. However, the fish are quite small, with a three-quarter-pounder being considered a good fish.

→ Fishingpassport.co.uk 52.8647, -3.9264 £10 Fly BT

39 LLYN TECWYN ISAF

This lake is renowned for rare dragonflies. We're told that you can see Downy Emeralds (only site in North Wales), Keeled Skimmers, and Hairy Dragonflies. It's predominantly a coarse lake with carp, rudd, and perch, but you can also find wild brown trout here too.

→ Fishingwales.net 52.9144, -4.0397 £12.50 Fly, bait, spin, led BT, carp, perch

37

47

40

40 LLYN EIDDEW-BACH & EIDDEW MAWR

A tarn in the remote northern Rhinogs, with cliffs for jumping and fabulous views of the sea. You might have to share the water with wild swimmers, so be nice. 40-minute hike to get there, but well worth it. Stone circles are round and about, giving the area a haunting, mysterious air. Plentiful small wild brown trout.

→ Fishingwales.net 52.8909, -4.0149 £12.50 Fly BT

41 LLYN Y FEDW

A longish walk of forty minutes to get to these wild mountain lakes. It's 1,000 feet above Harlech. The wild brown trout are superbly and vividly marked. It's worth the effort just to catch one to see a trout at the height of its beauty.

→ Fishingwales.net 52.8763, -4.0436 £12.50 Fly, bait, spin, led BT

42 LLYN CWM BYCHAN

There's an old school honesty box at the old farmhouse. I don't know how much they charge; currently, it is £5. I've made it up to £10 for this book, so you can't be caught out. It can be crowded at peak tourist times. Has native trout, but I've never seen them rising. That doesn't mean they can't be caught, of course. A terrestrial might do the trick.

→ Fishingpassport.co.uk 52.8615, -4.0259 £10 Fly BT, ST

43 LLYN DU-BACH

The water is clear but with a slightly peaty hue, reminiscent of some Scottish lochs. Free rising fish, and there are some shallow areas that might reward wading. The second part of the lake, bisected by a stone causeway, is too shallow and weedy to hold much angling interest.

→ Cambrianangling.com 52.8449, -3.9967 £20 Fly BT

44 CREGENNAN LAKES

Beautiful lake setting in the shadow of the legendary Cader Idris. In August, bring as many ant flies as you can fit in your box; the trout gorge on them. If the wind picks up a little and you have a long rod and fine leader, you could try dapping with them. Magical (if it works), I've never been successful.

→ Cregennan.co.uk 52.7108, -3.9834 £15 Fly, spin, worm BT

45 LLYN MWYNGIL/TAL-Y-LLYN

Lovely lake surrounded by mountains, including Cadair Idris. The lake is very shallow, formed after the last ice age, and as a result, can be mirror still. The lake is abounding with wild brown trout averaging a lb or slightly less. Originally, the native population was enhanced by stocking, but this was some time ago.

→ Ffermcedrisfarm.wales 52.6671, -3.9061 £20 Fly BT

46 TRYWERYN RIVER

The flow of this river is governed by Llyn Celyn, so beware of sudden rises and don't get caught out. This is a small, classic wild brown trout stream with good grayling fishing in the lower reaches. Don't bother on the weekend when the canoeists will be out and about.

→ Balaangling.co.uk 52.9166, -3.5815 £17.50 Fly, worm BT, Gr, Sa

47 DEE/LLANDDERFEL

Excellent grayling water and, of course, salmon. The Dee is such a distinctive river, so much so, and to quote Craig Somerville, "If you were to show an experienced angler a photograph of any part of the river, and say nothing, they'd recognise the character of the runs, glides, pools, and landscape and know for sure it was the Dee. The Dee is unique."

→ Balaangling.co.uk 52.9185, -3.5105 £17.50 Fly, Worm BT, Gr, Sa

CONWY

48 LLYN DULYN

A twisted country lane brings you to a valley flooded with light and surrounded by slopes, the imposing Carneddau crags to the west, and, in amongst all this, is Llyn Dulyn. In extreme droughts, the wreckage of a crashed WW2, US Dakota C-47 transport aircraft can be seen. The lake is lightly fished because the almost three-mile hike from the road deters all but the most dedicated angler.

→ Fishingpassport.co.uk 53.1797, -3.9454 £7.50 Fly, bait, spin, led BT, Ch

49 LLYN MELYNLLYN

High up the side of the Carneddau mountains, you'll find this splendid llyn. The bronze and red of the trout here speak of the peaty water they live in. It can be a trifle windy here, which will suggest the best places for you to fish (out of the damn wind).

→ Fishingpassport.co.uk 53.1717, -3.9436 £7.50 Fly BT

50 LLYN EIGIAU

Fittingly, the name Eigiau is thought to refer to the shoals of fish that once lived here.

→ Fishingpassport.co.uk 53.1652, -3.9171 £7.50 Fly, bait, spin, led BT

51 LLYN COEDTY

Llyn Coedty is on the edge of the Snowdonia National Park. Easy to drive up to, and parking is free on the verges just before the reservoir. If you're very lucky, there have been sightings of short-eared owls and hen harriers in these mountaintops moving across the valleys and hunting on the moorlands. The llyn contains brown trout, relatively easy to catch.

→ Fishingpassport.co.uk 53.1819, -3.8638 £7 Fly, bait, spin, led BT

52 LLEDR/DOLWYDDELAN

Night fishing for sewin (sea trout) is the name of the game here. You'll need to do it at night to have any chance of success. The association was formed in 1940 for the locals but has now expanded to include visitors. Thankfully - because it's good fishing.

→ Dolwyddelan.org 53.0546, -3.8833 £15 Fly ST, Sa

53 LLYN ALWEN RESERVOIR

Close to its cousin water, Llyn Brenig. You can fish all disciplines here, and as it's a stocked water, it's a good place for beginners to build their confidence and get the feel of catching fish. And it is a feel, almost an intuition; once you possess it, you can recall it in all angling situations.

→ Llynbrenig.com 53.065, -3.5668 £19 Fly, bait, spin, led RT, BT, Pe

54 LLYN BRENIG

Llyn Brenig has all the amenities, including a café, and you might be sharing the water with a windsurfer or two, but it offers excellent fishing for trout and, at certain times of the year, pike fishing.

→ Llynbrenig.com 53.0788, -3.5326 £24 Fly, bait, spin, led BT, Pi

DENBIGHSHIRE

55 ELWY RIVER/DDOL FARM

Classic spate river will have you hopping over stones and boulders. Salmon and sea trout can be encountered later in the season. As in all spate rivers in this book, please follow the weather forecast. There is little point in making the trip if the river is not fishable.

→ Valeofclwydanglingclub.org 53.2401, -3.5202 £15 Fly BT, Sa, ST

56 CLWYD RIVER/LLANDYRNOG

You can fly fish here, but it's probably better suited for the worm angler or spinning with a tiny mepps (the smallest they make). It's really challenging fishing with many long slow-moving pools, deep holes, and lots of tree and bank cover, as well as in-stream obstacles, but well worth the effort to fish.

→ Valeofclwydanglingclub.org 53.169, -3.3504 £15 Fly, bait, spin, led BT

57 CLWYD/RUTHIN PARK

The river is slow and deep by Ruthin Castle. The two short stretches above and below the Corwen road bridge are again beautiful stretches of small pools and runs. Can get crowded with children and families.

→ Valeofclwydanglingclub.org 53.1122 -3.3157 £15 Fly BT

58 LLYN DERWEN

Two lakes, both stocked with trout of almost every description: rainbow, blue, tiger, brook, blond, golden, and brown trout. One is fly-only; the other is any method that tickles your fancy. There is also coarse fishing available, including carp. It's a serene, peaceful location.

→ Facebook.com/llynderwen 53.0429, -3.4115 £7 Fly, bait, spin, led BT, Coarse, carp

59 CAMDDWR RIVER

Anglers have been coming to the Tregaron waters for over a century, and this little gem of a brook is why we have been making the trek for so long. This delight is set deep within the Cambrian Mountains and is as wild fishing as you can possibly get.

→ Tregaronangling.com 52.9781, -3.405 £13.00 Fly BT

60 DEE/LLANGOLLEN MAELOR

Regarded as one of the cleanest rivers in Europe, and you will be fishing in an area of Outstanding Natural Beauty. It is internationally renowned for brown trout and grayling fishing and has good runs of salmon and sea trout throughout the season. Hawker Overend have produced a detailed guide for each of the nineteen pools.

→ Llangollen-maelor-angling.com 52.9939, -3.2191 £22.50 Fly BT, Gr, Sa, ST

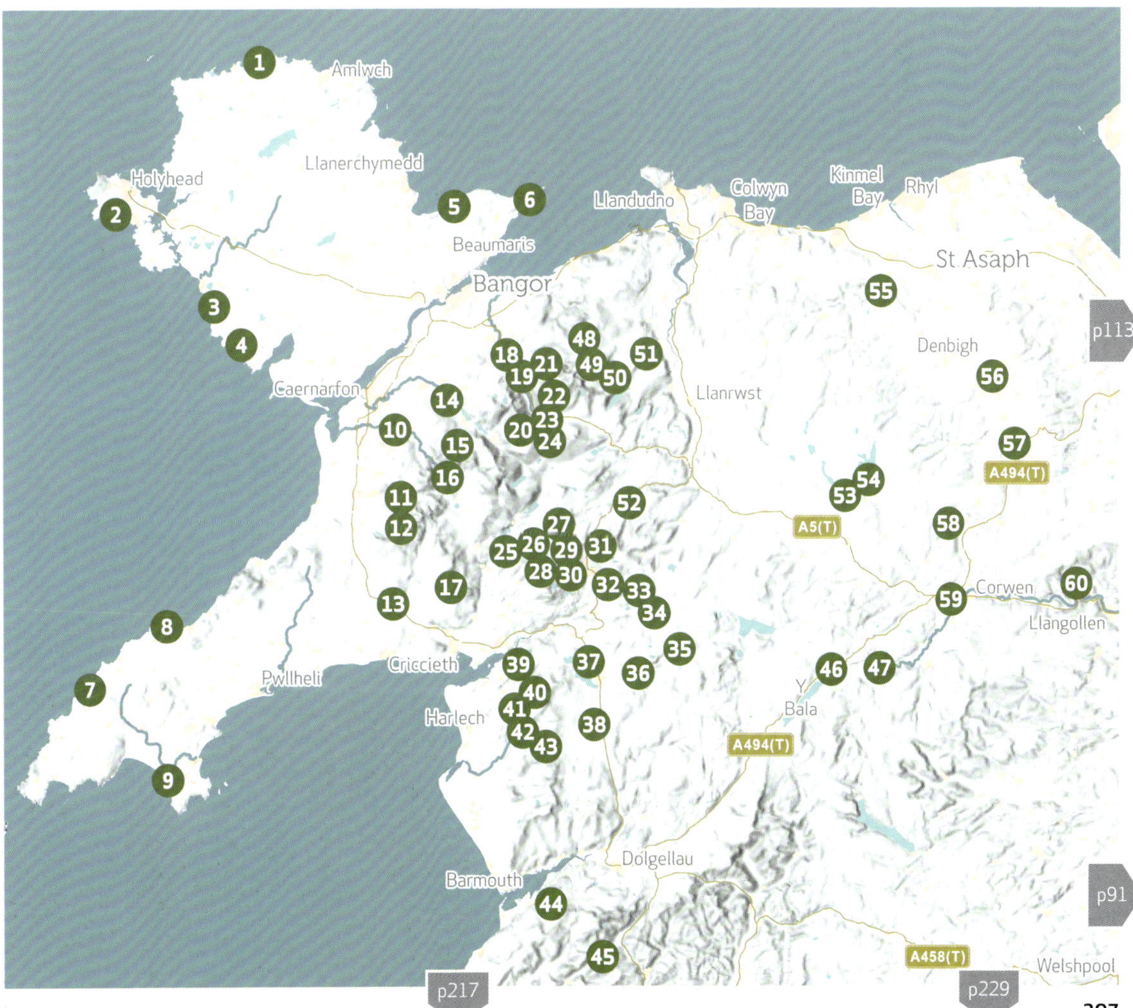

Ceredigion

Ceredigion is home to some of Wales's best freshwater fishing, especially for sea trout (or sewin), salmon, and wild brown trout. The county's best-known rivers are the Aeron, Rheidol, Ystwyth, and Teifi. Sea trout begin running in April or May and continue until the end of the season. The runs are generally water-dependent, with the best fishing usually coinciding with higher water levels. It's true that sea trout are running in smaller numbers than they used to, but there are still plenty of fish for you to angle for. Ideally, sea trout are fished for at night. This can be quite daunting for the novice, especially as we select quite out-of-the-way places to fish. However, I would urge you to give it a go. Nothing sharpens your senses more than being outdoors fishing in the pitch black, or with only the moon for illumination. You'll never forget the experience, and if you follow sensible precautions, it is quite safe.

Alternatively, you can go stillwater fishing in many of the countless llyns. For example, feature-packed Llyn Teifi; all the sides are steep, some almost sheer, but it has many points and bays to stand and cast from and into. It's normally quite generous in catches. Abundant spawning is provided by the many small streams that feed the lake. Half a pound would be a fair average here, although some larger specimens are sometimes caught, weighing over 1lb. We have even heard tell of somebody catching a fish of over 4lb here. If true, that is superlative fishing.

And finally, Ceredigion has some magnificent beach fishing. While the commercial fishermen are concentrating on lobster and crab, you can fish for mackerel, bass, and bream straight from the shore. All you need is your rod, tackle, and a sense of adventure. We suggest a number of excellent beaches for you to try.

For example, we feature the beautifully named Cwmtydu Cove, or Seals Bay in English. This secluded little cove was once a favourite for the local smugglers who would hide French brandy and salt in the cliffs surrounding the cove. Nowadays, you can fish for a variety of species, including codling, wrasse, and tope, in a lovely, peaceful environment – just as the smugglers would have wanted it.

1 TEIFI, NEWCASTLE EMYLN

The Teifi is the longest river in Wales and offers superb fishing for trout, salmon, and, famously, sea trout. The Teifi Trout Association has thirty miles and six beats available. On the lower beats, you can expect to catch salmon and sea trout straight from the sea. For trout flies, the TTA recommend March Browns, Grannom Sedge, small Mayfly, Alder, Stoneflies, and Pheasant Tail Nymphs. For sea trout, Teal Blue & Silver, Medicine Fly, Dunkelds, Butchers, Teifi terrors, and Black pennels. For salmon, a variety of tube flies might do the trick if the fishing gods smile on you.

→ Teifitrout.co.uk 52.0446, -4.4813 £30 Fly BT, ST

2 CWMTYDU COVE

The car park is right next to the beach but it doesn't detract from this delightful little cove. We're told that it was a favourite of local smugglers because of its quiet location. French brandy and salt, it is speculated, would have been hidden in the cliffs surrounding the beach. The fish that can be caught include dogfish, bass, flounder, plaice, dabs, codling, wrasse, and tope.

→ There's a car park at the beach. 52.1921, -4.4072 Free Beach Codling, wrasse, tope

3 ABERAERON NORTH

This rocky beach is about a mile north of Aberaeron. This beach and surrounding lowlands are well known for bird spotters. In the winter you might have the company of golden plovers along with oystercatchers, curlews, and dunlin. The fish caught here include, according to their various seasons, bass, codling, coalfish, whiting, dabs, garfish, dogfish, flounder, eels, rays, and mackerel.

→ There's a car park at the beach. 52.2422, -4.2658 Free Beach Bass, codling, coalfish

4 AERON RIVER

An excellent run of sea trout, typically from June onwards. There are also plentiful brown trout which will take the edge off while you wait for the sewin to come up. This is a spate river, so nothing is guaranteed, but salmon are here too.

→ aberaeron-angling.org 52.2322, -4.2519 £15 Fly, spin, worm ST, BT, Sa

5 WALLOG BEACH

This is a remote beach between Borth and Aberystwyth. Remains of an old lime kiln are visible just behind the beach, which is shingle and fishes onto mainly clean ground. The causeway is the favourite fishing spot. You should run into bass, dogfish, plaice, and pollack.

→ Simplest is to park at Clarach and walk to the beach. 52.4551, -4.0754 Free Beach Bass, pollock, plaice

6 YNYSLAS/NORTHERN GROYNE

At very low tide, you can see the petrified remains of a prehistoric forest. This beach has rapidly incoming tides, so keep an eye out and don't get caught out. Always know what is behind you as the tide approaches. Fish caught around here include bass, flounders, mullet, eels, plaice, dogfish, rockling, whiting, and turbot.

→ You can park with a view of the beach. 52.514, -4.0565 Free Beach Bass, dogfish, turbot

7 RHEIDOL RIVER

Internationally renowned as one of the premier sea trout and salmon rivers. The association has sixteen miles of fishing on both banks. Be aware that the river level is governed by the hydroelectric scheme, which means that the river can go into spate on even a dry summer day. Watch this if you're night fishing.

→ Aber-angling.co.uk 52.4014, -3.9923 £22.50 Fly, spin, worm. BT, Sa, ST

16

7

13

14

8 YSTWYTH RIVER

The River Ystwyth is one of the great sea trout rivers of Wales. When it's good, it's very, very good, and the fish run throughout the season. You can wander the river at your leisure and, best of all, pursue the sea trout throughout the night. One of the great thrills of British angling, chasing sea trout with the moon providing your only illumination.

→ Fishingpassport.co.uk 52.3536, -3.9929 £20 Fly, spin ST, Sa

9 UPPER TEIFI

The three raised bogs of the Cors Caron National Nature Reserve, at just over 2,000 acres, fill the valley of the upper Teifi. Undoubtedly, some of the best brown trout fishing in Wales, which, of course, is saying a lot. There are also grayling present but not in sufficient numbers to directly target. Additionally, there are sea trout and salmon later in the season.

→ Fishingpassport.co.uk 52.2453, -3.9165 £13 Fly BT, Sa, Gr, ST

10 RHEIDOL RESERVOIR

The Rheidol Reservoir is the largest of the Aberystwyth AA lakes and the lake levels fluctuate depending on the hydro power generating system. A good amount of trout with sewin and the occasional salmon present too.

→ Fishingpassport.co.uk 52.396, -3.9121 £22.50 Fly, spin, worm BT, Sa, ST

11 POND RHOSRHYDD

It's quite a shallow lake but of great interest to the fly fishing entomologist is the Great Red Sedge, which is prevalent(ish) here and during June there's the famed coach-y-bonddu beetle hatch. Morning and evening rises tend to be the best. The fish here are clever but are catchable with the correct fly.

→ Aber-angling.co.uk 52.3659, -3.9038 £22.50 Fly BT

12 POND GLANDWGAN

A minor hike to get here, farm track and then across some fields but you'll probably be on your own to soak up the solitary atmosphere. Excellent fishing when the coch-y-bonddu are about. Almost all the trout are under a pound but great fun.

→ Aber-angling.co.uk 52.3575, -3.8999 £22.50 Fly, spin, worm BT

13 FRONGOCH

This lake is a beaut and close to both Trisant Rhosrhydd and Glandwgan, so you can make an excellent day of it. Boat anglers can catch trout all over the lake, but bank anglers seem to do best on the dam wall.

→ Aber-angling.co.uk 52.3591, -3.8791 £22.50 Fly, spin, worm BT

14 LLYN OERFA

Boggy in parts, you can have your boots sucked right off your feet but firmer footing can be found. We have heard reports of large fish being taken here, five pounders. Dress warm, though. Llyn Oerfa translates as the cold place.

→ Aber-angling.co.uk 52.4, -3.8695 £22.50 Fly, spin, worm BT

15 LLYN RHOSGOCH

It's a short walk from the parking spot and when the coch-y-bonddu and sedges are on the wing, you can have great imitative fly fishing, some argue the highest form of the fishing arts. The trout here are trickle stocked up to 1.5lbs. The lake sits in a treeless hollow which can amplify the brooding quality of the place.

→ Aber-angling.co.uk 52.431, -3.8948 £22.50 Fly BT

20

16

19

22

16 LLYN BLAENMELINDWR

As the season goes on, the lake can become quite densely weeded in places but also offers excellent dry fly fishing to free-rising trout. It would be wise to check before venturing here from too far afield. It's close to a road, which makes getting here a simple exercise, and I find it makes a nice change having a car close by, rather than toting your own stuff up hill and dale.

→ Aber-angling.co.uk 52.4344, -3.8902
£22.50 Fly, spin, worm BT

17 LLYN SYFYDRIN

Amazing views and here you will catch one of the most beautiful wild brown trout in Wales with vivid markings. The water has a noticeable peat stain and we did wonder if this contributes to the vibrant colouring of the fish. The evening sedge falls can be jaw-dropping.

→ Aber-angling.co.uk 52.4453, -3.8813
£22.50 Fly, spin, worm BT

18 LLYN CRAIGYPISTLL

A large thin reservoir, giving you two miles to walk and fish. The wild brown trout are superbly marked and will be a treat for the accomplished angler to appreciate. Usually weighing in at a little under a pound but, of course, it's not the size, it's the beauty of these fish.

→ Aber-angling.co.uk 52.4549, -3.8843
£22.50 Fly BT

19 DINAS FISHERY

Dinas is supplementary stocked with rainbows and brown trout but it also enjoys a good head of wild brown trout. It's easy fishing with little forestry to bedevil your backcast. There are good falls of terrestrial insects in the summer months including coch-y-bonddu beetles. Fly, spinning, and worming are permitted making this a good place for fishing with the family.

→ Pumlumon.org.uk 52.4226, -3.8459
£20 Fly, spin, worm Trout

20 NANT Y MOCH RESERVOIR

A number of ancient cairns were removed to make this reservoir in 1964. Set in a remote part of the Cambrian Mountains, the Pumlumon (Five Peaks) Ridge offers wonderful wild mountain scenery. This is classic 'step and cast' fishing to rising fish, of an average of 10oz, or so. Classic wet flies will be productive too. Many perch abound but all are small, as far as we know.

→ Fishingwales.net 52.465, -3.8386
£14 Fly BT, Pe

21 LLYN LLYGAD RHEIDOL

This is remote fishing, and we mean remote. Two miles up a track, but when you finally get there, the lake is very clear and depending on the time of year can be teeming with midge, damselflies, and sedges. The fish are quite voracious, and having not often been fished for, will take most offerings. Particularly worth a visit when terrestrial insects such as the coch-y-bonddu, flying ants, or autumn daddy long-legs are around. Also, very close to the source of The Wye. Pop over and pay your respects if you have a minute.

→ Aber-angling.co.uk 52.473, -3.7814
£22.50 Fly, spin, worm BT

22 LLYN BUGEILYN

Lace up your walking shoes, it's a 2.2 mile hike to get here but when you are, it's truly wild fishing. You will be fishing for the unique black-finned trout of Bugeilyn. Are these trout a unique strain or have they adapted to the peat-stained water? Don't know but they are very good fun to catch.

→ Fishingpassport.co.uk 52.5153, -3.7373
£20 Fly BT

25

24

23

29

23 LLYN BERWYN

Surrounded by quiet woodland, you can spend the day fishing for wild brown trout in beautiful solitary surroundings. You'll need to be stealthy, as the water is shallow on the edges and crystal clear. If the wind drops, beware of midges, and bring protection.

→ Fishingpassport.co.uk 52.1951, -3.8399 £13 Fly BT

24 TEIFI RIVER

The Tregaron owns and manages a variety of quality wild brown trout fishing in the headwaters of the River Teifi. For your £13, you get to fish all their waters, so wander wherever fancy takes you. A few days up here and you will come back changed after this splendid, remote experience.

→ Tregaronangling.com 52.2769, -3.838 £13 Fly BT

25 LLYN TEIFI/TEIFI POOLS

Another of the Teifi Pools that gets a special mention. This is the source of the Teifi. Access is easy on the west side and if you come in June you'll see a spectacular fall of coch-y-bonddu beetles and the fishes' undying love for them.

→ Tregaronangling.com 52.2909, -3.7876 £13 Fly BT

26 LLYN HIR/TEIFI POOLS

One of the Teifi Pools but deserves its own separate entry. It has a cracking coch-y-bonddu fall in June. It's worth the trip and will linger in your memory. Bank fishing is all you need to do. Typically, this water has larger trout than the other Teifi pools.

→ Fishingpassport.co.uk 52.2914, -3.7777 £13 Fly BT

27 LLYN EGNANT/TEIFI POOLS

Llyn Egnant is arguably wild fishing in Wales at its best. Set in a remote location, it's one of the three lakes that make up the famed Teifi Pools. The waters are naturally peat-stained and there is a good balance of one lb plus fish.

→ Fishingpassport.co.uk 52.2872, -3.7716 £10 Fly BT

28 LLYN GYNON

Golden heavily spotted fish make the long, somewhat arduous hike worthwhile. Keep thinking about the fish as you labour through the tussock grass. We've heard tell of monster ferox trout of six pounds, never proven to my knowledge. Not even a photograph? Or, am I a doubting Thomas? Prove me wrong.

→ Rhayaderangling.co.uk 52.2655, -3.7606 £12 Fly BT

29 LLYN CERRIGLLWYDION ISAF

Big old hike to get here, four miles or so, up the 'Monks Trod' (ancient trackway). Numerous wild, but small fish. However, the fish are obliging here, which rewards your walk, even if small. It can be quite boggy in parts and the water is usually gin clear, which equals spooky fish.

→ Rhayaderangling.co.uk 52.3146, -3.6982 £12 Fly BT

30 LLYN CARW

Carw is placed within the 'Great Desert of Wales', not an official nomenclature, you understand. Rather, it illustrates the open moorland. It's a hike to fish, ninety minutes or so, not allowing for any stops to get your breath back. Spooky fish, so proceed with caution, or you'll be hiking back for another ninety minutes fishless. Good sedge hatch.

→ Rhayaderangling.co.uk 52.2367, -3.6765 £12 Fly BT

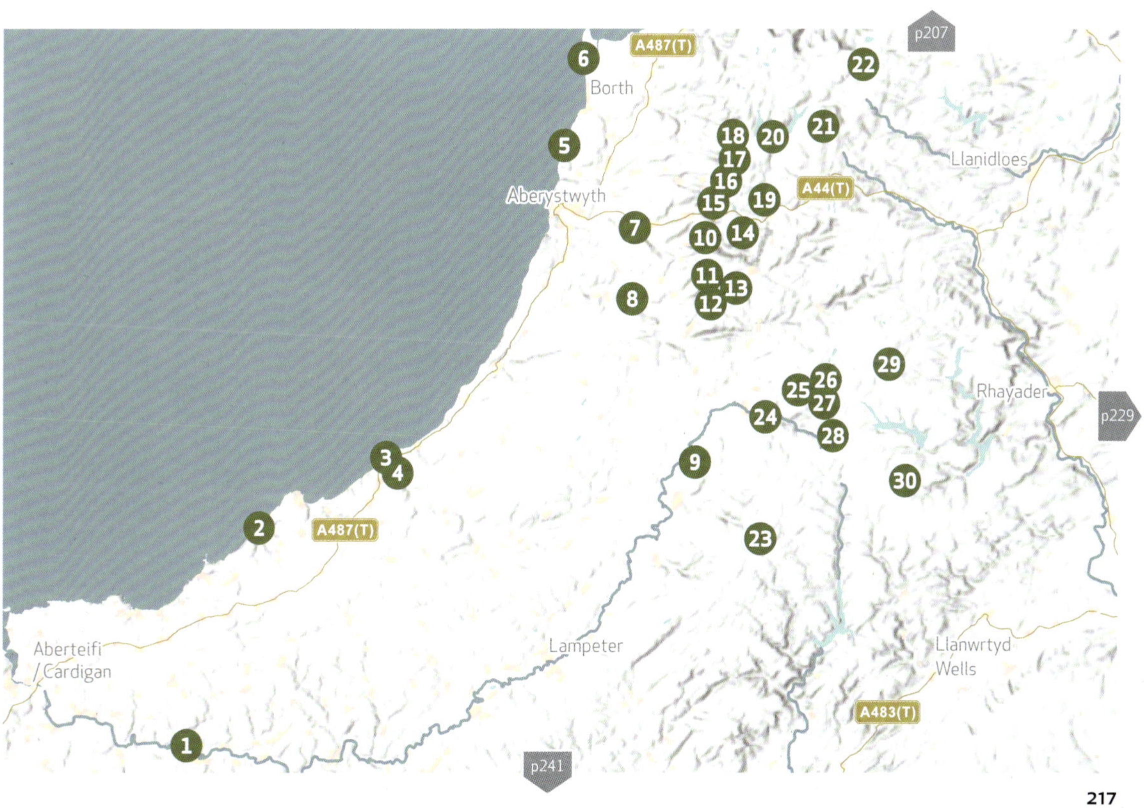

Powys

Powys changes abruptly from the rolling countryside in the south to the wide, open spaces of the Brecon Beacons National Park and then to the rugged beauty of the Berwyn Mountains in the north. Between these two mountain ranges lie many rivers and mountain streams.

The Elan Valley Reservoirs, to the west of Rhayader, are tailor-made for the wild fishing experience. These Victorian reservoirs, high up in steep-sided valleys, have a brooding magnificence, with kites wheeling above you to complete the picture. The access, unlike a great deal of wild fishing, is simple, and the brown trout are plentiful. It is easy when you fish in these grand spectacles to feel underdressed in your fleece and battered jeans. The Victorian builders would be amazed at how scruffy you look; perhaps, as in shooting, you should wear a tie? I seem to recall that on the Wye in the sixties, fishermen would wear jackets and ties to fish for salmon. Perhaps we should bring it back? Perhaps couple it with only fishing the flies that were in use when the reservoir was built: Tups Indispensable, Diawl Bach, Woolly Bugger, Butcher, and, of course, the Zulu.

Plynlimon is the highest point in Mid Wales, rising out of the Cambrian Mountains. Far more importantly, at least for this book, the Plynlimon area is the source of the Rivers Wye, Severn, and Rheidol. The sources are only a few miles apart. The exact source of the Wye is on the eastern slopes of Plynlimon. Sadly, as it wends its way down to the Severn Estuary, it has attracted many chicken farmers to ply their trade close to the banks. It is widely believed that unless immediate and meaningful remedial action is taken, the Wye ecosystem will suffer irreversible ecological damage.

I don't want to end the Mid-East Wales section on this depressing note because Powys presents many wild fishing opportunities. Let's instead celebrate Pant-y-Llyn. At 1,400 feet above sea level, it is found on the north-eastern edge of the Epynt Mountains, in the shadow of the nearby peak Banc y Celyn. After you walk half a mile from the parking spot (I wouldn't recommend driving unless you have a 4x4), you reach the eight-acre lake where you can fish for wild carp and, so I'm told, even chub. How did they get there? The Wye and Usk Foundation, which manages the ticketing, quotes the current landlord, who says he has no idea how they got there. Can you catch the most mysterious fish in the British Isles? Yes, it seems they're rather partial to single grains of corn.

1 USK RESERVOIR

The Usk Reservoir is a Dark Sky Discovery Site, an officially recognised place where anyone can stargaze. We've never been here at night, but it feels like a prime spot. It's generally regarded as one of the best still water fisheries in Wales. Standard reservoir nymphs are recommended for the most success.

→ Fishingpassport.co.uk 51.9442, -3.6986
£24 Fly, bait, spin, led BT,RT, Pe

2 CRAI RESERVOIR

3kms of shoreline to fish in the beautiful Crai valley. We're told the fish respond well to both dry and wet flies. One of four sights in all of Wales that has been designated as excellent for Stargazing, another one being its sister Reservoir, The Usk. Fish all day and marvel at the night skies at night? Not a bad way to spend a summer's day.

→ Cnewrestate.co.uk 51.8813, -3.6247
£15 Fly BT

3 CRAI RIVER

This stretch will reward you if you keep your casting accurate. This wide, fast flowing stream has plenty of holding spots for trout but beware there's quite a bit of tree cover to snag the careless cast. The boulders and pocket water will provide an interesting challenge for the angler too. By comparison, the wading is relatively easy.

→ Fishingpassport.co.uk 51.9435, -3.6041
£11 Fly BT

4 USK/PANTYSGALLOG

Wading is not easy here and care must be taken. Felt or studded waders are essential. This is a beautiful and secluded beat with a series of dramatic falls, flats and gutters. You can try your hand at all kinds of fly fishing here, dry or perhaps sending a nymph through the deeper channels. Some of the trout are large, we've been told up to 4lb. Later in the season both salmon and sea trout should make an entrance too.

→ Fishingpassport.co.uk 51.9503, -3.5966
£17.50 Fly BT, Sa

5 CILENI/PARC FISHERY

This is a remote tributary and is a beautiful mile long section, or so. It hasn't been fished often but should be – it's a gorgeous spot. However, there will be a lot of clambering up and over trees and banks, it's wild fishing. The vegetation can get quite thick. Jungle warfare, in parts.

→ Fishingpassport.co.uk 51.9642, -3.5792
£12 Fly BT

6 USK/SENNYBRIDGE

For the price of the day ticket you can also fish two tributaries, the delightful Senni and Cilieni. Over a mile in length, this beat has both open and shaded sections. Or, tree hazards and no tree hazards, depending on your point of view.

→ Fishingpassport.co.uk 51.9466,-3.5724
£17.50 Fly BT, Sa

7 YSTRADFELLTE RESERVOIR

This reservoir was started building in late Victorian times and was completed just before WW1 started. This is true wilderness fishing in the Brecon Beacons. Plentiful wild brown trout ranging from 12oz to 1lb. Occasionally, larger fish are hauled out.

→ Mountainashflyfishers.yolasite.com
51.8477, -3.5305 £20 Fly BT

13

8

14

12

8 BEACONS RESERVOIR

Brown trout and a few Rainbows too. Beacons is the smallest of the three reservoirs that make up the Taff Valley complex. Many shallow areas around the island and the top end, that provide lots of food for the trout and they hold there. This is where to fish, undoubtably.

→ Fishingpassport.co.uk 51.8545, -3.4693
£13 Fly BT, RT

9 CANTREF RESERVOIR

One of the well-known Victorian reservoirs. I always feel like I should be wearing a tie and a jacket to fish these large, formal places. A bit like fishing in a church. The water here is usually tannin-stained and the pretty native fish have vivid red spots.

→ Mtaa.co.uk 51.8331, -3.4609
£40/week Fly RT, BT

10 TARRELL RIVER

The Tarrell is an important Usk spawning area which can produce some very large trout indeed. Fish of 2lbs and more have been recorded, with fish of 12 inches being the average. You can fish most of the beat in thigh waders but if you want to complete the project you'll need chest waders to explore the deeper pools.

→ Fishingpassport.co.uk 51.94, -3.4139
£11 Fly BT

11 USK/BRECON

About a mile upstream of Brecon. Very good trout fishing with the occasional salmon. The river flows mostly over gravel which makes the wading a great deal easier. Best Flies; CDC Comparadun, Brook Dun Emerger and Twinkle Tag.

→ Fishingpassport.co.uk 51.9497, -3.4069
£15 Fly BT, Sa

12 TAL-Y-BONT RESERVOIR

Fantastic wild brown trout abound in this windswept masterpiece of a reservoir. The fish average a pound or so and it's nothing remarkable to catch a two pounder (well, it is for me but not for most anglers). Best months? We're told it's September and October, with Daddy Long Legs being particlularily productive.

→ Fishingpassport.co.uk 51.8614, -3.3117
£13 Fly BT

13 LLANGORSE LAKE

If you want to try fly fishing for pike this is one of the best venues around. It's home to very large pike and has been fished enthusiastically for centuries. A premier spot. It might be a bit too enthusiastic to try and catch one on a fly but, nothing ventured...

→ Llangorselake.co.uk 51.9361, -3.2705
£10 Fly, bait, spin, led Pike

14 GRYWNE FAWR

Studded soles will be very helpful in wading this bedrocked stream. It's slippery and the older I get, the less I enjoy it unless I have the correct wading boots on. Delightful little stream, with a good diversity of features.

→ Fishingpassport.co.uk 51.9315, -3.0828
£14 Fly BT

15 HONDDU/LOWER HENLAN

For the angler looking for true remoteness, surely the Honddu takes the crown in Wales. However, even up here, neighbourly disputes disturb the peace. Halfway up the beat is a stone arch, started in the 1800s and intended as a bridge but stopped because of a quarrel between adjoining landowners. Good fishing though.

→ Fishingpassport.co.uk 51.9336, -3.0261
£11 Fly BT

16 WYE/LLANTHOMAS FISHERY

A truly gorgeous spot with a lovely weather vane atop the fishing hut. The deep sense of peace and "rightness" in the valley will linger with you, long after the fishing. Primarily known as a premier late-season salmon fishery, it's also excellent for brown trout, which fits far more comfortably in our budget.

→ Fishingwales.net 52.0678, -3.1671
£15-£25 Fly, bait, spin, led
BT, Sa, coarse

17 CLETWR BROOK

Clettwr is Welsh for rough water and this sparkling stream earns its name. It's a rough and ready mix of gorges, riffles, pools, and minor falls making it a challenge to navigate. You need to be fit to make the most of this stream. It's got a good population of trout that are not often bothered by anglers and you can see why.

→ Fishingpassport.co.uk 52.0741, -3.3262
£13.50 Fly BT

18 UPPER WYE/ABERNANT

Easy wading for this section of the upper Wye, just below Builth Wells. You can coarse fish here for the large chub of the Wye but also there are pike, barbel and dace. Or, trout on the fly. The choice is yours. Chest waders are required to get the best out of the fishing on this stretch.

→ Fishingpassport.co.uk 52.1128, -3.3501
£23 Fly, bait, spin, led BT, Gr, coarse

22

19

21

19 EDW/ABEREDW

Legend has it that the last Welsh Prince of Wales hid in caves at Aberedw in 1282. He then escaped the forces of Edward 1 by turning the shoes of his horse the wrong way round, thus evading capture until he met his end by the River Irfon. Five popular beats are available, however the Aberedw beats offer the most classical mountain stream fishing because it flows over bedrock. Best fished on light tackle for the best sport.

→ Fishingpassport.co.uk 52.1163, -3.3434
£13.50 Fly BT

20 PANT-Y-LLYN

Set on a blustery hilltop with gorgeous scenery and far-reaching views, Pant-y-Llyn is Britain's most remote carp fishery. For a chance to hook up with hard-fighting wild carp, it's well worth the half-mile hike from the car park. You'll probably find it's weedy, so fish the gravel margins and/or use surface bait. It's windy up here, even on sunny days, so dress appropriately.

→ Fishingpassport.co.uk 52.1097, -3.4044
£12.50 Surface baits Carp

21 CAMMARCH RIVER

One long beat of over three miles, it can be divided into two parts, above and below Beulah. Above Beulah, it's a classic upland stream, fast flowing over rock and gravel and below the Cammarch is slow and meandering. Both sections have their fair share of wild, hard-fighting brown trout.

→ Fishingpassport.co.uk 52.1492, -3.5774
£11 Fly BT

22 IRFON/GOFYNNE

This stretch of about one km runs through some beautiful and remote countryside. You'll be fishing for both wild brown trout and grayling. There are chub too, which might be enticed by your fly.

→ Fishingpassport.co.uk 52.1462, -3.4618
£20 Fly BT, Gr, chub

23 UPPER WYE/THE ROCKS

This beat is upstream from Builth Wells and offers excellent grayling and trout fishing. Care must be taken when wading, as the pools are very deep. The best months for grayling fishing are September, October, and the first half of November. If you luck upon a winter hatch of large dark olives, grayling will be rising everywhere.

→ Fishingpassport.co.uk 52.1619, -3.4253
£22.50 Fly BT, Gr, Sa

27

24 CABAN COCH/GARREG DDU

Caban Coch is the lowest of the four reservoirs that contribute to Rhayader Angling clubs' water, also the most functional in decoration. It looks just like a natural waterfall when it is full and water is pouring from it. A beautiful site. Like the other three reservoirs in the Elan Valley, it's fly only, so be prepared with your double haul. You'll need to get the fly out some distance to be effective.

→ Elan-valley.co.uk 52.2567, -3.5875 £12.00 Fly BT

25 CLAERWEN RIVER

The river Claerwen connects the Claerwen Dam to Dolymynach Reservoir which is only a two-mile run. I don't believe this river is fished much at all, which, of course, gives you a blank canvas – fishing to untutored fish. It could be very good on the right day.

→ Rhayaderangling.co.uk 52.2518, -3.6373 £12.00 Fly, spin, worm BT, coarse

26 CLAERWEN RESERVOIR

One of the Elan Valley reservoirs, the Claerwen needs a special mention. It has 900 acres of wild brown trout fishing in the very heart of the Cambrian Mountains. While fishing, occasionally keep an eye on the sky. Red kites, buzzards, peregrine falcons, kestrels, and sparrow hawks are all plying their trade above you.

→ Rhayaderangling.co.uk 52.2721, -3.6777 £10 Fly BT

27 ELAN VALLEY RESERVOIRS

Coming in at 850 acres of fishing, the Elan Valley Reservoirs is a massive and beautiful place to fish. All the reservoirs hold a plentiful supply of hard-fighting wild brown trout. Perhaps not something one would want to do frequently, but for a special experience, it should be attempted at least once by any serious angler.

→ Tom Jones: 01597 810383 52.2722, -3.6889 £12 Fly BT

28 ELAN RIVER

The Elan supports a good head of brown trout and has a run of spawning salmon in the autumn. It's a nice, bright clear stream with plenty of riffles for you to dab a fly about. There's also an array of coarse fish here too for you to practise targeting coarse fish on a fly.

→ Rhayaderangling.co.uk 52.2829, -3.5221 £12.00 Fly, spin, worm BT, Sa, coarse

24

28

32

29

29 LLYN GWYN

This is a stocked lake, but it's such a lovely place it has to be included. They're also putting some much larger fish in, in their words, to spice it up. So, to avoid disappointment, check your knots before you start fishing and keep a landing net to hand.

→ Rhayaderangling.co.uk 52.2729, -3.4492 £22 Fly BT, RT, Ca

30 UPPER WYE (RHAYADER)

This water, along with the Dee, is prime winter grayling water. Times past, we used to go shooting on Boxing Day, it was a hoary old tradition. I've replaced it now with grayling fishing. Once seen as a nuisance species, they are now treasured, as they should be. Catching a grayling, right after Christmas, with a heavy frost on the ground, is a lovely thing to do. The Lady of the Stream, indeed.

→ Rhayaderangling.co.uk 52.2989, -3.514 £12 Fly BT, Gr

31 WYE/RHAYADER

The Wye's character changes through its length. Typically, it is divided into five sections of which this section is labelled as above Builth Wells. This section is known for its pools and streams and when the

Wye was a famous salmon river, many large springers were caught on famous beats such as Llysdinam and Doldowlod. This section is stocked every other year to supplement the native head of brown trout.

→ Elan-valley.co.uk 52.3102, -3.5209
£12.00 Fly BT, Sa

32 CRAIG GOCH RESERVOIR

Set comfortably in the Lakeland of Wales, this series of four reservoirs; Craig Goch the top dam, Pen-y-Garreg, Garreg-Du, and Caban Coch have 850 acres of wild fishing water. Built to stock Birmingham with water with work starting in 1897. The plentiful wild brown trout are supplemented with stocked fish.

→ Rhayaderangling.co.uk 52.3116, -3.6177
£12 Fly BT

33 MARTEG RIVER

Like its sister, The Elan, which is on the other side of Rhayader this smaller stream supports a good head of brown trout and is well known for its run of spawning salmon in the autumn. There are coarse fish present too. You could fish both rivers in a day if you get a move on.

→ Rhayaderangling.co.uk 52.3401, -3.4881
£12.00 Fly, spin, worm BT, Sa, coarse

34 ITHON/LLANBADARN FYNYDD

This is a short section of the Upper Ithon downstream of Llanbadarn Fynydd. Shallow and with some lovely riffle sections winding through the lovely Ithon Valley. We're told it's an excellent spot for a beginner to learn fly fishing.

→ Fishingpassport.co.uk 52.3901, -3.3272
£7 Fly BT

35 WYE/TY MAWR

Pretty well as far up the Wye you can go and still catch fish. There's brown trout and grayling here and few trees to snag your flies. I've heard this beat described as having a more Highland character. You'll have no cover from the wind (or to spot the fish spotting you). Like all streams of its ilk, stealth is mandatory if you want to catch any fish at all. They'll scatter at the slightest disturbance.

→ Fishingpassport.co.uk 52.4093, -3.6421
£11 Fly BT, Gr

36 UPPER SEVERN/LLANIDLOES

Just above Llanidloes, the Severn here is a very special and free 800 yards of fishing. This half a mile is blessed with both brown trout and grayling. It has good hatches of fly and the trout can at times be free rising, but late

evenings provide the best opportunities during the summer months or at times of low water.

→ Fishingwales.net 52.4513, -3.539 Free Fly, spin, worm BT, Gr

37 CLYWEDOG RIVER

What a delightful stretch of water. Wild brownies supplemented with stock fish. It's small river fishing, so probably nothing more than a 5wt rod will suffice. We're told by the club that occasionally a migratory fish will turn up in these waters which will wake you up if you are fishing at dusk onwards.

→ Valeofclwydanglingclub.org 52.4663, -3.5968 £15 Fly BT

38 LLYN EBYR

Magical 30-acre lake, heavily forested. Brilliant farm lake, plus. I was debating keeping this for myself but both my publisher and my wife said that it was unfair. I'm still undecided. If you do go, I would suggest concentrating on pike. Bring your own life jackets to fish by the provided boats.

→ Luke Williams: 07502.355.461 52.4835, -3.5136 £10 Fly, spin, worm Coarse, pike

39 LLYN CLYWEDOG

Superb and haunting Llyn to fish. The shallow part is the most productive. There are wild brown trout, but please be aware, the lake is also enthusiastically stocked with all manner of other trout from their farm. We're told they're putting in rainbows, browns, blues, goldies, and tigers. Not very wild I know, but still a beautiful lake.

→ Clywedogtroutfishing.co.uk 52.5115, -3.6348 £25 Fly BT & other trout

40 LLYN COCH HWYAD

Lake of the Red Duck in English, and you need to have a duck's webbed feet to fish here for most of the year; it's very boggy. Apart from, we're told, early in the season. Perhaps try a float tube? Best flies - dragged Bushy Bob flies.

→ Emyr Lewis, glantzj_uk@yahoo.co.uk 52.6865, -3.5952 £20 Fly BT

41 LLYN GWYDDIOR

Beware driving here in a normal car in wet conditions. Gwyddior is accessed through rough forestry tracks and involves crossing a ford, so a 4x4 vehicle is advisable in wet weather. When you arrive at Llyn Gwyddior, it is a 31-acre mountain lake with wild brown trout in May. Olives will work best.

→ Fishingwales.net 52.6539, -3.5735 £15 Fly BT

42 SEVERN/NEWTOWN FISHERY (URBAN ANGLING)

Free fishing on an excellent stretch of the Severn in Newtown. Trotting with maggot will provide reasonable nets of dace, chub, brown trout. And the cost is excellent, of course. You can also try a fly for the trout and chub too. Big pike up to 20lb have been caught here and chub up to a whopping 6lb.

→ Plenty of parking in Newtown. 52.5229, -3.2717 Free Fly, bait, spin, led BT, coarse

43 SEVERN/ABERBECHAN

Close to the free stretch of the Severn in Newtown. It gets a mention here because of the salmon that are taken. I'm not sure where else you can seriously fish for salmon as inexpensively as the annual membership of the BAA. Over a mile of left bank fishing with shallow runs, deep glides, and weir pool.

→ Baa.uk.com 52.5307, -3.2641 £40/year Fly, bait, spin, led Sa, coarse

44 CAMLAD RIVER

Much of the Camlad forms the boundary between England and Wales. In times past, this would have been an extremely tumultuous area, now it's serene. Good head of trout here, nothing large but they will rise to the correct fly, presented well.

→ Montgomeryshireanglingassociation.co.uk 52.585, -3.1463 £22.50 Fly, bait, spin, led BT, coarse

45 SEVERN/FORDEN

Both salmon and coarse fish can be discovered in the deep pools of this stretch of the Upper Severn. The many bends of this twisted stretch will also hold fish. There are three miles to fish on this beat, so travel light.

→ Baa.uk.com 52.6129, -3.1568 £40/year Fly, bait, spin, led Sea, coarse

46 SEVERN/HAMPTON

Gorgeous, unspoilt upland river stretch. Lots of pools and rapids, twists and turns, excellent salmon, trout, and coarse fishing for chub, dace, pike, barbel, and grayling. It is really remarkable that you can fish for salmon for £40 a year and get dozens of other waters to fish too.

→ Baa.uk.com 52.6948, -3.1002 £40/year Fly, bait, spin, led Sa, coarse

36

38

39

46

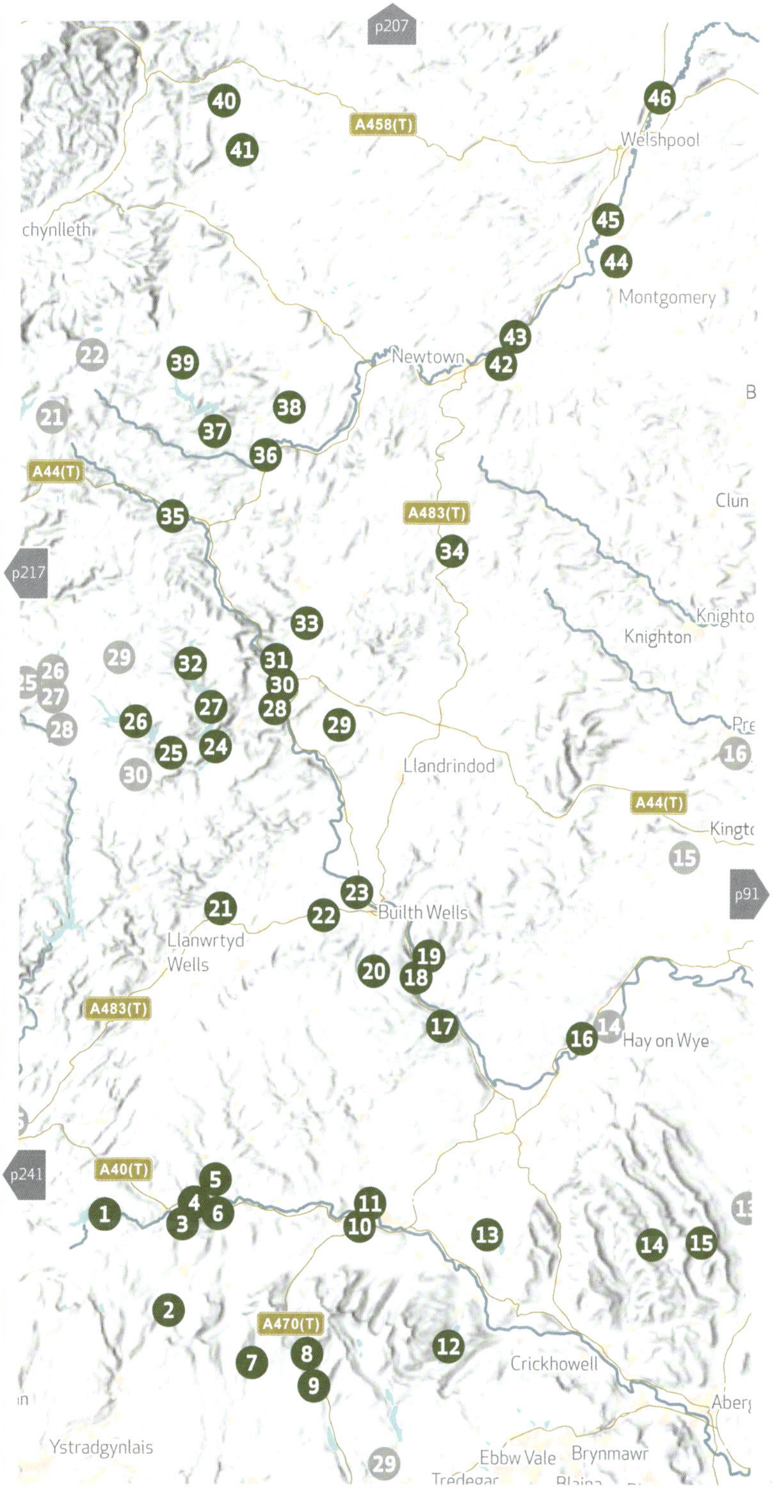
p207
40
41
A458(T)
46
Welshpool
chynlleth
45
44
Montgomery
43
22
39
Newtown
42
21
38
37
36
A44(T)
35
A483(T)
Clun
34
p217
33
Knighton
29
32
31
26
30
27
28
29
28
26
25
24
30
Llandrindod
A44(T)
15
23
p91
21
22
Builth Wells
Llanwrtyd
Wells
20
19
18
A483(T)
17
16
14
Hay on Wye
p241
A40(T)
5
4
1
3
6
11
10
13
14
15
2
A470(T)
7
8
12
9
Crickhowell
Ystradgynlais
29
Ebbw Vale
Brynmawr
Tredegar

South
Wales

Nowhere in Pembrokeshire is more than fifteen miles from the sea. Few places can top this county, not only for the quality of its fishing, but also the scenery that you'll be fishing within. Just as sommeliers tell you that drinking wine isn't only about taste – it's also the aroma and the mouthfeel – angling too is a multi-sensory experience. Our surroundings, while secondary to the activity itself, do contribute to the day. Whether you're fishing with friends or in spectacular environs, it all adds to the enjoyment.

The rugged shores of Pembrokeshire, a graveyard for tackle owing to the rough ground covered in kelp, are, in the final cost/benefit analysis, worth the effort. Monster conger eels lurk in the depths and will take squid baits as will bull huss and pollack. And what is a summer without mackerel? They're still here in numbers.

The River Usk is regarded by many as the premier trout fishing river in Wales. It rises in the Black Mountains and flows among bucolic scenery through the heart of Wales to the sea – we're told that the count of fish per mile rivals some of the top rivers in the world. The River Teifi, known as the "Queen of Game Fishing Rivers," whose upper reaches have been described as a Welsh chalk stream (but at considerably less cost than her southern English brethren) is wild fishing heaven.

In most years, the section of the River Wye below Monmouth is the one that adds most to the Wye's overall salmon catch. The salmon run on the River Usk is slightly later than the Wye, with the bulk of the catches coming from May/June onwards. Salmon fishing is generally outside the purview of this book, but it is always a good indicator of the health of a river and, if a river is healthy, there will be many other fish to interest us. It is commonly the case that the fishery owner will offer one price for salmon fishing and another, considerably less, for trout, sea trout, or coarse fishing. For example, the Wye at Wyebank costs £37.50 per day to fish for salmon or £27.50 to coarse fish. And it's not like the coarse fishing on this beat is poor; in fact, it's excellent: the barbel and dace fishing is particularly good. Chub fishing can be superb on this stretch with specimens to 5 and 6lb.

The Vale of Glamorgan is particularly good for shore fishing, notably the Bristol Channel, which has the second highest tidal range in the world. This sucks the fish in, and due to the powerful currents here, commercial fishing is kept at bay. This means great catches for us when the commercial boys are kept out. You can fish a huge variety of species throughout the year, including smoothhounds, tope, spurdog, congers, bull huss, bass, and many species of ray.

7

PEMBROKESHIRE

1 PORTHMELGAN BEACH

St. Davids Head is noted for its wildlife and flowers and for remains of human settlements. It splits the Irish Sea from the Celtic Sea. Float fishing for pollock and mackerel is productive when they move close to the shore. We're told that sharks sometimes follow.

→ Park at Whitesands and walk over. 51.9038, -5.3041 Free Beach Pollock, mackerel

2 DALE BEACH

A sheltered wide bay with a pebbled beach. Good for bass fishing but any number of other fish are a possibility, including flounders, dabs, whiting, dogfish, mackerel, garfish, and the occasional ray depending on the time of year. If you want to get amongst the rays, you'll need to cast a long way out.

→ Has its own car park. 51.7087, -5.169 Free Beach Flounders, dabs, whiting

3 ST. BRIDES HAVEN

A mixed sand and rocky beach, it's popular with divers. The whole bay is dominated by the 19th-century baronial residence of St Brides Castle, which is now a self-catering complex. We're told the most popular marks are on the west side. Expect to encounter bass, pollock, and wrasse.

→ Limited free parking, get here early. 51.8378, -5.1144 Free Beach Bass, pollock, wrasse

4 CLEDDAU, EAST & WEST

Designated as a Special Conservation Area, these waters provide a haven for wildlife, including otters and a wide variety of bird life. This is prime fishing water: double-figure sea trout are caught here each year, and beautifully marked wild brown trout too, sometimes up to a pound and a half. Even the salmon are weighty here, 15lbs is not uncommon.

→ Fishingpassport.co.uk 51.7868, -4.9426 £15 Fly, spin ST, Sa

5 LLYS-Y-FRAN RESERVOIR

Gorgeous location in the foothills of the Preseli Mountains. Due to its beauty, it can get quite crowded but with seven miles of bank, you can always find a secluded spot. There's plenty of room for everyone. However, its clean deep water with no tides does attract the paddleboarders.

→ Llys-y-fran.co.uk 51.8831, -4.8551 £15 Fly/Worm BT, RT

6 NEVERN RIVER

A beautiful spate river starting in the Preseli Hills and then winding through ancient, wooded valleys before meeting the sea at Newport Bay. The River Nevern has miles of prime sea trout fishing. The sea trout normally start to run the river from the beginning of May, peaking in July, with grilse appearing from July and salmon from August to the end of the season in October. If you can, schedule your time so you can fish for sea trout at night. We're told that the butcher, teal blue and silver, and black pennell are all effective flies.

→ Nevernanglingassociation.org.uk 52.0229, -4.7931 £30 Fly, spin,worm BT, Sa, ST

7 CEIBWR BAY

A minuscule inlet of sand and rocks surrounded by tall cliffs. You should see some porpoises on this remote and wild beach. Be alert to the incoming tide; don't

8

9

get caught out. The southern side can yield mackerel, pollock, and wrasse either side of high tide, while flounder can be caught on ragworm and lugworm baits.

→ Parking on the roadside but it's narrow. 52.0783, -4.7608 Free Beach Mackerel, pollock, wrasse

8 POPPIT SANDS

From March through September, the beach hosts a chance of salmon and sea trout, primarily on the incoming tide. Then switch to flounder, cod, and whiting in the winter. It's attractive to families with its low-formed dunes and loose sand - so, plan your trip accordingly.

→ Poppit Sands car park. 52.1045, -4.6999 Free Beach Salmon, ST, cod, whiting

9 MONKSTONE BEACH

Acclaimed for its rock pooling. Beautifully formed pools are at either end of the beach. Monkstone Point is very good for bass fishing, and we're told that both peeler crabs and fresh sand eels are excellent baits at this location.

→ Roadside parking is available on the verge of the lane to Trevayne Farm camping site. 51.696, -4.6812 Free Beach Bass

CARMARTHENSHIRE

10 TAF/ST. CLEARS TO DDOLERWYDD FARM

The St. Clears Angling Club controls the River Taf from Ddolerwydd Farm to the tidal waters in lower St. Clears. It also has a superb stretch on the River Cowin at Bancyfelin. This is, to my mind at least, sea trout waters. The mystical silvery fish that is best fished for at night. You needn't go after them with a fly exclusively; certainly, casting a spinner is less tiring over the hours of hunting this elusive fish than casting a fly.

→ Permits from Texaco Station in St. Clears 51.793, -4.4755 £20 Fly, worm, spin ST, Sa, BT

11 TYWI - DAN YR ALLT WATERS

The river is famous for its sea trout fishing with double-figure fish being taken regularly on the River Towy. However, there are also good runs of salmon, especially from July. The river is a spate river and benefits from a heavy rain - just to get everything fishy moving again.

→ Fishingpassport.co.uk 51.8255, -4.3261 £30 Fly, spin BT, ST

12 PEMBREY BEACH

Pembrey (Cefn Sidan) is a long, wide, unspoilt, sandy beach, backed by sand dunes, stretching for approximately 8 miles. A wetland ecosystem known as Pembrey Burrows can be found behind the eastern end of the beach and is a good destination for bird watchers. This is a very popular spot for targeting tope in the summer months. Tackle needs to be strong, as even a small tope will put up a great fight, especially if it can use the strength of the tide to its advantage.

→ The beach has its own parking at £8 a day. 51.6695, -4.3008 Free Beach Tope

13 BURRY PORT

Look for the Whiteford Lighthouse, a hotspot for large bass. Crab or spinning a lure is best for this mark. To the right of the outer slip, you have the north channel which you can see to the left of a stone wall, and further out on the Gower side is the south channel; both areas can be good fishing for bass, flounder, and plaice. Here, the best baits are maddies, closely followed by lug and crab.

→ Burry Port has its own parking. 51.674, -4.2654 Free Kayak Bass

14 BRAN RIVER

A heavy rain and the resultant rise in the waters can bring this stream to fishing excellence. The River Bran has good wading

15

19

21

and a variety of different waters from riffles to relatively deep pools. The name Bran means Crow in Welsh, which may be a reference to the colour of the water.

→ Fishingpassport.co.uk 51.9395, -3.8345 £11 Fly BT

15 TOWY/ABOVE LLANDOVERY

Above Llandovery, the Towy is narrower and cuts through rock faced gorges, laced with deep holding pools. Many of these pools, unchanged for centuries, are rightly famous for holding large number of salmon and sea trout. Dolauhirion, Tairheol and Divlyn are probably the most famous. It is recommended to work upstream with a running worm, or spinner.

→ Llandoveryaa.co.uk 52.0043, -3.8051 £25 Fly, bait, spin, led BT, Sa, ST

16 TOWY/BELOW LLANDOVERY

The Towy is prolific with diverse birds. Among the more distinctive species found along the river are sand martins, common sandpipers, little ringed plovers, dippers, kingfishers and grey wagtails. Red kites and buzzards are numerous. Goosanders and cormorants prey on sea trout and salmon. The main run of sea trout, often averaging four to five pounds, usually appear from the middle of June onwards. July, August and September can be good for the smaller shoal sea trout and salmon become more numerous as the season progresses.

→ Llandoveryaa.co.uk 51.9763, -3.8216 £25 Fly, bait, spin, led BT, Sa, ST

GLAMORGAN

17 RHOSSILLI BAY

Long regarded as one of Wales's most scenic beaches, however, you'll still probably be fishing alone because it's a very sharp descent to the bay. You have an enormous selection of possible fish to target here including bass, mackerel, flatfish, whiting, codling, garfish, dogfish, wrasse, conger, bream, triggerfish, mullet, pollock, and plaice.

→ Has its own parking at £6 a day. 51.5776, -4.2885 Free Beach Bass, mackerel, flatfish

18 WORMS HEAD

Famous for bass (especially from the causeway), other fish include flounders, pollock, turbot, conger, rays, dabs, spur dog, plaice, pouting, wrasse, gurnard, tope, dogfish, monkfish, mackerel, rockling, scad, whiting, codling. The western side of the Worm is steeper and deeper than the eastern side and is preferred for angling.

→ Worms Head has its own parking. 51.5688, -4.2917 Free Beach Bass

19 FALL BAY

This is a rock and sand beach that is almost always empty of people because it's hard to reach. The best way is to park at Rhossili Village Hall and follow a path through fields before you commence a steep descent into the bay. You'll be able to target bass, mackerel, dabs, garfish, dogfish, pollock, and plaice.

→ Pay at the honesty box at Rhossili Village Hall. 51.5621, -4.2894 Free Beach Bass, mackerel, dabs

20 MEWSLADE BAY

Close to Fall Bay, I think this represents my favourite sort of beach fishing. In summer months, you can merrily spin for mackerel and bass (school bass really) that come into range fora beach caster. I have also heard of far larger bass being caught here too.

→ The car park is 400 metres from the beach. 51.5612, -4.2804 Free Beach Bass

21 PORT EYNON

Kayak fishing is gaining in popularity all the time. There are now even European

22

23

25

Championships which, in my ignorance, I knew nothing about until recently. There are good bass to be caught along the right-hand side and around the point fishing the ledges and drop-offs. You can drift for plaice over the sandy bottom around the bay.

→ Port Eynon has its own car park. 51.5432, -4.2046 Free Kayak Plaice, gurnard

22 SLADE BAY

Slade Bay is set in a relatively inaccessible location - being reachable only on foot and climbing over some large rocks but it's eminently doable and, of course, it will also increase your chances of having the beach to yourself. You can do well here for flatfish while the bass come in well on a rising tide.

→ Park in Slade and walk over, it's fifteen minutes or so. 51.5475, -4.1813 Free Beach Flatfish

23 THREE CLIFFS BAY

This is a spectacular shoreline of sand dunes, salt marsh, and limestone cliffs. It's a small sandy beach framed by rocks at each end. The fish present are flatfish, whiting, dogfish, pollock, and plaice. The best way to fish for whiting is to use long shank hooks with green or red beads to attract them. I have no idea why this works.

→ Three Cliffs has its own car park. 51.5716, -4.116 Free Beach Flatfish, whiting, dogfish

24 KNAB ROCK BEACH

This easily accessible beach is just outside Mumbles and you can begin fishing straight out of the car park. It can get crowded with jet skiers and the like, so avoid the holidays and sunny weekends. Ideally, it's suited for autumn winter fishing for codling, whiting, and dab.

→ Knab Rock has its own parking. 51.5709, -3.9837 Free Beach Codling, whiting, dab

25 NEATH RIVER

17 miles of beautiful gin-clear water, dotted with wonderful waterfalls. The river is topped up with stocked fish throughout the season. We're told that there are also good sea trout and salmon runs. To help you navigate the river, these pools have been recommended: Langi, Rock Pool, Pontwalby Bridge, Water Bridge, Ynys-y-Nos Rock Pools, and the Potato Pool. Night fishing will pay dividends when the sea trout start running.

→ Fishingpassport.co.uk 51.7293, -3.6534 £22 Fly BT, ST, Sa

26 LLYN FAN FAWR

Humans inhabited this area from about 8000 years ago and it's from here that the Llyn Fawr Hoard was discovered. Twenty-one bronze and iron objects were found, including swords, spearheads, and horse harnesses. There is a resident stock of brown trout which are supplemented by rainbow and blue trout from the club's own hatchery.

→ Fishingwales.net 51.7187, -3.5669 £12 Fly BT, RT, blue

27 PENDERYN RESERVOIR

Please be aware that the boats here are only for members. That's not to rule out a member taking pity on you as you labour away on the bank and invite you aboard. In these waters, there are brown trout, some perch, and yes, it's stocked with rainbow trout. Could be a good place to attempt taking a perch on a fly.

→ Mountainashflyfishers.yolasite.com 51.7532, -3.5392 £20 Fly BT, RT, Pe

28 NANT MOEL RESERVOIR

We're told that 81 species of birds have been recorded within a five-mile radius of the reservoir. It's situated in over 12 acres of idyllic countryside at the top of the Cynon Valley, between Aberdare and Merthyr

31

29

33

32

Tydfil. Regular stocking with large rainbow trout with an average weight of 2lb and with the occasional monster of 7lb thrown in. Brown trout are also there.

→ Nantmoel.co.uk 51.7538, -3.4757 £13 Fly RT, BT, blue trout

29 TAF FECHAN

Runs through deep countryside for the first mile or so with deep water at the Taf Fechan Gorge. The next three kilometres start with deep gutters and then it tends to be a smaller stream with only wild natural brown trout. If you can fish this little river when the reservoir is overflowing slightly, you will have every chance of success on flies fished up or downstream.

→ Fishingpassport.co.uk 51.7824, -3.3806 £11 Fly BT

30 LLYNFI/BRIDGEND

The Llynfi is a small river but prolific, packing a large punch for sea trout. Large fish flow upriver from March, and you'll find weighted nymphs are frequently successful. The golden hours are, as is frequently the case, if you fish in the early morning or later in the evening.

→ Sgll.co.uk 51.5516, -3.5942 £20 Fly BT, Sa, ST

31 MONKNASH BEACH

This beach takes a little effort to visit but it's a beautiful beach with a sheer cliff backdrop. A brook tumbles onto the rock platforms creating gushing waterfalls and, when the tide is out, golden sands. You will expect to encounter, depending on your fishing style, codling, monkfish, ray, dogfish, and turbot.

→ Monknash has its own car park. 51.4175, -3.5638 Free Beach Codling, Ray, Turbot

32 LLANTWIT MAJOR

This area is comprised of three sites: Llantwit Major, Stoats Point, and Tresillian. The latter two are regarded as a little fraught (as in dangerous) to fish. So, perhaps really just concentrate on Llantwit Major, which is a good bass spot. Bass are extremely slow-growing – a 10lb bass could be over 20 years old. Bass are vulnerable to overfishing and there is a bag limit of 2 bass per angler per day in force in the UK.

→ Llantwit Major has its own parking. 51.3964, -3.5006 Free Beach Rays, dogfish, wrasse

33 LIMPERT BAY

Great views over the Bristol Channel to Minehead and Exmoor. The closer views are of the huge power station but, before you turn your nose up, the warm water discharge supports an array of sea fish who bask in the bath like waters. You can run into conger eels well into the autumn and ray, dogfish, wrasse, and rays throughout the summer.

→ Parking is available right next to the beach. 51.3883, -3.4175 Free Beach Rays, dogfish, wrasse

34 SULLY ISLAND

Sully Island is a small tidal island by Swanbridge. Apparently, it has been visited by the Romans and Vikings. Although the Monkey Pole is reputed to be the best mark on the island we've been told to beware of clambering down the rocks. So be careful, but it's worth it. Large cod and conger eel abound in these waters.

→ Park at The Captains Wife pub, sometimes it's even free! 51.3954, -3.1999 Free Beach Cod, conger eel

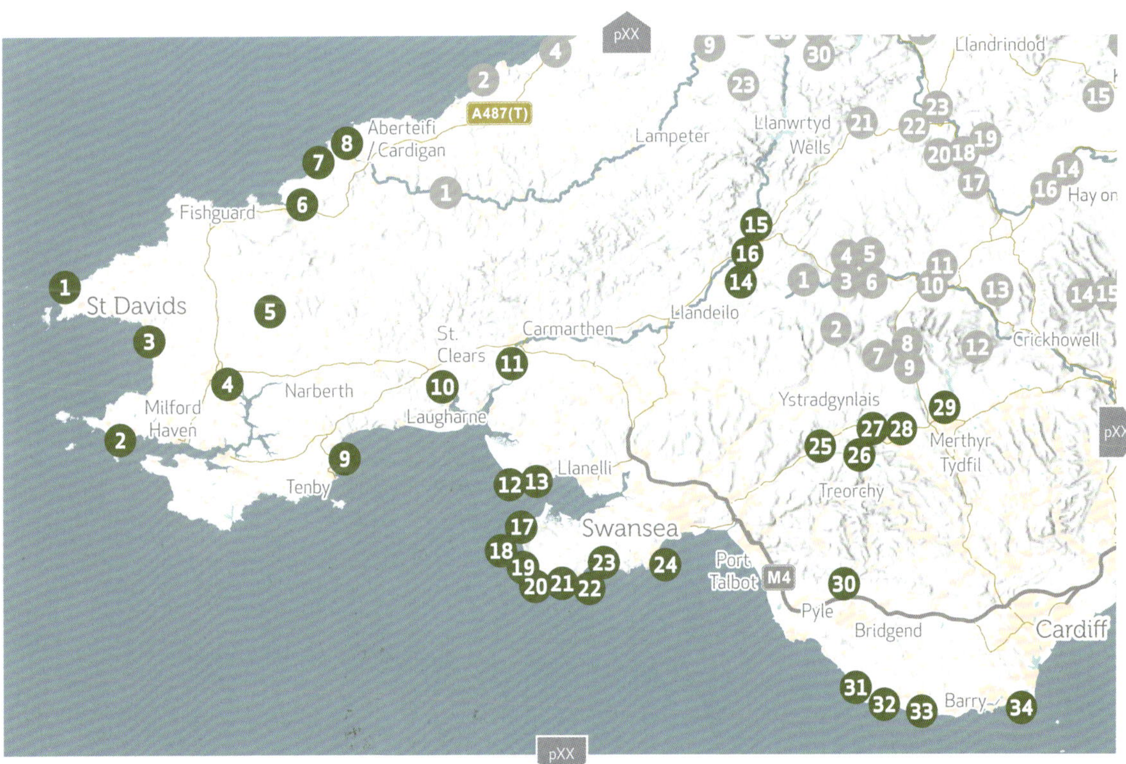

Loch Leathan, p189

Wild Fishing Britain

Words:
Kevin Adams

Photos:
Jill Adams
and those credited

Editing & Design:
Emma Stebbings

Distribution:
Central Books Ltd
50, Freshwater Road
Dagenham, RM8 1RX
020 8525 8800
orders@centralbooks.com

Published by:
First edition published in the United Kingdom 2025 by Wild Things Publishing Ltd. Freshford, Bath, BA2 7WG
ISBN 9781910636466

wildthingspublishing.com

Author acknowledgements:
Thanks to John Cheyne, The Angling Trust, Ceri Thomas, Fly Fishing Wales and Jonathon Muir, The Atlantic Salmon Trust.

 Maps contain data © Ordnance Survey 2016. All photos © Jill Adams, except the following, © to those named, used with permission or a CCBYSA licence: 19 & 21 wwwarjag, 32 MagicBones, 34 Grafxart, 38 Goodluz, 40 Bob Parker, 44 Susanna Lobb, 46 Dmitry Djouce, 49 Shutterstock Zoblinski, 50 Tim Green 50 Andrew, 51 Shutterstock Simon Burt, 51 Heather Cowper , 51 Shutterstock Tim Woolcock Photography, 52 Shutterstock Sarah2, 54 Derek Harper , 55 Andrew, 57 eff Collins, 58 Hannah, 58 Thomas Guest, 58 Richard-Dorrell, 59 Martin Bodman, 60 Getty Images/iStockphoto Thomas Faull, 62 George Keast, 62 GeorgeKeast, 62 Lewis Clarke, 63 Dulverton Angling Association Christopher Guest, 64 Phil Williams , 64 Rick Crawley , 65 Richard Szwekkowski, 65 George Keast, 66 Adrian Farwell, 66 Shutterstock Chris Dorney, 66 GeorgeKeast, 66 Shutterstock jimmonkphotography, 67 Shutterstock Joe Dunckley, 68 Shutterstock David Jarrott, 68 BVI4092, 68 Gary-Rogers , 70 Shutterstock Hwa Cho Yi, 72 Chris J Wood, 72 Shutterstock BasPhoto, 72 Trish Steel , 73 Shutterstock Kirk Fisher , 74 Leimenide, 74 Jim Champion , 75 Amanda BH Slater, 75 ITookSomePhotos, 75 Jim Champion , 75 Nicola Dunkinson, 76 Peter V Banyard, 77 Brett Jordan, 77 Nigel Cox , 77 Shutterstock Richard Paterson, 78 Jonathan Billinger, 79 grassrootsgroundswell, 79 Andrew Bowden, 79 Colin Smith, 79 Paul Hitchcock , 80 Kate R, 80 Natalia Romanovszka , 80 Shutterstock Jake Lilley, 80 Peter Watson, 80 Tony Atkin , 81 David Anstiss, 81 Robin Webster, 82 Shutterstock David Hughes, 84 Jonathan Billinger, 84 Bill Boaden , 84 Shutterstock Wirestock Creators, 86 Shutterstock Nicola Pulham, 87 Philip Halling , 87 Stephen McKay, 87 Jaggery, 88 Shutterstock Christine Dodd, 89 Roger Davies , 89 P-L Chadwick, 90 Jeff Gogarty, 91 John M , 91 Philip Halling, 91 Philip Halling, 91 P-L Chadwick, 92 Matthew Hartley, 94 Chris Wood, 94 Chris Wood, 95 Shutterstock Ben Molyneux, 96 Kevin Adams , 96 Amie Nimmo, 96 Chris Reynolds, 97 Shutterstock David Hughes, 98 Chris Morgan, 98 Shutterstock Stephen Richard McAdam, 99 Shutterstock J and S Photography, 100 Shutterstock Keith Bath, 100 Brian Pallett, 100 Tim Regan , 101 Judy Mackenzie , 101 Shutterstock AA creators, 101 Raffaella Barker, 101 Brian Pallett, 102 Zorba the Greek, 102 Blue Print Dave, 102 Shutterstock yackers1, 104 Shutterstock Rob Thorley, 106 Jaggery, 106 Martyn Wright, 106 Marilyn Peddle , 107 Shutterstock Phil Kieran, 108 Mat Fascione, 108 Roger Kidd , 108 Mat Fascione, 109 Roger Kidd , 110 Andy and Hikart Alder, 110 Elliott Brown , 110 Its No Game, 110 Shutterstock lortek, 111 Tony Monblot , 112 Brian Fagan, 112 Shutterstock Lucian Milasan, 114 Shutterstock Pete Stuart, 116 David Dixon, 117 Shutterstock Kevin Eaves, 118 Shutterstock jimmonkphotography, 118 Chris Hearn , 118 Shutterstock BobbyJean, 119 Shutterstock Christopher Chambers, 120 Shutterstock Peter is Shaw 1991, 120 Shutterstock Rodney Hutchinson, 120 Colin Gregory, 120 David Smith , 121 Shutterstock Jack Cousin, 122 Scott Robinson , 122 Shutterstock LFM Visuals, 122 Shutterstock WillJackson 7, 124 James Johnstone, 126 James Johnstone, 126 morebyless, 126 Doug Sim, 127 Ian Carroll , 128 Jake Cook, 129 Michael Bryan, 130 Colin Gregory , 130 Craig Bullock, 131 Jake Cook , 131 Shutterstock Jan Bray, 132 Audrey Gray , 132 UpSticksNGo , 134 Cole Gregg, 136 Tom Curtis, 136 Andrew Smith, 136 Shirokazan, 131 Anthony Parkes, 137 Jon Burrell, 138 Stephen Richards, 138 Andrew Curtis , 138 Paul Franks , 138 Alljengi, 138 Andrew Curtis , 139 Doug Belshaw, 139 Getty Images/iStockphoto jeangill, 139 Shutterstock Dave Head, 140 Graeme Churchard, 140 Shutterstock coxy58, 140 Peter Mulligan , 140 Shutterstock H Athey, 141 Andrew Curtis , 141 Robert J Heath, 141 Peter McDermott , 142 Shutterstock PointLabs, 142 Dennis Lovett , 142 Jake Cook , 144 RFPhotography PH3 1FY, 146 Billy McCrorie, 146 Walter Baxter, 146 Ann Cook, 147 Shutterstock Rodney Hutchinson, 148 Andrew Bowden, 148 Carol Ann Brown , 148 James Johnstone, 149 James Johnstone, 149 Billy McCrorie , 149 Colin Kinnear , 149 James Johnstone, 150 Anne Burgess , 150 Jim Barton , 150 Phil Williams, 150 James Johnstone, 151 Chris Wimbush, 151 Iain Thompson , 151 Ronnie Macdonald, 151 Steven Anderson , 152 John Ferguson , 152 Jonathan Cruickshank, 152 Alistair McMillan , 152 Shutterstock Mariusz Olszak, 153 Paul Farmer , 153 Claudia Audley, 154 Charlie Marshall, 154 Simon Allardice , 155 James T M Towill, 155 Patrick Mackie, 155 Tim Regan, 155 William Craig, 156 Andrew Wood , 156 Patrick Mackie , 156 Patrick Mackie , 156 John Ferguson , 157 Richard Webb , 157 Richard Webb , 157 John McLinden, 157 Julian Paren, 158 Ian Cranman, 158 Scott Oxford, 160 Getty Images/iStockphoto ditruter, 162 Richard Webb , 162 Scott Oxford, 162 Scott Oxford, 163 Fergus King, 164 Scott Oxford, 164 Scott Oxford, 164 Karin Lorvik, 164 Scott Oxford, 165 Gordon Baxter, 165 Gordon Baxter, 165 Lynn Wishart, 165 Fergus Fleming, 166 John Loach , 166 Markus Trienke, 167 Neil Williamson, 167 Paddy McCann, 167 Russel Wills, 168 Neil Williamson, 169 Iain Cameron, 169 Lucia Walker, 170 Scott Oxford, 172 Bob Jones, 172 Tad Turski, 172 Rowena Red Ruby Rose, 173 Shutterstock grafxart, 174 Ron Baldwin, 174 Flying Stag, 174 Ben Walmsley , 175 David Greer , 175 Rachel Maclennan, 175 Graeme Shimwell , 176 Clive Giddis, 176 Graeme Churchard, 176 Graeme Shimwell , 176 Nigel Brown , 177 Peter Moore, 178 John Ferguson, 178 Graeme Shimwell , 178 Suzie.Vestri, 179 Graeme Shimwell , 179 John-Lucas, 179 Shutterstock imageBROKER.com, 180 Alastair G, 181 Peter Van den Bossche, 181 Anabel Baranowska, 181 David Bremner, 182 Shutterstock Helen Hotson, 183 Shutterstock Alan Morris, 184 Shutterstock Charlesy, 184 Rupert Fleetingly, 184 Les Ellingham, 185 Shutterstock katerina12605, 187 Jennifer Budd, 187 Mike Dunn, 187 Shutterstock Kaca Skokanova, 188 Peter Moore, 188 Shutterstock Swen Stroop, 188 Shutterstock jack perks, 188 Manuel Osdoba, 189 Steven Rae, 190 Getty Images Chunyip Wong, 190 Andy Farringdon, 190 Colin Wilson, 191 Andy Farringdon, 191 Shutterstock 13threephotography, 191 John Halsam, 192 Shutterstock tony mills, 192 anne burgess, 192 Ronnie Robertson, 194 Shutterstock Helen Hotson, 196 Shutterstock Dave Harrison-Ward, 196 Sara Florence, 196 Bob Linsdell, 197 Sarah Franklin, 198 Shutterstock Matt Gibson, 198 Eric Jones, 198 Peter Barr, 199 Shutterstock Rob porter, 199 Helfin Owen, 199 Masa Sakano, 200 JJ Jones, 200 Jimmy Davies, 200 John Jackson1935, 201 Hanno Rathmann, 202 Peter S, 203 RichardO, 203 David-Medcalf, 203 Daniel Start, 203 Peter S , 204 Daniel Start, 205 Alan Fairweather , 205 Daniel Start, 206 Benedict Mason @sarkadventures, 206 Shutterstock Rob Thorley, 206 Terry Hughes, 208 Vicki Woolven, 210 Steve Fareham, 210 Humphrey Bolton, 210 Shutterstock Iolo ap Gwynn, 211 Shutterstock ieuan, 212 Nigel Brown, 212 Ian Capper , 213 Shutterstock David Dennis, 214 John Lucas, 214 Shutterstock Wozzie, 215 Shutterstock Iolo ap Gwynn, 216 Daniel Start, 216 Rob Davies, 216 John Lord, 216 Alan Richards, 218 Getty Images/iStockphoto birdsonline, 220 Nigel Davis, 220 Rachel Chapel, 221 Shutterstock Pete Holyoak, 222 Shutterstock Richard Whitcombe, 222 , 222 Phil Dolby, 222 Gareth James, 222 Shutterstock Anna Jastrzebska, 223 Stuart Wilding, 223 Jonathan Billinger, 223 Jeremy Halls , 224 Jaggery, 224 Nicholas Keeble, 225 Shutterstock David Hughes, 225 Derek Veller, 225 Guilhem Vellut, 226 Shutterstock valerie holloway, 227 Andrew Hill, 229 Phillip Halling, 230 Shutterstock Billy Stock, 232 Andy F, 232 Richard Williams , 232 David Joyce, 233 Susanna Lob, 234 Shutterstock Steve Wall, 234 Alistair Hare, 235 Shutterstock jax10289, 236 Getty Images/iStockphoto AlasdairJames, 236 Shutterstock Andy Williams photos, 236 Anne at Clyne Farm, 237 Stewart Black, 238 Philip Pankhurst, 238 Georgie Hoffrock , 239 RichardDowling, 240 Shutterstock Greens and Blues, 240 Shutterstock steved_np3, 240 Shutterstock Kenneth Evans, 243 Shutterstock Daniel Kay

WILD THINGS PUBLISHING

hello@wildthingspublishing.com